RAVES FOR *ALL-AMERICAN MURDER* AND JAMES PATTERSON

"Ripped from the headlines…Combining in-depth, investigative reporting and fresh interviews, the authors effectively tabloid-proof this shocking, celebrity-driven story by lining up the facts and labeling rumors." —*USA Today*

"The rapid-fire tale of one of the most infamous true-crime stories of the past decade…As can be expected in any book with Patterson's name on the cover, the authors tell the Hernandez tale in page-churning fashion." —*Kirkus Reviews*

"Patterson has mastered the art of writing page-turning bestsellers." —*Chicago Tribune*

"A must-read author…a master of the craft." —*Providence Sunday Journal*

"No one gets this big without amazing natural storytelling talent—which is what James Patterson has, in spades." —Lee Child

"James Patterson is the boss. End of." —Ian Rankin

"The page-turningest author in the game right now." —*San Francisco Chronicle*

"Patterson is a master." —*Toronto Globe and Mail*

A complete list of books by James Patterson is at the back of this book. For previews of upcoming books and information about the author, visit JamesPatterson.com, or find him on Facebook.

ALL-AMERICAN
MURDER

THE RISE AND FALL OF AARON HERNANDEZ, THE SUPERSTAR WHOSE LIFE ENDED ON MURDERERS' ROW

JAMES PATTERSON
& ALEX ABRAMOVICH WITH MIKE HARVKEY

GRAND CENTRAL
PUBLISHING

NEW YORK   BOSTON

Grand Central Publishing
Hachette Book Group
1290 Avenue of the Americas, New York, NY 10104
grandcentralpublishing.com
twitter.com/grandcentralpub

Originally published in hardcover and ebook by Little, Brown & Company in January 2018
First trade paperback edition: September 2018

Grand Central Publishing is a division of Hachette Book Group, Inc. The Grand Central Publishing name and logo is a trademark of Hachette Book Group, Inc.

The publisher is not responsible for websites (or their content) that are not owned by the publisher.

The Hachette Speakers Bureau provides a wide range of authors for speaking events. To find out more, go to www.hachettespeakersbureau.com or call (866) 376-6591.

Library of Congress Control Number: 2017958901

ISBNs: 978-1-5387-6085-7 (trade paperback), 978-0-316-41268-1 (ebook)

Printed in the United States of America

LSC-C

10 9 8 7 6 5 4 3 2 1

To Bill Robinson, who got this thing cooking

ALL-AMERICAN
MURDER

PROLOGUE

Matthew Kent ran track and played football at a high school in Attleboro, Massachusetts. After school, he worked out at a gym called Answer is Fitness. Then he would run, two miles north, to his house on Homeward Lane. The route went through an industrial park and into a clearing. The path turned to gravel, then dirt. On the far side of the clearing, at Landry Avenue, it turned into pavement again.

On June 17, 2013, Matthew did not get as far as the pavement.

It was a Monday. The day before the last day of school. Matthew had gotten to the gym at four. By the time he got out, an hour later, the weather—which had been beautiful all day—had started to turn. Clouds were gathering. The wind had started to gust. Matthew was running through the industrial park.

Suddenly, at the far end of the clearing, he stopped.

There was a man, lying on his back near a dirt pile.

Matthew called out to him: "Are you all right?"

The man did not answer. Matthew walked a bit closer, until he was about twenty feet away.

"Are you all right?" he asked again.

Once again, there was no answer.

Detective Mike Elliott was nearing the end of his eight-hour shift at the station when the transmission came over the radio: A guy down. A "possible sudden" behind the Corliss Landing industrial park.

Lieutenant Michael King, of the Massachusetts State Police, was coaching his son's little league team when he got the call—he was already on his way down to the clearing. Assistant District Attorney Patrick Bomberg would arrive shortly after, along with uniformed police officers and members of the North Attleboro fire department. But North Attleboro PD Captain Joseph DiRenzo beat everyone else to the scene.

The captain had left work at four. He was less than a mile away from Corliss Landing when the call came in, and he showed up, in shorts and a T-shirt, at 5:38.

DiRenzo saw right away that they were dealing with a homicide.

"There were rounds, and what appeared to be bullet wounds to the torso," he says. "When I knelt down and touched the body, I could clearly tell that rigor mortis had set in."

The man on the ground was lying faceup. His left fist was clenched over his chest—one of several places he had been shot. He was young. He was black. His eyes were half-open.

Flies were buzzing around the man's nostrils.

DiRenzo made note of the sneaker prints that had been left in the dirt. He saw a baseball cap, a white towel, and a partially smoked marijuana blunt lying on the ground. When he looked up, he saw something else: Dark, menacing clouds. A storm coming in from the west.

Soon, it would rain—heavy rain, which would wash away crucial pieces of evidence.

"It could not have come at a worse time," DiRenzo recalls. "We have the body itself, tire marks, shoe prints, and rounds. All of a sudden you could see the trees bending over, clouds moving in in slow motion. It was a moment of, 'Holy shit, we've gotta do something here!'"

The fire department had brought tents and tarps that the police could use to cover the crime scene. The cops worked quickly, trying to stay ahead of the storm. They measured, logged, and photographed as much as they could. But they also had to be careful not to contaminate the location.

Everyone had to park one hundred yards away from the body, in order to preserve the tire tracks. Everyone, including the firemen, had to wear boots and gloves, or have the bottoms of their shoes photographed for comparison purposes in preparation for the eventual homicide investigation.

The man had been standing when the first shot hit him. The detectives made note of the dirt the man's heels had kicked up as he fell—it was the kind of detail that a rainstorm would wash away.

The man had been shot several more times after falling.

Boom, he goes down, the cops thought. *Then, when he's down: Boom, boom, boom. You could definitely tell, somebody wanted to make sure he was dead. And the shell casings are right there—one in the dirt and three more in a little indentation in the ground right next to the body. They're all right there. Whoever did this was brazen. It's crazy—not even bothering to pick up the brass?*

The police put tarps over the tire and sneaker prints, set a tent up over the body, and covered the body itself with a tarp, placing rocks around the tarp's circumference to keep the wind from blowing it away.

There was nothing more they could do before the storm passed.

The rain lasted for twenty minutes—a half hour at the most—but it was heavy. Forty-mile-an-hour gusts shook the trees that stood around the clearing. The temperature dropped by twenty degrees. When the rain stopped, a state trooper named Michael Cherven removed the tarp and went through the dead man's pockets:

Sixty-four dollars and seventy-five cents in cash. Two sets of keys for an Enterprise Rent-A-Car. A cell phone.

"His *cell phone?*" one of the officers said. "For Christ's sake, you're gonna kill someone, take his cell phone!"

In the man's wallet, they found an ID: Odin Lloyd. Twenty-seven years old. The face in the photograph matched the victim's.

Back at the North Attleboro police station, Detective Elliott and Elliott's colleague, Detective Daniel Arrighi, waited outside of the room as a state trooper named Eric Benson called the car rental company and spoke with a manager named Edward Brennan.

"I'm investigating an apparent homicide in North Attleboro," Benson said. "We've recovered two sets of keys to a black Chevy Suburban, Rhode Island registration 442427. We have reason to believe that the person who rented it may be in danger."

Brennan looked up the number.

"Oh, no," he said.

Outside of the room, the detectives strained to hear Trooper Benson's side of the conversation. A few moments went by.

Benson opened the door.

"You're not going to believe this," he said when he saw Elliott and Arrighi. "The car was rented by Aaron Hernandez."

PART ONE

CHAPTER 1

I t was November 23, 2006, and Aaron Hernandez's high school football team—the Rams—was suiting up for the Battle for the Bell.

Played annually on Thanksgiving mornings, the Battle was a grudge match between Aaron's school, Bristol Central, and its crosstown rival, Bristol Eastern.

Bristol, Connecticut, is a working-class town—football country in the middle of a state where soccer and crew are the suburban sports—and the Battle drew thousands of people to Muzzy Field, an ancient, minor-league baseball stadium that had hosted Babe Ruth at one time, and had been scouted as a film location for *The Natural*.

Every year, going all the way back to 1959, bragging rights had been at stake: Would the Rams get to lord it over the Lancers for twelve more months?

This year, the stakes were especially high. If the Rams won, they'd advance—for the first time in nineteen years—to the state championship. If they lost or tied, it would be the end of their season, and the end of Aaron Hernandez's high school football career.

The Rams were confident as they ran out onto the field in their red-and-white uniforms. They had good reason to be. With Aaron Hernandez as their team captain, the Rams had won all but one of their games. Everyone favored them over the Lancers, who had bigger players on their team but had lost four of their games that season. Everyone knew that, on this day, a win by the Rams would push them into the playoffs.

Once again, all eyes were on Aaron Hernandez.

Aaron was a quadruple-threat athlete. He ran track, and was the best player on the school's basketball team. He had speed, dexterity, good reach, great hands. When he played baseball, he was the pitcher. On the basketball court, his dunks were legendary. And on the football field, he ducked, dodged, and stutter-stepped like a basketball star.

At 6'1" and 245 pounds, Aaron already had the body of an NFL player. Big and fast, he was the kind of tight end who'd *always* be the offense's primary option.

He was the best athlete that Bristol Central had ever produced.

"Bristol Central had become the powerhouse of the state," says Armando Candelaria, who was coaching high school football nearby in New Britain. "And Aaron Hernandez was the big name in Connecticut football. New Britain is a bigger city than Bristol. Our rivalry goes back to 2001, when Aaron's brother, DJ, was on Bristol Central's team. Our rivalry went from there to Aaron's own rise in football. In 2005, I remember game planning for Aaron. Planning *just for him*.

"He was like something you'd see on ESPN's *30 for 30* series. A man among boys, even as a junior. When we played him the second game of his junior year, he caught four balls for a hundred and eighty yards—on a losing effort. In college, he could have played tight end *or* defensive end—it didn't matter. You knew who the best player was when he walked onto the field. He was. Definitely.

"I was the defensive coordinator, the secondary coach. It was my responsibility to stop Aaron. But he was very, very hard to block. He'd run away from the whole game. There was nothing you could do about it. From the coaching point of view, his numbers were unbelievable. As a senior, on both sides of the ball, he was dominating. His junior year as a tight end put him on the map. He would give you two hundred yards receiving as a tight end. I remember one game: DJ was a senior. Aaron was a freshman, but he didn't look like a fourteen-year-old kid. He ran a shallow cross, coming across the middle, and turned it up against seniors. To do that at fourteen against varsity kids speaks volumes.

"In his junior year, we started calling him 'The Big Guy.' We started to play a tough man underneath him—whoever got at his feet—and then we'd have a man eight yards on top of him, in case he got free of the first guy. Double coverage the whole time. That was easier said than done because my staff and I did not anticipate how physical he was. He was a lot faster in person than he was on film, and he would get free from the first defender and get open in front of the second defender. That made the game plan difficult during his junior year. We still got the win, but he made it known that you weren't going to double him.

· "Everyone talked about his size. No one talked about his feet. He had really good basketball feet. His athleticism and speed took over. His footwork and balance. When you saw it live you understood, the kid was a born athlete."

"The thing that stood out to me," says Ian Rapoport, who covered football for the *Boston Herald,* "was the first time I saw a guy fall down. He was the first football player who played like a basketball player, making defensive backs fall down. The kind of player who made the press box go, 'Wow!' An incredible, freakish athlete, with unbelievable versatility and talent. The first time I saw him, I thought, *This guy's got game.* He could start and stop on a dime. It was amazing."

CHAPTER 2

Aaron knew that the Lancers' coach would double-team him at every turn, just as every other opposing coach had all season long.

"From a coaching perspective, the philosophy had to be to figure a way to take Aaron out of the game plan," says Sal Cintorino, who ran the football program at Newington High School and went on to coach Bristol Central. "That was what everyone tried to do. We'd try to put two guys on him, try to influence Matt Coyne, who was their quarterback at the time, to go in a different direction. But Coyne had so much confidence in Aaron. He didn't care who covered him. He'd throw right *into* the coverage. Somehow, Aaron would come away with the football."

Given how well Aaron had been playing, Bristol Central should have steamrolled the Lancers straight back to their side of town. But, just after kickoff, dark clouds full of rain, slush, and snow filled the sky.

Although it was just a few degrees above freezing, the cold did not bother Hernandez. He had played beautifully in the cold in last year's Battle, making seven catches for 112 yards, scoring a touchdown, leading the Rams to a thirteen-point victory. More troubling was the fact that the Rams were a passing team—and, Aaron knew, passing teams did not do well on rainy, windy football fields.

The Lancers took a 7-0 early lead in the game, moving fifty-five yards on eleven plays. In the second quarter, the Rams' coach, Doug Pina, adjusted for the rain and moved Aaron into the backfield. Hernandez did not disappoint. He ran straight up the middle, plowing straight through the other team's players. He made a short but explosive touchdown run that opened up a 14-7 lead. But stripped of their passing game, playing in the mud, the Rams struggled to maintain their advantage.

"It was a bad day," Pina recalls. "The field was a mess. Our quarterback was having a lot of trouble throwing."

"It was the coldest I'd ever been," one of Aaron's teammates remembers. "I remember being out there, just stepping in puddles when I was on the field. Down in the line your hands would sink into the mud."

"The downpour was torrential," says Cintorino. "The rain was sideways."

Aaron's teammates on the sidelines wondered if Bristol's Parks Department had let the game go forward because the department employee who had made that call was biased toward Bristol Eastern.

"Physically, the Lancers were bigger, and the conditions

would have given them an advantage there," a player on Aaron's team says.

"Paul Philippon, the head coach at Bristol Eastern, was adamant about playing that game," Cintorino remembers. "Everyone else was like, 'It's a terrible game in this weather!' But Phillipon said, 'We're playing this game.' The reason was, Central was not going to be able to throw the ball. The weather was that bad. And if you couldn't throw, you had to figure out some other way to get the football to Aaron."

Aaron battled through freezing rain in the third quarter. The Rams held the Lancers to seven points. But midway through the fourth quarter, the Lancers capitalized on the advantage the weather had given them. Rallying, they ended the game in a tie at fourteen.

Given the Rams' reputation, that tie—one of only two in the decades-long history of the Battle—felt more like a loss. ("Probably the biggest upset anyone could think of," Cintorino says.) It knocked Bristol Central out of contention for the upcoming state championship, ending Bristol Central's season as well as Aaron's high school career.

But if Aaron was disappointed, he did not show it that day. As a high school player, he was known for his composure.

"Mature before his time," Cintorino recalls. "A lot of kids at seventeen would have been very angry after a loss like that. But in the football arena, where I saw him, he was very mild, very humble, and very mature. He carried himself in a way you'd appreciate."

*   *   *

What changed?

Blows sustained on the football field were already altering the structure of Aaron's still-developing brain.

Celebrity status, drug use, and criminal associations would help to make Hernandez unstable, paranoid, and dangerous.

But some of those who knew Aaron in Bristol suggest that, even then, his humility was a put-on. The only *real* change, they say, had to do with Aaron's ability—or his desire—to hide his true character.

CHAPTER 3

The formation of Aaron Hernandez's mask began at home, in a cottage on Greystone Avenue.

Growing up, Aaron shared a bedroom with DJ— Dennis John—who was three years his senior. Sometimes, it felt as if everyone in the family was living right on top of one another. But Aaron's parents, Dennis and Terri, were proud of the home and took even more pride in DJ and Aaron. They were determined to keep the boys on the straight and narrow.

"I met the Hernandezes in second grade, or third grade, when I began to play football," a family friend named Tim Washington remembers. "Aaron and DJ lived near the high school, in a rural type of area off of Union Street. They had a nice house with a nice finished basement. Their dad had a little gym set up down there for them to work out. It had some weights and a weight bench. There was an in-ground pool and the basketball court right behind that.

Aaron and DJ played basketball and home run derby in the woods off to the back of the house.

"Dennis and his brother, Dave, were on the coaching staff for the Bristol Bulldogs and the Pop Warner league. Dennis was the janitor at my middle school. And in high school and college, I dated Dave's daughter, Davina. We were very close. Dennis would always tell me, 'My boys are coming up! You need to watch out for my boys. You need to protect my boys.'

"Dennis knew that those boys were going to be special in any sport that they played. And Aaron was driven to make his dad proud."

Dennis woke DJ and Aaron at dawn so that they could work out. The boys practiced their layups for hours on end. They ran countless suicide drills up and down the hills around their home. All the while, lessons their father had instilled in them rang in their heads:

If you do anything great in life, it will come from within, Dennis would tell them. And, *If it is to be, it is up to me.*

Aaron and DJ worshipped Dennis. And if Dennis was overprotective of them, it was because he had come close to living out his own dreams.

Dennis Hernandez had played for Bristol Central back in the 1970s. Like his son, he'd been triple-varsity, running track and playing basketball as well as football. Along with his twin brother, David, he'd been big and fierce: a dominant player. For decades to come, Dennis held on to his high school nickname—"the King."

Along with David, Dennis had gotten a full football scholarship to the University of Connecticut. But, in his youth, he had also gotten into a fair deal of trouble.

As one of the only Puerto Rican kids in a hardscrabble, Irish-Italian town, Dennis had spent his youth proving his mettle, on and off the football field. A wild kid with a chip on his shoulder, Dennis drank and partied. Along with his brother, and a friend and teammate named Rocco Testa, he got into fights, broke into strangers' houses, and stole. Surrounded by friends from the wrong side of town, both twins ended up dropping out of UConn.

Testa came to a bad end. A few days before Thanksgiving, in 1977, he and his uncle, a petty criminal named Gary Castonguay, were burglarizing a house in Plainville, Connecticut. When a police officer named Robert Holcomb arrived, responding to a call about a burglary in progress, Castonguay shot him four times and left him to bleed to death. Officer Holcomb was twenty-eight, with a three-year-old son. Castonguay was thirty-three, with a long rap sheet. Testa was twenty. When Castonguay was arrested, two weeks after the shooting, Testa was given immunity from murder and burglary charges in exchange for testifying against his uncle.

For David and Dennis, this story would serve as a cautionary tale. But fatherhood was the thing that straightened the brothers out for good. David became a corrections officer. Dennis got his job as a janitor at Bristol Eastern. Dennis's wife, Terri, who'd been a majorette, a few years behind him at Bristol Central, became an administrative assistant at a Bristol elementary school.

The young couple scrimped and saved to buy the cottage

on Greystone Avenue. They had their boys, and a white German shepherd named "UConn." They loved their lives. But money would always be an issue for them.

Dennis and Terri saw to it that Aaron and DJ had everything that they needed to be safe and comfortable. Still, they couldn't afford the designer clothes and fancy toys that other parents bought for their kids. Watching her boys go without, and suffering for it, caused Terri to make poor decisions. In 2001, the Bristol police came to the house and placed her under arrest: Terri had gotten involved in a bookkeeping operation run by a local restaurant manager named Marty Hovanesian.

"She was the phone operator," Hovanesian's lawyer told the *Boston Globe*. "A minor player, not the brains." But the operation was serious enough that Hovanesian was convicted of felony racketeering and professional gambling. "I'm not saying it was right, what she did—at all," DJ would tell *Sports Illustrated*. "I don't think it is. But this woman did this because I was crying every single night. She didn't do it for the thrill. She didn't do it to pocket the money. She did it to provide for me and Aaron."

The case against Terri never went to trial. But in Bristol's close-knit community, word got out. Before long, the whole town seemed to know about Terri's arrest.

Aaron was twelve at the time—an innocent, outgoing kid who liked pranks and practical jokes. But despite his popularity, and DJ's, Aaron and his brother were teased about the incident, and if DJ was quick to forgive, Aaron was more of a cipher. He kept his feelings to himself. But try as he did to mask his embarrassment, Aaron's relationship with his mother grew strained as he entered his adolescence—and decisions Terri made as the years went by only increased the distance between her and her younger son.

CHAPTER 4

By all accounts, Aaron kept up appearances. His former classmates describe a likable, well-behaved teenager. The worst thing that Bristol law enforcement has to say about Aaron, in his youth, is that once, at a party, he ran up onto a car and put a slight dent in the roof.

On that occasion, the Bristol police had called Dennis Hernandez.

"Dennis came down and rode a hard line on him," an officer remembers. "The old man made him do the right thing. Made the kid apologize. And the kid wouldn't say 'boo.' He was reserved. Not a bad kid at all."

Now, as Aaron finished out his last year of middle school, there was no doubt that he would be joining DJ on the BCHS varsity squad. Aaron's grades up to this point had been good. (In high school, Hernandez would make the honor roll.) His football game was already exceptional.

Though he preferred basketball, Aaron seemed to have a

sixth sense for the sport, leaving spectators with the feeling that he was seeing the field from above.

Dennis Hernandez watched everything that Aaron did on the field from the stands, just as he had with DJ.

Whenever one of his boys scored or made a beautiful play, Dennis was not ashamed to cry tears of pride. But back at home, the family dynamic was changing.

Dennis's brother, David, was struggling with cancer, and the family had braced itself for bad news.

His son DJ, who had preceded Aaron as a superstar player for the Rams, was heading off to UConn (where he would excel as a quarterback and wide receiver for the Huskies).

His wife, Terri, had become romantically involved with a married man named Jeffrey Cummings.

Cummings's wife, Tanya, was the daughter of Dennis's sister, Ruth—which made Aaron and Tanya first cousins. Because the Hernandezes were a tight-knit family, Terri and Jeffrey had to be extra-careful. At first, they were, and no one found out about their relationship. But, in September of 2005, an ugly incident occurred at a UConn football game.

While DJ was down on the field, Tanya came up to Terri and slapped her, right there in the stands.

Now, the family affair was pried open for Aaron and others to see.

Given the chance, Aaron's parents might have gotten past the unfortunate incident, patched things up, and moved on with their lives and their marriage.

Instead, tragedy struck.

CHAPTER 5

It was January of 2006. Tim Washington, who had played football with DJ in high school, had gone on to college. But, during the winter break, Tim had gone to work out with his old high school running backs coach.

"One day, I was in the car with the coach," Washington recalls. "He got a call: 'Hernandez died.'"

Washington's first thought was that David Hernandez had died.

"Dave had been battling cancer for as long as his daughter, Davina, and I were together," he says. "He had been in remission, and then the cancer came back."

A moment later, the coach's phone rang again.

"No," the coach said, "it's not Dave! It's Dennis!"

Why would anyone have thought it was *Dennis?* Dennis *couldn't* die. Too many people in Bristol loved him. DJ and Aaron needed him.

Dennis hadn't even been ill.

"What the hell happened to Dennis?" people said when they found out.

"Everyone was devastated," Washington remembers. "Every time you'd say, 'Dennis died,' they'd look at you and say, 'You mean Dave?'"

A few days earlier, Dennis Hernandez had gone in to the hospital for a hernia repair. Immediately afterward, he contracted a fatal bacterial infection. The death was stupid, shocking, out of the blue, and impossible to process.

The largest funeral parlor in Bristol was too small to host the thousand-plus people who turned out for the man who was known around town as "the King."

"The funeral was absolutely gigantic," Washington remembers. "I waited in line for over an hour just to get in—and I was there pretty early. There was a line for as long as you could possibly see. Dennis was that well-respected.

"They were a staple in Bristol, the Hernandez family. They always had been. Good people, they'd give you the shirt off their backs. They'd give you a ride if you needed it. Get you something to eat if you needed it. Give you advice. Talk to you about sports, how you could get better. They were great, down-to-earth people."

CHAPTER 6

DJ was nineteen at the time. He was a few inches shorter than his younger brother, and thirty pounds lighter, but Aaron and DJ had the same strong jaw, the same dark, piercing eyes, the same wide, toothy smile. It wasn't hard to mistake one for the other.

But the brothers were not the same.

At the funeral home, DJ broke down and sobbed over his father's coffin.

Aaron, who was sixteen, had trouble expressing his grief.

"He was lost," DJ would tell *Sports Illustrated*. "He cried, but [only] at moments. Crying is not always the answer, but being an emotional family, for him to put up a wall during the services...He was holding everything in. Our bodies just reacted differently."

On the night after the funeral, Aaron scored thirty points in a basketball game against Windsor. The following night, in a game against South Windsor, he scored thirty-one.

"That night after the funeral, when he decided to play in his basketball game, it ended up being very emotional," says Tim Washington. "He dunked. The whole crowd went crazy. Aaron made the best of it, but it was a tough time. A very tough time, that's for sure."

Hernandez continued to work out. On the football field, he was unstoppable. As a sophomore, he had begun to feel more comfortable inside his oversized body. As a junior, he'd set the state record for receiving yards in a single game. The following year, Aaron would tie the state record for career touchdowns. Two ranking services would rate him as the nation's number-one tight end. Aaron already had a verbal agreement with UConn's coach, Randy Edsall. He told fans and reporters that he could not wait to play football with DJ again.

Scouts from powerhouse teams like the Florida Gators were also beginning to show up at Aaron's games. But at home, Aaron began to rebel. "It was very, very hard, and he was very, very angry," Terri told *USA Today*. "I didn't know what to do with him. He wasn't the same kid, the way he spoke to me. The shock of losing his dad, there was so much anger."

The silence left by Dennis's absence created its own series of shocks. It was just Terri and Aaron at home—and the comfort that Aaron could take in his mother was undercut by the knowledge that, a few months earlier, she had betrayed his father with Jeffrey Cummings.

With DJ and Dennis *both* gone, Aaron did not know who to turn to. He did not know what to do with himself. "Everyone was close to my father, but I was the closest," Aaron would say. "I was with him more than my friends. When that happened, who do I talk to, who do I hang with?"

Before long, Aaron was hanging out on the wrong side of town, at a house on Lake Avenue that belonged to Tito Valderrama—"Uncle Tito," who had married Dennis and Dave's sister, Ruth. There, he bonded with his cousin Tanya, the woman who had slapped Terri at DJ's UConn game.

He grew close to Thaddeus "TL" Singleton, a drug dealer Tanya had taken up with after Cummings left her for Terri Hernandez.

He picked up new running mates: a drug-addled townie named Carlos Ortiz and an older man named Ernest Wallace.

Narcotics officers in Bristol knew Wallace (whose nickname was "Bo") as one of the petty criminals they'd seen around a housing unit on Lillian Road and Lake Avenue. The police believed that Ortiz—who went by "Charlie Boy"—had ties to a Bristol gang called the Doo Wop Boys, who were themselves affiliated with the Bloods.

Aaron still held it together in public. His mask stayed intact. But privately, friends and mentors like Coach Pina grew worried.

They knew that there was a dark side to Bristol, Connecticut, and it seemed to them that Aaron Hernandez was hell-bent on working his way to its center.

CHAPTER 7

"Hernandez Still on Track for UConn"
—*Hartford Courant,* February 8, 2006
"Misdirection Play: Hernandez to Gators"
—*Hartford Courant,* April 23, 2006
"D.J. Hernandez Tries Draw Play; But Brother Stands By Choice"
—*Hartford Courant,* September 10, 2006

Football fans across Connecticut were stunned: three months after his father's death, Aaron announced his intention to back out of the verbal agreement he'd made, as a sophomore, with Huskies coach Randy Edsall.

Although that commitment had been publicized, Aaron had never stopped getting calls—from Boston College, Georgia, Illinois, Indiana, Iowa, Michigan, Miami.

At first, Aaron had been firm about his commitment to Edsall.

"They've most all been sending stuff, but they've been calling more lately," he told the *Hartford Courant*. "They call my coach and he tells me. I just tell him to tell them I'm going to UConn.

"It's my dream to play with my brother in college," Aaron said. "But it's not a huge thing. I think I would still be going to UConn even if my brother wasn't there. Since he's there, it just makes it a better fit. Whether my brother is starting or not, he's still going to push me and make me be better just being there. He's a big motivator for me.

"Since my freshman year, UConn has been coming after me. They offered after my sophomore year. That was before anybody was going after me. So that makes me feel better.

"UConn is like family. They were there for me when my dad passed away. It's tough, though. I wish my dad was here now that more schools are coming. Notre Dame just came on recently and it really makes you think. It just makes me think more. My dad would have been able to help me out even more. But I'm pretty sure he would have wanted me to go to UConn. My family wants me to go to UConn and my heart's at UConn."

Then, the Florida Gators made their full-court press.

"We don't typically recruit in Connecticut," says Urban Meyer, who was the head coach in Florida at the time. "But I remember watching the videotape. I'm always looking for that hybrid player. We're not looking for a big, slow tight end. We want a guy that can do a lot of things."

At first, Meyer did not see anything special in Aaron. "That was more our staff," he says. "I'm the ultimate decision maker, but I didn't know enough about him. He looked like a very athletic guy. But to say that I saw something special—I did not."

Nevertheless, in April, the Gators had flown Aaron down for a meeting. Aaron told his brother that he was only going down for a vacation. But down in Gainesville, the Gators' freshman quarterback, Tim Tebow, showed Aaron around the campus and football stadium. Sitting beside Heisman Trophy candidate Chris Leak, Aaron took in a spring game. He met with the team's other coaches, who had done their best to convince Urban Meyer that Aaron truly *was* special.

Aaron had spent his whole life in Central Connecticut. Florida might as well have been a different planet.

He made his intentions known then and there. In a video posted on the GatorCountry.com website, he said, "I'm going to be a Gator. This is what I want. They can compete for a national championship, and that's what I want to be in."

"It was hard," Aaron said of his decision. "I was close with Coach Edsall, the coaches, and the UConn players. They're a great building program. It was something I thought I wanted to be around. But then I became the number-one tight end in the country, so I wanted to play at a top school against the top kids. My dad always said to be the best you have to play against the best."

DJ had become an integral part of Randy Edsall's organization. He tried everything he could think of to get his brother to reconsider. "I think it's still up in the air a little bit. He talks about Florida and everything, but it's not over until it's over," he told the *Hartford Courant*. "I think when it comes down to crunch time he's going to really think about the family and put everything in perspective and just really realize that maybe Florida is a little too far. We're such a close family. If I put myself in his shoes, I know that would be really tough for me to do. I just see him doing the same, in the end finding it really difficult to go there."

But Aaron felt that, short of winning a national championship, there was nothing UConn could do to get him to change his mind.

Aaron had grown up watching the Patriots quarterback, Drew Bledsoe. He had his sights set on the NFL.

Playing for the Gators would give him the opportunity.

"I really did always want to play with my brother," he told the *Courant*. "But I also have to think about what's best for me and my career, and what's best for me I think is Florida."

Down in Gainesville, Gators were treated like royalty wherever they went. Hernandez found that appealing. But there were also compelling reasons for him to move far away from Bristol.

According to a family friend, "Aaron started to get mad at the dumb things that Terri was doing." The desire to get away from his mother is "what really drove the Florida decision. He wanted to get the fuck away from her. She'd been a problem for a long time. And a lot of people were very disappointed with how Terri carried herself after Dennis passed—even shortly before. Her affair with Jeff Cummings. People did not like the decisions that she was making at the time. They felt as though she had started to tarnish the Hernandez name. Even friends who were tight with the family got to a point where they wouldn't invite her to things anymore, because of the things she was doing or what they had heard about her."

If Terri had been more of a steadying influence—if Urban Meyer and Tim Tebow had been less persuasive—or if DJ had succeeded in changing his brother's mind, everything might have turned out differently for Aaron. Like their father, who had done all he could to keep his sons on the right course, DJ wanted nothing more than to keep Aaron close and keep him safe.

But Aaron had settled on another path. Up in Bristol, he'd kept up his friendship with people like TL Singleton, Carlos "Charlie Boy" Ortiz, and Ernest "Bo" Wallace.

Down in Florida, he would begin to act like a thug.

PART TWO

CHAPTER 8

Aaron graduated from Bristol Central a semester early, in December of 2006.

In January, the University of Florida's second-ranked football team trounced the top-ranked Ohio State Buckeyes in the BCS National Championship game.

When Hernandez arrived in Gainesville that month, the Gators were being feted all over town. Aaron had only just turned seventeen. According to Urban Meyer, he was still deeply affected by Dennis's death.

"Everybody was walking around on eggshells," the rangy, plainspoken coach explains. "I knew he'd lost his father. I didn't realize how *sudden* it was. And when Aaron got to us that spring, I realized the impact that loss had on him."

"He was very young, coming out of high school. We tried to counsel him through that. He tried to quit at least a dozen times. My wife's a psychiatric nurse. She met with him. I would talk to his brother at least every other week. I felt like he was trying to grab hold of something. And I wanted to make sure that he was going to grab hold of the right thing."

Meyer recalls that Aaron would pull himself together, seem "to get everything under control." Then he would have visions—"visions of his dad," Aaron would say—and try to quit, yet again, and go home to Bristol.

"Decimation," Meyer says, when asked about the impact of Dennis's death. "I mean, it just destroyed him. There were times he would melt down in my office—break down and start sobbing about his dad. How much he missed him. It happened so fast he never had a chance to say good-bye.

"I lost my father when I was forty-eight years old. I was a grown person when my mom passed away. For me to give advice on something I've never walked in those shoes—but I did walk in those shoes, a little later in life. My relationship with my mom was very similar to Aaron with his father. So we would talk about that nonstop. And it seemed like it would comfort him. He would often ask me about that: 'Tell me when you lost your mom...' And uncomfortable as that was, I understood. That was his grieving. His opportunity to release a little bit and talk about it."

If Aaron was in pain, he took care not to show it outside of Urban Meyer's office. Despite his age, he was quick to find his place on campus. Friends Aaron made as a freshman describe him, today, as kooky, outgoing—a class clown.

"First time I met Aaron, he was on campus with a long pink T-shirt all the way to his knees, blue gym shorts, and bedroom shoes," Aaron's friend Markihe Anderson remembers. "He always wanted to be around people. Hang out. Do anything for fun. Anything for excitement. He was always goofing off, making everybody laugh."

When Anderson went home to Fort Meyers, Aaron would tag along.

"He brought the energy like he already knew my family," Anderson says. "First time he met them. Ask him for a handshake, he'd give you a hug. He called my ma 'ma.' He called my grandma 'grandma.' He called my brother 'brother.' He had that personality. He swept everyone off their feet." But a few months after Aaron's arrival in Florida, an ugly, off-campus incident provided a glimpse of the demons that lurked behind the mask.

CHAPTER 9

It was midnight on the last Friday in April. Aaron was upstairs at a campus restaurant and bar called the Swamp, drinking lemonade with Tim Tebow and hanging out with his new friend Shaun Young—a tennis player who was the only one of the three who was old enough to drink alcohol.

Classes were over. Finals were set to begin the following week. The Swamp—which was packed to the gills every weekend—was full to overflowing.

The bar was a perennial favorite with students at the University of Florida. It had a prime location: Ben Hill Griffin Stadium, where the Gators played (it, too, was known, to one and all, as "the Swamp"), was just a few blocks away. The beer the bar served was cheap and ice-cold, the waitresses all wore short shorts, and the tree-covered patio had just enough shade to keep the Florida sun at bay.

The Swamp was also a good place for the school's star football players to see, be seen, and be admired, and although

Aaron was still a freshman, he already had admirers of his own.

Before long, a waitress appeared with two shots someone had sent over.

Not carding Aaron was a natural mistake on the part of the waitress. "Hernandez looked like a thirty-year-old man," the Swamp's owner, Ron DeFilippo, recalls. "Like LeBron—a man-child at seventeen. If you saw him walking your way you'd cross the street."

There was also the fact that, in Gainesville, the drinking age did not always pertain to underage Gators.

When Tim Washington flew down to visit Aaron in Florida, he was struck by the way players were treated in town. "If you're a Gator, you can do no wrong," Washington says. "I remember, after a game, we went and pulled up at the liquor store. Aaron walked in and got what he wanted to get. I was just sitting there like, 'Yo, you're a freshman! They know you're a freshman. How can you buy this? How can you even do this?' It was not normal. We went to after-parties where some of the DJs had water bottles for players when they came in because they needed to hydrate—except the bottles were full of vodka."

Aaron Hernandez was not a big drinker. Back in Bristol, marijuana had become his drug of choice. And in any case, he didn't like the way that *this* alcohol tasted. He dumped the shots that the waitress had brought into his lemonade. An hour later, at around one in the morning, he went downstairs to head out. But as Aaron made his way toward the exit, a manager stopped him, waving a bill for twelve dollars.

"What about *this?*" the manager said.

Tim Tebow and Shaun Young would both say that the manager—a man named Michael Taphorn—was aggressive. Taphorn was right up in Hernandez's face, they recalled, and "irate." Tebow stepped in to resolve what was rapidly turning into a conflict. A woman standing nearby offered to pay Aaron's bill. But Taphorn ignored her, waved Tebow off, and ordered Hernandez out of the bar.

Ron DeFilippo remembers things differently: according to him, when Hernandez was confronted with the bill he said, "'I don't pay for anything in this town'—like he had celebrity status."

All parties agree that Hernandez walked outside of the bar with Taphorn following close on his heels. Then, accounts diverge. According to Hernandez, Taphorn stayed up in his face. According to Taphorn, Hernandez pushed him a few times on their way out of the bar. Then, standing out on the gray wooden patio, Hernandez lost his temper completely.

"He sucker-punched me," Taphorn would tell the police. Having done so, Hernandez bolted, losing one of his shoes as he ran away.

Taphorn was in terrible pain. The blow had exploded his left eardrum—an injury that would take six weeks to heal. Still, he ran after Aaron. Along with some of the bar staff, who had come outside to back their manager up, he called out to Hernandez: "Come back!"

Aaron did not come back. Taphorn picked up the shoe—a black sneaker. It was still in his hands when the police arrived.

CHAPTER 10

Hernandez had been in Gainesville for less than four months. He was a Gator, but hadn't played in an actual game yet.

Michael Taphorn had recognized him all the same.

"The freshman tight end," Taphorn told Sergeant Rowe of the Gainesville Police Department.

After taking the manager's statement, Rowe placed a call to Tim Tebow.

"It will be in Hernandez's best interest to give us his side of the story," he said, and Tebow agreed. He was relieved when Sergeant Rowe went on assure him that no one would alert the press, and that his own name would be kept out of the media.

Two hours later, at three in the morning, Rowe got a call back: Hernandez, Tebow, and Young were waiting for him a few blocks away from campus. Upon arrival, the sergeant informed Hernandez of his Miranda rights, but Hernandez chose to tell his side of the story.

Aaron was calm and collected. Mask firmly in place, he told the sergeant he didn't know that the woman who'd brought him the shots was a waitress. He had thought she was a fan. And since he had not ordered the drinks, or liked them, he did not see why he had been asked to pay for them.

But, Hernandez said, Taphorn had "kept advancing" on him. Aaron had called out to Tebow for help. Then, outside of the bar, just to get Taphorn out of his face, he had thrown a punch.

Aaron gave Rowe his Connecticut driver's license. He gave the officer his mother's telephone number. He told Rowe that he and Tebow had already called their coach, Urban Meyer, and described the incident.

Rowe was impressed with the young man. Hernandez was polite and professional. He seemed to be sober. Rowe decided against charging him with underage drinking—that was a matter the university could handle internally. But Aaron was also facing a felony battery charge.

It was up to Taphorn to decide whether he would press the matter.

In the days that followed, Taphorn and Ron DeFilippo both heard from the university. "A couple of people who worked for Urban Meyer, but never really identified themselves, said, 'It's in everybody's best interest if we reprimand the kid, get him under wraps, and let him go his own way,'" DeFilippo recalls. Then, according to DeFilippo, a handler who worked for Meyer rang him up and said: "Let this thing go. Anything you ever need for the Swamp, just give us a call."

In the end, Taphorn changed his mind about pressing

charges. Part of the deal that was struck was that Hernandez would have to come back to the bar to apologize.

Hernandez never did. But he did make another appearance at the bar. According to DeFilippo, sometime after the night of the incident, members of his staff saw Aaron drive by the Swamp, making shooting gestures with his hand. DeFilippo called the university, yet again. He told the official he talked to, "Get the kid under wraps."

But, at the time, school officials had bigger headaches to deal with.

CHAPTER 11

Earlier that month, a few days after April Fool's Day, Aaron Hernandez's teammate Ronnie Wilson had made his way through XS, a nightclub in Gainesville.

Wilson was a sophomore, an offensive guard, and—at 6'4" and 315 pounds—one of the team's biggest players. He was a man who drew glances wherever he went, and on this night, not long after midnight, Wilson got sucked into a nasty exchange with a young man named Frank Fuller.

Despite the way Gators were treated in football-mad Gainesville, it wasn't unusual for tensions to arise between UF players and locals. All around town, and especially in tough neighborhoods, there were thugs, or wannabe thugs, who liked to try the players, or test them. Getting in a player's face gave you a lot of cred in the neighborhood.

Fuller, who was enrolled at a nearby community college, was not a thug. But as tensions rose, Wilson spat on Fuller, slapped him, and punched him. Then he walked out of the club.

Fuller followed, dialed 911, and stayed on the line as he tailed Wilson's BMW down University Avenue. At 13th Street, Wilson made a right. Fuller turned with him. A few blocks later Wilson turned right again and pulled into a UF parking lot. There, he got out and popped the trunk of a blue Crown Victoria.

Fuller expected Wilson to turn around with a baseball bat—or maybe a tire iron—in his hand. That would have been bad enough. What he saw instead was much more frightening.

"He's got, actually, an automatic weapon!" Fuller shouted into his cell phone. "I am extremely fearful for my life right now," he said.

Wilson had taken a step forward and pointed an AK-47 at Fuller's car.

The dispatcher told Fuller to get out of there, fast. "I'm trying to," Fuller shouted as he slammed his car into Reverse. "I'm trying to get away as fast as possible. Oh, shit!"

As he peeled out of the parking lot, Wilson raised the AK toward the sky and fired.

"Oh, shit! Did you hear that?" Fuller yelled.

Wilson would tell the police he had fired the weapon because he had been "afraid for his life." Then, after being suspended by Coach Urban Meyer, the offensive guard copped a plea: Two years' probation and one hundred hours of community service—service that Wilson performed while on suspension. Once he was done, Meyer let him back on the team.

This was the sort of thing that gave Urban Meyer a bad name in certain circles in Gainesville. In Gator Country, it was said, being an actual Gator brought you a boatload of special privileges. It was not that you were *encouraged* to behave badly, *per se*. It was just that, if you *did* behave badly, the odds were better than decent that you would be given another chance.

It was a state of affairs that explained a few of the chances that Aaron Hernandez would get as a Gator. But there was another side to the stories told around town about Urban Meyer and his troublesome players.

Years earlier, while coaching at Utah, Meyer had seen exactly what second chances could mean to troubled kids who had never caught a fair break.

There, a tailback named Marty Johnson had plowed his car into another car and fled the scene. The arrest for drunk driving that followed was Johnson's second—it landed Johnson in jail and brought pressure on Meyer to kick him off of the team. Meyer did that, but he and his wife, Shelley, whose psychiatric speciality was addiction, also visited Johnson in jail. Their eleven-year-old daughter, Gigi, wrote Johnson encouraging letters. Upon Johnson's release, Meyer gave the kid a second shot on the team. He brought Johnson into his home and his life. And, against all odds, Johnson ended up abstaining from alcohol, playing in the Fiesta Bowl, finishing college, and turning his life around.

"Once I got away from my old lifestyle for a while," Johnson said, "it wasn't hard. I have the Meyers and my teammates to thank for that."

But Marty Johnson did not keep assault weapons in the

trunk of his car. He did not threaten people's lives, shoot people in the head, try to strangle women, or deal cocaine outside of the stadium on game days—all incidents involving Gator players that Meyer would have to contend with in 2007.

When he addressed the UF Alumni Association Gators Clubs, Coach Meyer used a certain phrase to describe his team: "The top one percent of one percent," he would say. When it came to the 2006 season, he wasn't wrong: The Gators ended up 13–1, setting a school record by winning both the SEC *and* BCS Championships. The last game of the season was a stunning upset over the number-one ranked Ohio State Buckeyes—the team Urban Meyer now coaches.

But that was the year before Aaron's arrival in Florida. In 2007, Aaron's first year on the team, Meyer's players brought home a record their coach had never asked for and didn't want.

They brought him the NCAA record for most players arrested in the course of a single year.

CHAPTER 12

Coach Meyer did what he could to minimize the damage. What that meant for Aaron Hernandez, in particular, was that Tim Tebow was assigned to keep an eye on the hotheaded player.

Tim and Aaron could not have been much more different. Tebow was the youngest of five children, all of whom had been homeschooled by their deeply religious parents. While Tebow's teammates in Florida partied, fought, got high, and spent time in strip clubs, he stuck to the straight Christian path he had followed since boyhood.

The quarterback was clean-cut, clean-spoken, open about being a virgin and saving himself for marriage. Tebow sang hymns on the sidelines, and on the field he dropped down to one knee, bowed his head, and prayed after victories.

Before long, the phrase "Tebowing" would enter the national vocabulary. It involved striking the same kneeling pose.

Tim wrote references to Bible verses in his eye black. When the NCAA passed a rule that banned players from writing such messages, it became known as "The Tebow Rule."

Like Hernandez, Tebow was an especially versatile player—6′3″, physical. A dual-threat quarterback who was as likely to run with the ball as he was to pass it. And if Hernandez had been an exceptional player in high school, Tebow had been even better. ESPN had aired a documentary about his senior year, and his decision to play for Florida over Alabama, called *Tim Tebow: The Chosen One.*

Now, at the start of Aaron's first full school year in Florida, Aaron and the Chosen One were living next door to each other. On the road, Urban Meyer put them together as roommates. And on the field, Tebow was a constant inspiration. Aaron knew all about a famous game Tim had played as a high school sophomore, in 2003. In the course of that game, a bad tackle broke Tebow's leg. Tim heard the pop and felt the bone moving. But his team was down seventeen points.

"Don't take me out," Tim told his coach, before fighting back against the deficit and tying the game, running for a twenty-nine-yard touchdown *on his broken leg.*

As a Gator, Tebow showed just as much heart. Playing against the Kentucky Wildcats, in October of 2007, Tebow separated his right shoulder but continued to play, beating a tackler and running in the winning touchdown.

Hernandez also scored in that game—it was his first touchdown as a college player. Urban Meyer could see Tebow's influence rubbing off on the tight end. "Aaron used to text me all the time," Meyer recalls, "about him and Tim going to train in the evenings: 'While you're sleeping, I'm working out. We gotta go win a national championship!'"

But in other respects, Aaron was failing, in heroic fashion, to live up to Meyer's expectations.

The coach was especially concerned about Aaron's friends from Bristol. He noticed a difference in Aaron whenever he returned from Connecticut. "It would almost take us a few weeks to get him back to thinking about the team and thinking about what to do right," Meyer says. Time and again, the coach told his players: "You know, we've got to be very cautious about outside influences. Cautious of people who maybe should not be in your life."

Aaron would ignore the advice.

"It wasn't healthy at all," Meyer says of the Bristol influence. Players that Aaron was close with would tell the coach, 'He shouldn't go home. Don't let him go home anymore.'"

DJ told the coach the same thing: "He needs to be around people that are good for him."

But Aaron was loyal to his friends on Lake Avenue. Loyal to his cousin Tanya, and her man, TL, loyal to Carlos Ortiz, and to Bo Wallace. They were the friends who had taken him in after his father's death. No matter the consequence, he never turned his back on any of them.

CHAPTER 13

For all the trouble that Hernandez would get into up in New England, Aaron's teammates on the Gators would always remember him fondly.

"Let me tell you right now, there's not one person in this world who didn't like Hernandez," Ahmad Black says. "We called him 'Chico,' and everybody loved Chico. Everybody in Gainesville. Everybody in the division. Everybody."

Black, who went on to play for the Tampa Bay Buccaneers, came to Gainesville at the same time as Hernandez. Like Aaron's high school friends, he remembers Hernandez as a class clown—someone who'd make funny faces to trip his friends up in public speaking, or pop Ziploc bags in the back of the class to make his professors jump.

"Seven people from my high school, Lakeland High School, came here at the same time," Black explains. "Me, Chris Rainey, Paul Wilson, John Brown, Steven Wilks, and the Pouncey twins, all in one year. "Me, Wilson, and the Pounceys came early, Hernandez came early as well, along with Joe Haden and Cam Newton. Those are the guys that you tend to hang out with. And that was a hell of a class. We arrived right after our team had won the 2006 National Championship. We got to go to the White House and met Bush.

"The Pouncey twins moved in with Hernandez on campus. I moved in with Markihe Anderson. But my best friends on the team were the Pouncey twins. I was always over there. Hernandez was always there. Hernandez went back home to Lakeland with us a couple of times.

"Then our tight end, Cornelius Ingram, got injured.

"Ingram tore his ACL at camp, going into the 2008 season. Hernandez played some significant minutes freshman year, but he wasn't the starter. When Ingram got injured, Aaron picked up right where Ingram had left off and probably was even better. He grew up very fast. We saw a lot of great plays out of him. He was like two totally different people, off the field and on the field.

"Off the field everybody was always together, always joking, having fun. To this day, ninety percent of the guys I talk to are from that team. But that's one of the things that gave us an advantage over other teams. We trusted that the man next to us would get his job done. And we never let anybody down. Hernandez was a significant part of our championship runs. Big plays. But Aaron *always* did big plays. Miami, Tennessee, in that 2008 season. He was the best tight end in the country—and he went hard.

"We had to go hard. Those of us on defense had to be better than the offense. The offense stressed that they had to be better than us. Ultimately that made us a better team.

"But Hernandez was also in there with Percy Harvin. We had Louis Murphy, Riley Cooper, David Nelson, Brandon Frazier, and Harvin at wide receiver. All those guys are NFL players today. We had Tebow at quarterback. We had one Pouncey on the O-line. We had another Pouncey at the O-line. We had Chris Rainey in the backfield. We had Jeff Demps, the fastest eighteen-year-old in the world—*in the world*—at running back. All those guys are first-round, second-round picks. We had studs all over the field. Who wouldn't want to bring it to the offense? We had to show our best stuff.

"But Aaron's thing with me was, he'd say something weird that made zero sense. He'd come up to me and say, 'If the hamburger eats the ketchup and climbs the tree, who's going to come to the ocean?'

"He would just bust out laughing. I'd think of the most random thing to say to him. Then he would say something back. Everybody loved Chico. We laughed together. We went to the White House together, again, after winning the 2009 National Championship. We met Obama. We ate together. Hamburgers. Pizza. Whatever we wanted. It's catching up to me now, but back then we burned it off super-fast. And Chico was always the life of the party."

Others who knew Aaron in Gainesville would speak about him in similar terms. After a rocky start as a freshman, Aaron became a ferociously driven football player. As a member of Florida's student body, he was quick to make jokes, polite and deferential when he had to be, and disruptive when it served his purpose.

"He had a beautiful smile on his face," Urban Meyer recalls. "Later in his career, it seemed to change."

Even in Florida, it came down to this: Aaron loved to be the center of attention. But he was also impressionable and eager to please, and when the people around him made questionable decisions, he tended to go along.

"Here's the thing about being around violence," a person who encountered Aaron up in New England would say. "One time is bad luck. Two times, you have bad habits. Three times, you're a goon. Violence is only around you so often *by mistake*. After a while, you are who you hang out with. And Hernandez did not have the best taste in friends."

CHAPTER 14

Cops in Gainesville called it "the procession." Every Saturday night, hordes of people spilled out of the clubs and made their way down University Avenue, stopping here, stopping there, partying, fighting, causing trouble for three blocks, five blocks, or more. It was not unusual for thirty or forty cops to occupy a two-to-three-block area, babysitting the college students for hours on end, doing all that they could to get the kids home and keep them safe until Sunday morning.

Now, on the last Saturday in September of 2007, with school back in session, the procession was back in full force.

The day had gone badly for Florida—the Gators had lost 20-17 to the Auburn Tigers. Aaron Hernandez had played in the game and needed to blow off steam afterward. That night, he went to a nightclub called Venue.

Venue was a relatively new club in Gainesville, but it had already become a favorite with UF's football players. Previously, it had been some other club. Before that it had been something else—a restaurant called Shakers. Students came and went, no one remembered. But what Aaron Hernandez knew, as a regular participant in the procession, was that when the doors closed, at two in the morning, the crowd would regroup in a parking lot behind the building. Sometimes there were fights.

Sometimes, arrests were made.

It was not the place a player as volatile as Aaron should have been. Certainly not on a day where the game had gone badly. But, try as he did to keep an eye out for his teammate, Tim Tebow couldn't be there for every minute of Aaron's life. And tonight, a former Gator named Reggie Nelson was back in town.

Nelson was in the NFL now—he'd been the Jacksonville Jaguars' first pick in that year's draft. Down from Jacksonville, he was riding high in Venue's VIP booth. Chris Harris, who had been drafted by the Chicago Bears in 2005, was with him. Mike and Maurkice Pouncey were also there, along with several other players and soon-to-be players.

A bouncer named Antwuan Hamm would recall that Nelson had not been seen at Venue for some time. But Hamm had already gotten to know the Pounceys, who were there *all* the time and—according to the bouncer—*always* spoiling for a fight. They weren't the only ones. A local man named Justin Glass had also gone to Venue that night. He had brought two friends along to the club: a man named Randall Cason and an older friend, Corey Smith, whose nickname was "Squirt."

Squirt had two kids, a good job, and a white Crown Vic.

There was nothing thuggish about him. In fact, he had taken Glass under his wing and done his best to keep him off the streets. But Glass was caught between Squirt, the good father, and Cason, who was more of a negative influence.

According to Gainesville PD, Cason and Glass had gone to the club looking for trouble.

Neither man wanted to listen to anything Squirt had to say.

According to Randall Cason, everything that followed stemmed from an incident that had taken place the previous week—an altercation Cason's brother had gotten into with several UF football players. Now, in the dark, crowded club, Cason found himself in the middle of a similar altercation.

Words were exchanged, and menacing glances. A football player reached out and tried to grab a chain Cason was wearing around his neck—but the chain was too thick to break.

Reggie Nelson would say that, when he arrived at the club, Aaron Hernandez told him about an incident involving the Pouncey twins: according to Aaron, *Cason* had snatched a chain away from one of the Pounceys.

According to Hamm, the club bouncer, it was Justin Glass—and not Cason—who got into a confrontation with the Pounceys. Hamm would say that one of the twins approached Glass and said, "I want my motherfucking chain."

"What chain?" Glass had replied. "I ain't got no damn chain."

At that point, Hamm said, club security escorted both of the Pouncey twins out of the club. Having done so, they also ejected Glass.

The Pouncey twins would say that, afterward, out in the

club parking lot, a "black man" who had snatched a chain away from Mike Pouncey had taunted them, tugging at his shirt as if to indicate to the Gators that he had a gun in his waistband.

The accounts contradict one another, to an extent. But the involved parties seem to agree that Reggie Nelson stepped in to defuse the increasingly tense situation, getting in between the Pouncey twins and the locals.

Nelson knew Cason socially. Trying to broker a peace, he told Cason that the players didn't want any trouble.

Cason told him that the chain had already been given away.

Cason and Nelson ended up shaking hands and hugging. Then, Cason and his friends took off in Squirt's car. The football players took off in their own cars. Aaron Hernandez went with them.

The whole affair might have ended then and there, peacefully.

But, as it turned out, the night was just starting.

CHAPTER 15

The traffic was thick as Squirt's Crown Vic inched its way down University Avenue. The clubs were all closed now. The streets were full of people.

The three men were headed to see a couple of women they knew. The night was warm and the car's windows were down. They had just passed a McDonald's on their right. On the opposite corner there was a sign that welcomed visitors to the UF campus.

Glass was driving Squirt's car. On the floor next to him, hidden under a black T-shirt, there was a gun—a Taurus 9mm that had been stolen from the Jacksonville sheriff's office.

Randall Cason was in the back seat. On the floor, under his foot, he had a Smith & Wesson .40-caliber pistol—a gun from which the serial number had been filed.

Squirt, in the passenger seat, was the only unarmed man in the vehicle.

Stopping at a red light, Glass noticed some girls driving in the next lane. He pointed them out to Cason. But what Cason saw when he looked over was Reggie Nelson's Tahoe, a few cars behind their own.

Cason thought they had settled their argument back at the club. Now, he guessed they had not.

"They're following us," Cason said. But the light was still red, the traffic still bumper-to-bumper.

If they *were* being followed, there wasn't much they could do about it.

Suddenly, Cason would say, he noticed two men on the sidewalk: Reggie Nelson and the freshman, Aaron Hernandez. Cason would claim that Hernandez walked up to the Crown Vic and looked inside. Then, Cason says, Hernandez raised his hand, shoved a gun through the open car window, and pulled the trigger.

"Oh, my God!" Cason yelled as blood splattered all over the Crown Vic's upholstery. Squirt slumped forward, slowly. Glass yelled out—he'd been hit, too, in the arm. Glass jumped out of the car and Cason jumped out after him, gun in hand, and racked the weapon. A bottle of Coors Light that Cason had been holding fell out of the car and rolled and rolled down the street as Cason yelled: "You killed my friend!"

According to Cason, Hernandez was already too far away to hear him, running through a Holiday Inn parking lot, toward the McDonald's. Nelson also appeared to have fled. But Cason could see the Tahoe—someone else must have been driving it now—heading northbound on 13th.

At that very moment, a stranger in some other car

tossed a full pack of Black Cat firecrackers out into the street.

The firecrackers popped and smoked on the pavement. Pedestrians out on the sidewalk ducked. Drivers piled out of their cars, shouting and pointing in every direction.

The scene could not have been more chaotic.

CHAPTER 16

In Sandra Hines's Gainesville neighborhood, a phone ringing in the middle of the night only meant one thing: bad news.

On the morning of September 30, 2007, the call came at four in the morning.

Sandra jumped out of bed and ran to answer it, already expecting the worst.

"Hello?" she said.

"Is this you, Ma?"

Most of Squirt's friends called her "Ma."

"Yeah, it's me," Sandra said. "What's wrong?"

"You need to get to the hospital. He's been shot!"

Sandra took a deep breath.

"Is he dead?" she asked.

Squirt's friend paused before answering: "I don't know."

Sandra's niece, her other son, and her mother, Barbara, lived with her in the apartment. She woke her niece up but left her son and her mother sleeping.

Barbara had raised Squirt while Sandra worked evening shifts at South Florida State Mental Hospital in Miami. Sandra knew how upset her mother would be, so she and her niece left quietly. Slipping out of the apartment, they got into a Buick Century Sandra had recently borrowed from an out-of-town friend. The sky was still black and Sandra took the long route to Shands Hospital—a route that cut through UF's campus. The school was quiet at that hour, and Sandra prayed as she drove.

"Lord," she said, "whatever your will it will be done, not mine. I don't know what I'm going to face right now."

In the hospital, Sandra was led straight to Trauma One. There, in order to prove that she was Corey's mother, she told the doctors about a scar he had on his shin. "When I lived in Miami he would come visit," she said. "He loved mangoes, and next door there was a mango tree. He said, 'Can I ask the neighbor about the mango?' I said, 'If he's home.' He didn't ask. He got stuck on the fence and scarred his leg."

It was good enough for the doctors, who let her in to see her son. Corey was alive, but bandages covered his head and his face. *He doesn't look like my son,* Sandra thought. There were tubes everywhere and the doctors asked Sandra to agree to brain surgery. They had to cut open the skull, a doctor explained, in order to dig out the bullet.

The bullet had exploded part of Corey's brain. The doctors did not know if he would make it. If he did pull through, the doctors said, it was not clear that he would be able to walk, or talk, again.

CHAPTER 17

Back at the crime scene, witnesses interviewed by Gainesville PD said that the shooter was black. A thin man with cornrows, they said. About 5'10" in height.

But, at the hospital, Cason swore that he knew what he had seen. After the shooting, he'd jumped back into Squirt's Crown Vic. With Glass at the wheel, they had peeled off toward Shands Hospital, which had the nearest ER. On the way, Squirt bled, badly—the shooter had hit him in the back of the head. But Glass, who had been shot in the arm, thought that Squirt was still breathing.

The car's insides looked like something out of *The Texas Chain Saw Massacre*. There was blood and brain matter on the dashboard, blood on the windshield, blood on the seats and the ceiling. A few spent shells rolled around on the floor. One shell had lodged in the ashtray.

Blood poured down Glass's arm as he steered.

At the hospital, they carried Squirt in. Glass was taken to a trauma wing on the hospital's tenth floor. Cason went back outside, to where the Crown Vic was parked, and found the police there waiting for him.

"This is all my fault!" Cason yelled. He told the cops that Squirt had been shot because of the altercation he'd had at the club.

"It should have been me that was shot," Cason said.

That morning, Sandra signed off on her son's surgery. Corey was wheeled into an operating room, and doctors spent hours removing the bullet and performing a "bone flap" procedure, sewing the part of Corey's skull that had been removed into his stomach, where it would need to remain for the next nine months.

While the doctors worked, Sandra called her sisters to tell them about what had happened. There was hollering and crying. Sandra asked them to bring Barbara by. By nine thirty—Corey was still in surgery—the waiting room was full of family and friends. Corey's godmother was there, along with his ex-girlfriend, and they were *mad*—mad enough to tear up a garbage can in the waiting room.

After his surgery, Corey was wheeled into the hospital's trauma unit, where Sandra was finally allowed to see him. Corey was already coming to. He seemed to recognize his family. And he was able to speak.

"But he didn't call me Ma, which was strange," Sandra says. She and her sisters showed him pictures of people he knew to see if he recognized them. He did. But as he did so, he kept pounding his chest.

Sandra realized that he was hitting himself where he'd been defibrillated—Corey's heart had stopped more than once.

Sandra asked her son a question: "Who shot you?"

Corey told her: Two men were involved. Then, to indicate the skin tone of one of the men, Corey started to flip his hand over, from front to back. "It was like this," he said, showing the palm of his hand. Then he flipped his hand around: "Not this."

To make sure Sandra understood, he flipped his hand over again and showed his palm: "He was this color," Squirt said.

Light-skinned. Like Aaron Hernandez.

PART THREE

CHAPTER 18

Patty Nixon's phone rang at two thirty in the morning. Her husband slept through the ringing—Nixon's husband slept through *everything*—but Nixon, a detective in Gainesville's police department, sensed that the call was important.

It was.

A shooting had occurred on the 1200 block of West University Avenue.

Nixon knew the location—right across the street from a sign marking one of the entrances to the University of Florida. She was told that there were two victims. One had been shot in the arm. The other had taken a bullet to the head. The man who'd been shot in the head was alive but "circling the drain," Nixon recalls.

The detective got dressed and woke her husband. He'd have to get the kids to school that morning. For now, Gainesville PD was treating the case as a homicide, and Nixon knew from experience that homicide calls could keep her out in the field for twenty-four hours, or more.

Nixon made a quick stop at the crime scene on her way down to the hospital. *Of all the places to do something like that,* she thought when she saw the site of the shooting.

The street would have been mobbed with students at the time that the crime had occurred. *Whoever the shooter or shooters had been, they were not the smartest tools in the shed,* Nixon thought.

By the time Nixon got to the hospital, at half past four in the morning, a crowd had gathered in the parking lot. The police were there, along with Randall Cason, who had been in the backseat of the Crown Vic at the time of the shooting. "It should have been me!" Cason was shouting.

Nixon had been told, over her police radio, that Cason was describing the shooter as a 6'3" or 6'4", 240-pound "Hawaiian" or "Hispanic" man. Cason had said that the man had been wearing jean shorts and a green collared shirt. He had tattoos. More likely than not, Cason had said, he was a member of the UF football team.

Cason had also told the police that Reggie Nelson had been standing out on the sidewalk at the time that the shooting occurred. Somehow, Cason said, the Pouncey twins were also involved.

Nixon knew who the Pounceys were. She knew who Nelson was. But she could not place the man Cason had identified as the shooter. She decided to drive Cason down to the station herself.

There, she put Cason in an interview room and called UF

Police Detective Brian Norman, who gave her the number for Coach Urban Meyer's personal assistant, Jon Clark. By six thirty in the morning, Nixon had Clark on the line. "We need to talk to the Pouncey twins about an attempted murder that happened tonight," she told the assistant. Then she asked Clark if he was aware of any white, Hispanic, or Hawaiian men that the Pouncey twins were hanging out with.

Clark gave the detective one name: "Aaron Hernandez."

CHAPTER 19

At seven o'clock that morning, Detective Nixon called Jon Clark again. The assistant had said that he was on his way to pick up Urban Meyer. He had promised to call her back about setting up an interview with the Pounceys.

But half an hour had passed, Clark had not called, and when Nixon called him again Clark said he was busy and told the detective, once again, that he would call her back.

Every minute counted in an investigation like this. Now, with the clock ticking, Nixon began to feel as if the university was stalling her. "It took an extraordinary amount of time to get those guys over there," the detective says. "We had to go through the University of Florida to find out who Hernandez was, and that took an excruciatingly long amount of time."

While waiting for Clark to arrive, Nixon called Detective Norman and asked him to send a photograph of Aaron Hernandez over e-mail. Then she turned her attention to Randall Cason.

According to Gainesville PD, Cason was a suspected gangbanger. According to Detective Nixon, the second man in the car, Justin Glass, "was a wannabe gangbanger." Squirt— Corey Smith, who had been shot in the head—was the only straight-up civilian who had been in the Crown Vic that night.

"Cason was the only one saying Hernandez was involved," Nixon says. "The shooter, according to every other uninvolved witness, was a black male. 5′8″, corn rows…Hernandez looks nothing like that. He's a very big guy. We knew we had a credibility problem right off the bat."

Once the e-mail with Hernandez's photo came through, Nixon showed Cason a photo lineup: six men, including Hernandez. When Cason pointed Hernandez out, Nixon called Clark yet again and told him she needed to question Hernandez, along with the Pouncey twins. Clark told her that the players were being called into the football office and would be brought to the station after that.

Nixon called Clark several more times that morning. Then, at around ten, another one of Urban Meyer's assistants—a man named Hiram de Fries—finally did bring the Pouncey twins and Hernandez down to the station.

Why the delay? As the detective understood it, the university had taken the time to call in its lawyer.

Nixon knew how things worked in Gainesville. "It's a big business and big money," she says.

"They can have lawyers, that's no problem. But the amount of time it took them to respond . . . This is a really serious case: a shooting where somebody was supposed to die. Thank God, he didn't. But, in my eyes, a four-and-a-half-hour response time was pretty extraordinary and unacceptable."

CHAPTER 20

Down at the station, Patty Nixon and other police officers were talking about the delay. When the Pouncey twins and Aaron Hernandez finally showed up, the conversation shifted.

"Cops who were football fans knew that the Pounceys were promising," Nixon says. "But I remember them talking about how soft they were physically, saying, 'Wait until the strength coaches get ahold of them.' They were big guys in stature, but soft. Hernandez, on the other hand, was a physical specimen—even at seventeen."

Mike Pouncey, Maurkice Pouncey, and Aaron Hernandez were placed in separate interview rooms.

Each room was small, with a tall ceiling, "just like you see on TV," she says. Each one had a desk, two chairs, and audiovisual recording equipment. Nevertheless, Hernandez felt comfortable enough, in this austere and threatening environment, simply to doze off.

"I was a little frustrated to walk in to see him sleeping," Nixon recalls. Instead of waking him, she went to question the Pouncey twins.

According to the detective's report, Maurkice told Nixon that "he, his brother, Aaron Hernandez, and a friend of theirs...went to the Venue. Around 0130 hrs, a man snatched his thick gold chain off his brother Mike's neck. The chain was thick with a large 'Jesus' head' as a medallion. Pouncey stated the club was so crowded that he didn't see who snatched it.

"After the club was closing, Pouncey said, they were standing outside. A male walked up to them and said, 'I got your chain' and pulled on his shirt like he had a gun. [Pouncey] said there was such a crowd, he couldn't be certain he had one but his actions were indicating he had one. The black male also said, 'I rule these streets.' [Pouncey] said he told Reggie Nelson about the chain incident. Nelson told him there was nothing he could do about it. Pouncey said Nelson spoke with the male later and told him nobody wanted any trouble."

Mike Pouncey told the detective that he had left Venue "somewhere around 0129 hrs. He said a male snatched his large gold chain. He didn't see who because the club was so crowded but he told an unknown bouncer. Pouncey said they went to the parking lot, where the black male who had snatched the chain approached them.

"He said, 'I got something for you. You need to stick to football.' He pulled the chain out and told him to come get it. The male kept backing up as [if] he had a gun. Reggie Nelson told us not to worry about it. We left the area at that time."

The statements lined up, more or less. Both twins told Nixon that, after the incident, they accompanied Nelson and Aaron Hernandez to a campus apartment belonging to their friend Markihe Anderson. Then, after twenty or thirty minutes at Anderson's place, they had gone to get some food at a Checkers restaurant—this would have been at two-thirty in the morning, or thereabouts. Afterward, they had gone back to Anderson's apartment.

There was just one discrepancy between the twins' statements: Maurkice Pouncey said that Hernandez had been with them the whole time.

Mike said Hernandez had left the Checkers before them, at around three in the morning.

CHAPTER 21

Down in the lobby, Patty Nixon's colleague Detective Michael Schentrup was interviewing Reggie Nelson.

Nelson told the detective that Aaron Hernandez had been the one who had told him about Randall Cason snatching Mike Pouncey's chain. Outside of the club, Pouncey himself had pointed Cason out as the chain snatcher. Because Nelson knew Cason, he spoke with the man. Cason told him that the chain had already been given away. Nelson told Cason that the players didn't want any trouble. According to Nelson, they had left, after that, on good terms, heading, with some other players, to Markihe Anderson's campus apartment, away from the school's football stadium.

Detective Schentrup relayed this information to Patty Nixon. He and Nixon read Nelson his Miranda rights. Then they questioned the NFL player again.

Nixon asked Nelson if he was covering anything up— anything pertaining to the shooting. Nelson denied it. He seemed to be open and cooperative. At around noon, Nelson was released.

Nixon released the Pounceys, too. Finally, at half past noon, she and Schentrup went to the interview room where Hernandez was sleeping.

Aaron woke up as soon as they entered. Although she had her doubts regarding Cason's statement, and his fingering of Hernandez, she read Aaron his Miranda rights before starting the interview. "I didn't want any gray area," Nixon recalls.

But Hernandez said, "I'm not going to say anything. I want my lawyer present. I'm sorry, my lawyer told me to say that."

Sorry or not, that was the extent of his cooperation with Gainesville PD.

That afternoon, Nixon and other detectives interviewed several eyewitnesses to the shooting. Every person they spoke with identified the shooter as a black man with corn rows and a green polo shirt—under six feet tall—slim. No one said anything about a Hawaiian, white, or Hispanic man— certainly not one who was as tall as Aaron, weighed 240 pounds, and had a buzz cut.

And so, at six in the evening, Nixon and Schentrup picked Randall Cason up at his apartment and asked to interview him again. Down at the station, Cason admitted that he had *assumed* Hernandez had been the shooter—assumed it because of the incident in the club. Cason also said that he hadn't seen *anything at all*. That he'd balled himself up inside the Crown Vic, trying not to get shot. By the end of the interview Cason had rescinded his initial identification of Aaron

Hernandez *and* Reggie Nelson, and blamed the chain snatching on someone else—"one of his boys," Cason said.

Fourteen hours into her investigation, Patty Nixon had gotten exactly nowhere.

That Monday, Nixon called Aaron Hernandez and warned him to be careful out on the streets. Cason had put it out there, she said, that Hernandez had done the shooting. Hernandez thanked the detective and said he'd be careful.

On Tuesday, Nixon visited Corey Smith at Shands. The shooting victim had trouble remembering words, but was much better off, overall, than expected. The detective told him about her investigation. She also asked him if he was holding anything back.

Squirt swore to her that he wasn't.

As far as the detective was concerned, she had hit a dead end.

That fall and winter, Nixon made several attempts to interview Cason and Glass.

"I continued to call Cason and continued to show up at his house," the detective says. "There were times I sat up on his house trying to contact him...I felt like they knew who the shooter was...I just felt like they were definitely holding something back—it felt like they either, not *knew* the shooter, but certainly could give me a better description of the shooter. But as far as being successful, getting that information out of either one of them—no. I got no additional information out of them, and no cooperation, which was frustrating."

The detective kept on the Pouncey twins, too: "I decided at one point to take a different approach with them and act like after hearing that these chains were being popped off of their neck—bless their heart, you know what I mean?—that to me says they were victims of robbery. I tried to approach them—'let me take care of you, let me arrest somebody who actually tried to rob you guys and let's talk about it'—and let me do it that way. They wanted no part of that. But then I ended up approaching them again at another point, where I actually met them at their lawyer's office, to see if I could appeal to their humanity. I described what the victim was going through and what he had to go through and what was in front of him in terms of surgeries and just not getting his life back, the difficulty he's having, and that sort of thing. I was pretty sure they knew what had happened. But again—unsuccessful."

Seven months later, Corey Smith came down to the police station, his head encased in the blue helmet he would have to wear for nine months following his surgery.

An E-FIT (Electronic Facial Identification Technique) computer program was used to make a composite of the man who had shot Smith in the head.

The man in the digital sketch looked nothing like Aaron Hernandez.

In Patty Nixon's estimation, the University of Florida remained less than cooperative as the investigation dragged on. The case had been frustrating enough from the beginning. Now it had reached a dead end.

Was Randall Cason lying when he fingered Aaron Hernandez for the shooter? Or was he lying when he recanted, and said that he had no idea who the shooter was?

Patty Nixon did not trust Cason at all. But the school had stalled her, the Pouncey twins had refused to talk. Aaron himself had refused to cooperate. The detective simply did not have enough information to connect the dots. Nixon did not believe that Aaron had been the shooter. She did not even believe that Aaron was *connected* to the shooting. But, given how little she'd been given to work with, there wasn't much she could do to disprove Cason's original accusation.

In the end, she could neither arrest nor exonerate. As a result, rumors about Aaron's alleged involvement in the shooting would never be put to rest.

CHAPTER 22

Patty Nixon had been disappointed by the "extraordinary and unacceptable" amount of time the University of Florida had taken before delivering Aaron Hernandez and his fellow Gators into police custody. But were the university's actions a part of a community-wide culture of impunity that had risen up around the team?

"It's Gator Country," Corey Smith's mother, Sandra, says, when asked about the climate in Gainesville and her own sense that, in Corey's case, justice has never been served. "When they say, 'Gator Country,' they *mean* it."

"We were national champions," a teammate of Aaron's recalls. "We were walking around with rings on. They had lists of our names at the clubs. If we wanted to get in, they just looked down the roster: 'There he is. Let him in.' It was very accommodating. We could do whatever we wanted to. Everyone knew us. We were celebrities. We ran the city."

No one could argue that, in Gainesville, the University of

Florida, and its 50,000-person student body, played an out-sized role. The university's 88,000-seat football stadium—which was often filled above capacity for Gators games—could fit two-thirds of the city's entire population. Around town, you'd see stores, shops, and companies with names like Gator Fever, Gator Mania, Gator Cuts, Gator Nails, Gator Cross Fit, and Gator Hydroponics. But, popular as the Gators were, there were those who bristled at the suggestion that UF's football players were given free rein in the city.

Bill Cervone, a University of Florida alumnus who is currently serving his fifth term as a State Attorney in Gainesville, says that, over the years, "way too many" Gators have gotten themselves into trouble—usually for "insignificant college kid stuff." But to him, "the idea that the university runs this town is way overblown."

"It's true to say that economically it's the engine that drives Gainesville," Cervone says. "We would be a much different community if the university wasn't here. Obviously. But it's way overblown to say that anyone around here, certainly law enforcement, kowtows to the university."

"The coaching staff you have asked about are no longer here at the University of Florida, and the incidents involving Mr. Hernandez did not occur on campus," university representatives say.

They continue: "UF has always and remains willing to cooperate fully with the Gainesville Police Department, which led all investigations regarding Mr. Hernandez while he was a student. We are not aware of any information—then or now—that requires action by the university.

"There was a time when the number of football player

arrests was unacceptable and we are mindful of that. Our highest priority is to help these young men succeed in collegiate football and academics while growing them as leaders along the way, and many of them do.

"But we don't always succeed. Some of our students— including student athletes—come from difficult backgrounds and bring with them lifelong problems. Sometimes it is not possible to overcome those challenges in the relatively short period of time these students are at the university."

To his credit, Urban Meyer did his best to mentor Hernandez, making himself available to Aaron day and night. It was an extraordinary investment of the coach's time—although, of course, Aaron was an extraordinary player.

"Aaron was unique," Meyer says. "In a thirty-one-year career, I've never seen one like him. His route-running and athleticism. I don't know if I *will* see another one. And I didn't see it at first. I was disappointed in the guy that recruited him. I was disappointed in the player. I didn't see the competitive spirit. But in the second year, in 2008 and 2009, we used him as much as we've ever used any player. He was the guy you would go into the game saying, 'He's one of the best players in America. Get him the ball.'

"He loved the game. He was extremely smart—a truly intelligent player. We're a very complicated offense. We did a lot of things with him. He was a shovel runner. He was a corner-out runner. He could run all the routes. We isolated him to run the wide receiver screens. We could do everything with him."

Meyer had a daily routine: in the mornings, he'd study the

Bible. Aaron asked the coach if they could do that together. "Absolutely," Meyer told him.

"So we'd sit there. That was every morning for quite a while. Then it started to be once a week. We'd usually take a scripture verse, or he'd read a part. I'd have him read it, and we'd talk about it: 'What's it mean?' Then we'd pray together and he'd go about his day. He was asking for help. It was very obvious. He was over at my house quite often. He was very close with my kids, with my wife. He would come over by himself. He just wanted to experience family. That was almost his catharsis, his time, his release. Once in a while, I would hear about his tough side. I'd confront it. But I didn't *feel* it until later on in his career. And then, you know—he just seemed to change. We didn't have the Bible studies later on. The deep conversations stopped—and I *would* try to have them. He had his own way of dealing with it. And that concerned a lot of us."

CHAPTER 23

It was August 30, 2008, the first game of Aaron's sophomore season at the University of Florida. UF was playing Hawaii, but Aaron was on the sidelines, dressed in the #81 jersey that marked his position as a tight end but wearing the kind of walking boot used by injured athletes. Among Gator fans, rumor had it that the walking boot was worn by players who had gotten themselves into trouble. Other players had worn it previously, and the word in those cases had usually been that the players had failed drug tests and been made to wear the boot as punishment.

Aaron had spent his freshman year protecting the kickoff returner on special teams (as units who are only on field when the ball is kicked off, punted, or returned, are known). "He'd be part of the wedge and just block," a teammate remembers.

As a sophomore, Aaron was determined to show Urban Meyer what he could do.

"Only so many can play, especially for Coach Meyer," the teammate explains. "Aaron was on special teams to start, but he just took off from there. He was an animal out there. A force to be reckoned with. He could block. He was strong. He was fast for his size, he could catch, and that package of awesomeness—they just exploited it."

And yet, despite all he had done to prove himself, here Aaron was, on the sidelines, wearing the boot, watching his team trounce Hawaii 56-10.

Luckily for Hernandez, Meyer believed in second chances. The following week, in a game against Miami, the coach finally put Aaron in. In the Gators' first possession, Hernandez caught a fourteen-yard touchdown pass from Tebow.

The roar that went up in the stadium set the tone for the rest of the game. The Gators went on to crush Miami, 26-3.

For their third game of the season—their first away from home—the Gators faced Tennessee. Hernandez read the Bible with his coach in the morning. Once again, Meyer had picked him to start in the game.

Football was big in Tennessee—Knoxville's Neyland Stadium could hold 100,000 people. The teams were evenly matched. In 2007, the Volunteers had won the SEC East title—whereas the Gators had come up empty, finishing the season at 9–4. But, the Gators had beaten the Volunteers in their last two meetings, the last time by a margin of just one point.

There was no part of this game that Urban Meyer was taking for granted.

The Gators' first possession against the Volunteers resulted in a forty-four-yard drive. Just over three minutes into the game, the Gators were positioned at 1st and goal. In the huddle, Tim Tebow—who had won the Heisman the previous year—gave out instructions: Fake pass to Percy Harvin, run right, touchdown. But Tennessee's defensive line was jumpy after letting the Gators' offense get so deep into their territory on the first drive. When Harvin broke right, he found himself up against a wall of orange jerseys.

Tebow faked the pass, but the Volunteer tackles rushed through cracks in the Gator line. The quarterback's options were running out fast. Dodging a tackle, Tebow spun and drove left to run the ball in himself.

Somehow, he saw, Hernandez had managed to get himself into the open.

Tebow jumped and made the toss.

The ball hit Hernandez square between the eight and the one on his jersey. For two games running, he'd scored the first Gator touchdown on passes from Tebow. Now, in the end zone, Aaron let the ball drop at his feet, spread his arms out like Christ on the cross, and felt the crowd roar all around him.

By the end of the season, the Gators were back in the number-one slot in the college rankings, having lost just one game (to Ole Miss)—by one point—in the season.

It had been a stellar showing for the team—and, especially, for Aaron Hernandez. The sophomore tight end was the talk of the town.

On January 8, 2009, the Gators traveled to Miami Gardens for the BCS National Championship Game against the second-ranked Oklahoma Sooners. Almost 80,000 fans jammed the stands of Dolphin Stadium—this was beyond capacity, and nearly twice the number of fans that would scream for Madonna, at the same stadium, later that year. The fifty million people watching at home set a record for a college game, and in eighty-two movie theaters in thirty cities across the nation, thousands of people paid to watch a 3D broadcast.

Tim Tebow, who been writing "Phil 4:13" ("I can do all things through Christ who strengthens me") in his eye black during the season, had switched to "John 3:16" for this game:

"For God so loved the world that he gave his one and only Son, that whoever believes in him shall not perish but have eternal life."

During the game, more than ninety million people Googled the verse, which also trended to #1 on Twitter and Facebook.

"John 3:16" made an even greater impression on Aaron Hernandez. Years later, when he was alone in his prison cell, it would come back to him in a way that continues to haunt his friends and loved ones.

The game got off to a slow start. By halftime, the score was still 7-7. Then, in the locker room, Tebow gave his teammates a motivational speech that Bear Bryant himself would have been proud of.

"Get in here!" he said. "Get in here right now! Thirty minutes! For the rest of your life!...I promise you one thing. We're going to hit somebody and we're going to move the ball down the field and score a touchdown. I guarantee you that."

Consciously or not, Tebow was quoting—and mangling—

James Van Der Beek's speech in the 1999 film *Varsity Blues*. But the quarterback's delivery was everything, and his teammates responded in kind.

"Look at me!" Tebow shouted. "Look at me! We got thirty minutes for the rest of our lives. *Thirty minutes for the rest of our lives! Let's go!*"

In the second half, Tebow made good on his promise. By the end of the game, he'd completed eighteen of thirty passes for 231 yards and two touchdowns.

Playing on a sore ankle, wide receiver Percy Harvin managed 121 yards and scored a touchdown.

Aaron Hernandez caught five passes for fifty-seven yards—another impressive showing.

The final score, 24-14, won the Gators their second National Championship in three years.

All in all, Aaron had finished the season with thirty-four receptions, 381 yards, and five touchdowns.

Eight days later, Terri Hernandez married Aaron's cousin Tanya's ex-husband, Jeffrey Cummings, in Las Vegas.

It appears that Aaron did not attend the ceremony.

CHAPTER 24

In the 2009 season, Hernandez led the Gators in receptions, with sixty-eight for 850 yards and five touchdowns—two of them in the same game, against rival Florida State. In December, he won the Mackey Award, given annually to the best collegiate tight end, along with the All-American and All-Southeastern Conference first-team picks.

After the Gators won the 2010 Sugar Bowl that January, there seemed to be no question that Aaron Hernandez had earned a spot as a first-round pick for the NFL. He seemed to have every reason to skip senior year and enter the upcoming draft. But Aaron also knew that there were questions about his behavior and his drug use—questions that he would have to address at the league's upcoming Scouting Combine in Indiana.

To prepare, Aaron spent several weeks on the West Coast, where Brian Murphy, the founder of Athletes First—the sports agency Aaron had signed with—oversaw his training for the NFL Combine and Pro Day.

"He flew out to California, with his brother, and lived here for two and a half months," Murphy says. "That's what we do with all our recruits. These days, we spend about $75,000, $100,000 on each person. We have our own training facility. They train there. They work out with our tight end coaches. We give them a physical therapist, a soft tissue specialist, a mental health specialist. We teach them the ins and outs of the NFL.

"We got to spend every day with Aaron. We talked about his past. We talked about where he grew up. We talked about his dad. We talked about his mom. We talked about everything. I really got to know him well.

"The idea is to get these players ready for the draft and ready for life. You're not in Florida anymore. You can't be late for meetings. You can't play by your own rules. And Aaron tried his hardest."

In February 2010, Aaron joined Tim Tebow, Maurkice Pouncey, Brandon Spikes, and six other Gators who had flown to the Combine in Indianapolis.

Aaron had torn a muscle in his back and stood on the sidelines as dozens of scouts, assistants, and coaches watched his teammates drill and work out. The prospects were tested for their speed, strength, and stamina, for their intelligence—even for the flexibility of their joints.

By the end of the testing, few of Aaron's teammates had impressed the scouts.

More than one scout voiced his doubts about Tebow, worrying about the quarterback's accuracy and release speed. But if the scouts were skeptical about Florida's star QB, they were fascinated by Aaron Hernandez.

"He weighed in, got measured, did the body test," Brian Murphy said. "Most importantly, he did all of the interviews. He had an inordinate amount of interviews with the teams. There's some physical testing he did not do. But the reality with Aaron was, no one in the NFL cared about watching him physically work out. Everyone knew he was a freak of nature. They didn't want to waste time. They didn't care. They wanted to spend time with him. They wanted to interview him in those fifteen-minute slots. Everyone wanted to see what he was like in person."

For all of his charm, Aaron did not do well in the interviews. The NFL scouts seemed to see right through his mask.

"Self-esteem is quite low," one would note. "Not well-adjusted emotionally, not happy, moods unpredictable, not stable, doesn't take much to set him off, but not an especially jumpy guy."

"It was pretty well known that he had failed some drug tests at Florida, and there were questions about his maturity that come along with that," another scout told *Boston Globe* reporter Shalise Manza Young. "You worried about the people he hung out with."

"The year before he came out, I was at their Pro Day, and I remember seeing the Pounceys, and then him," an AFC college director told NFL Network reporter Albert Breer. "It was very clear that they were the leaders, that they were the influential guys, and he was behind them, a tagalong, a follower in that sense. He was always following them. And they were trying to bring him along."

The Pouncey twins had a bad reputation among the

scouts. And Hernandez was already known for his drug use, and for his knack for getting himself out of scrapes.

"They couldn't pin a lot of stuff on him," another AFC college scouting director told Breer. "But people at the school would tell you, 'Every time there's an issue, he's around it.' He was a con guy. Very believable. Spoke well. A lot of things inside of you hoped you'd turn him around, but people that I talked to said they didn't trust him, that he'd burn you."

The perspective on Aaron Hernandez was simple: He was smart—smart enough to beat the system. But he could also be reckless, if not downright self-destructive.

"He was very, very immature," an NFC personnel executive told Breer. "Urban did him right by having him follow Tebow, and he was such a follower. He could go in any direction. Everyone knew that if you didn't keep an eye on him, he was an easy guy to persuade to do the wrong thing."

According to Jonathan Clegg of the *Wall Street Journal,* a psychological profile assembled by a North Carolina scouting firm called Human Resource Tactics, at the request of several NFL teams, suggested that Aaron enjoyed "living on the edge of acceptable behavior," and noted that he "may be prone to partying too much and doing questionable things that could be seen as a problem for him and his team."

Hernandez had scored 10 out of 10 for focus, motivation, and mental quickness, 9 out of 10 for self-efficacy and receptiveness to coaching, and 7 out of 10 for dedication. "Hernandez sees himself as a football player above all else," the report noted. "He will place a high priority on football and what it takes to be successful." But in the category of "social maturity," Aaron had scored an abysmal 1, and at the

Combine, Aaron was finally forced to admit that the persistent rumors about his drug use were true.

"He admits it," an NFL executive who spoke with Hernandez told Breer. "He had multiple positive tests, so he either had issues or he's dumb. One or two tests? Fine. But four, five, six? Come on, now you've got an addiction. He's not a bad kid. He just has an issue."

CHAPTER 25

Aaron's drug use was not the only strike against his character.

Scouts at the Combine traded rumors about gang activities Hernandez may have been involved in. According to Ian Rapoport, who covered the Patriots for the *Boston Herald*, Hernandez was "probably the most talented guy in the draft, but there were obvious questions going in. One was, is he in a gang? That was an obvious, legitimate concern. Did he have gang ties? What was his off-the-field life like? He definitely got into some trouble in Florida. And drug use was the other part of it. He failed a couple of drug tests in Florida. Florida said one. The Patriots said one. I was told it was four."

"He failed a ton of drug tests," says Albert Breer. "But look, 75 percent of the NFL smokes weed. The big thing is, is the guy going to be able to pass a drug test when he's in the pros?"

Nevertheless, the scouts had to balance rumors they were

hearing against Aaron's undeniable abilities, his potential, and his willingness to take responsibility for at least some of his actions. At the time, the perception was that, under Urban Meyer's tutelage, Aaron had begun to outgrow his destructive habits—although, in retrospect, it would look more like Urban Meyer had done an excellent job of *managing* Aaron's worst impulses, and shielding him from those who encouraged those impulses.

"The staff in Florida didn't want him going home on the weekends," Breer says. "They tried to convince him to stay during breaks. And there was a lot of uneasiness about home football weekends, because the guys from Bristol would come down for home games.

"His dad had always insulated him from those people in Bristol. His dad had associated with them, I believe, and when his dad died, he was broken. The guys who were there for him were the gang guys. And that's where the loyalty came in. Those guys had his back and it was important.

"There are probably a dozen guys in every draft who have gang ties. It's not uncommon. Sometimes it's serious. Other times, it's friends they're loyal to and they can separate— compartmentalize. Aaron's background wasn't completely bizarre. But it *was* enough to knock him down in the draft."

CHAPTER 26

Pro Day workouts were showcases for NFL scouts. Players drilled, ran, worked out, and stood stock still to be measured. For most, it was their last chance to show the scouts what they could do.

In 2010, Pro Day in Gainesville took place on March 17. For Gators who thought they had a shot at the pros, the pressure was on.

The draft was just one month away.

Inside the Swamp, it felt like a cattle call. A hundred scouts swarmed around the stadium. Their stopwatches ticked like mosquitos. Their eyes scanned the field for breakout stars.

Tim Tebow hoped to have a better showing than he had had at the Combine. Humbled by his performance there, he would not be taking anything for granted. "I don't know if I necessarily dreamed of this process ever being like this," he told the *Florida Times-Union*. "It's a little bit of a roller coaster."

Tebow was not the only one feeling whiplash. Aaron Hernandez posted good numbers in the forty-yard dash: 4.56, 4.61. Better than the numbers that Oklahoma's star tight end, Jermaine Gresham, had posted at the Combine. Hernandez beat Gresham in the speed drills and the bench press as well.

But teams still had serious questions about Aaron's character. Hernandez knew that he would have to get ahead of the scouts' reservations.

Growing up, Aaron had been a fan of Drew Bledsoe, the star quarterback for the New England Patriots. Now, he took his future into his hands. With the help of his agent, Hernandez wrote the Patriots' director of player personnel, Nick Caserio, a personal letter:

"I am writing in regards to some of the feedback I am receiving from my agents, Florida coaches, and other personnel," Aaron wrote. "These sources have indicated that NFL teams have questions about my alleged use of marijuana."

Aaron had no problem with these questions, he told Caserio. But he did want to address them directly, and counter them with a simple proposition: If the New England Patriots would consent to draft him, he would consent to biweekly drug tests throughout his rookie season. Aaron offered to tie his 2010 earnings to these drug tests, and promised to reimburse the team "a pro-rata amount" for any tests that he failed.

"If I fail a drug test," Hernandez wrote, "I do not deserve a portion of that money.

"I realize that this offer is somewhat unorthodox, but it is also the only way I could think of to let you know how serious I am about reaching my potential in the NFL."

In other words, Hernandez said, he was "literally putting my money where my mouth is," by shouldering the financial burden himself.

"Test me all you want during my rookie year," Hernandez said in conclusion. "All of the results will be negative while I am having an overwhelmingly positive impact on the field."

Hernandez must have known that, according to agreements the NFL Players Association had long since negotiated with the league, the Patriots would be prohibited from testing Aaron biweekly, or even bimonthly. Like all incoming NFL players, he would be tested yearly, on dates he would know about ahead of time.

Hernandez knew that, in practice, it was absurdly easy to smoke weed—even on a daily basis—while playing for the NFL.

But if Aaron's letter amounted to little more than a good-will gesture—a promise that could not, and would not, be enforced—it did speak to his willingness to at least address the rumors that swirled all around him.

Signing the letter "Sincerely," Hernandez sent it off to the executive, sat back, and hoped for the best.

There was nothing more that Aaron could do now but wait.

CHAPTER 27

NFL Commissioner Roger Goodell walked out onto the stage at Radio City Music Hall in New York City, looked up from his notes, and read out a name: "Sam Bradford."

It was Thursday, April 22. The start of the 2010 draft.

Dozens of fans in the audience booed, but Bradford ignored them. The Oklahoma quarterback was thrilled. He hugged his family and waved at those who were cheering him on.

Tim Tebow, who had defeated the QB every time they had faced off on the field, found himself clapping for Bradford as well. Then, he settled back in his seat and waited, nervously, to see if he would hear his own name.

Twenty-four picks would go by before he did. But when Goodell looked up from his notes and said, "Tim Tebow," the reaction was joyous: loud cheering, peppered just with a smattering of boos. Dozens of fans leapt to their feet for a standing ovation, and Tebow appeared to be overwhelmed.

He was a Bronco now.

Two Gators had been picked higher than Tebow: center Maurkice Pouncey (#18) had gone to the Steelers, and cornerback Joe Haden (#7) had been drafted by the Browns. On the following day, three more Gators made the second round: linebacker Brandon Spikes, who had recently served a half-game suspension for trying to gouge the eyes of a Georgia player, went to the Patriots (#62), as did outside linebacker Jermaine Cunningham (#53). Carlos Dunlap, a defensive end who had missed that year's SEC Championship game as a result of a DUI arrest, was drafted by the Bengals (#54).

In the draft's third round, UF safety Major Wright found a home with the Bears (#75).

Aaron Hernandez had to wait until the last day of the draft—Saturday, April 24—to hear his own name read out loud: the New England Patriots had taken him as the 113th choice of the draft. The *Boston Globe* said the Pats were "getting what many considered to be a player with first-round talent for a fourth-round price tag."

For Aaron Hernandez, it was a slap in the face: At the very outset of his professional career, the NFL seemed to be treating him as damaged goods. One failed drug test had already come to light. Some recruiters claimed to have heard that Aaron had failed as many six. (According to Urban Meyer, Aaron had only failed two.) But the overall consensus was that the Patriots knew what they were doing. After all, quarterback Tom Brady had been a *sixth*-round draft pick—and he had worked out pretty well for the Pats.

"Personally," Aaron's high school coach, Doug Pina, told

the *Hartford Courant,* "I've always had concerns. He graduated when he was seventeen. He'd just lost his father. He was going away from home. He's still a young man. He's leaving college a little early. He's still finding himself. With the right people around him, he keeps his head straight, he'll do very well. He's a good kid."

For his part, Aaron was gracious. "It's obviously a dream come true," Hernandez told reporters via conference call afterward. "I still can't believe it's real."

Six weeks later, on June 8, 2010, Hernandez got a Patriots jersey of his own, along with a check for $200,000. It was a lot less than second-round pick Rob Gronkowski, another tight end, had gotten from the Patriots. But it was more money than Aaron Hernandez had ever seen. It would have taken Aaron's father, Dennis, years to earn that amount. And $200,000 was just a signing bonus—the tip of the iceberg, if Aaron could manage to keep all his demons at bay.

PART FOUR

CHAPTER 28

Aaron's mother ran, bleeding, out of the cottage on Greystone Avenue.

It was June 29, 2010—one month before Aaron was due to report to his first Patriots training camp. Terri Hernandez's husband of eighteen months, Jeffrey Cummings, had just slashed her face with a kitchen knife.

Cummings, whose criminal record included arrests for assaulting women and children, had been drinking. He and Terri had argued, and he had shoved her to the floor.

"What did I *do?*" Terri pleaded as she pulled herself up. "Why did you do that?"

Terri went into the living room to sit down. Cummings disappeared into the kitchen.

When he came back, he was holding a butcher knife—one with an eight-inch blade.

Cummings held the knife to his wife's throat. "What are you doing?" Terri whispered, afraid for her life.

Dennis Hernandez had never acted like this.

Cummings began to stab at a stand-up fan, putting the knife through one of the fan's blades.

Then he turned and started to stab the chair Terri was sitting in, nicking her face in the process. Blood flowed down Terri's cheek and onto her arm as Cummings began to whirl around the room, smashing everything in front of him.

"I don't care if I go back to prison!" he yelled.

Although he was on probation for assault, Cummings had failed nineteen drug tests that year. He had also failed to complete a court-mandated anger-management course.

Somehow, Terri managed to run to the kitchen, out the side door, and over to a neighbor's house, where she called 911.

Jeffrey Cummings was in the backyard when the police arrived. The police ordered him to put his hands up—they didn't know if he still had the knife.

Cummings ignored them, and started to walk away.

The cops screamed at him: "Stop!"

When he finally did, Cummings said, "I didn't do anything."

He would not say any more. But after putting him in a police cruiser, cops entered the cottage. There, in the kitchen sink, they found a butcher knife. There was blood on it, and the blade was bent.

CHAPTER 29

The troubles brewing back home in Bristol had shown up in Aaron's face almost at the moment of his arrival at Gillette Stadium.

Just a few days after the draft, Hernandez was trying to watch film and growing frustrated as he tried, and failed, to figure out how to use the machinery. When wide receiver Wes Welker walked past the film room, Hernandez asked for his help.

"Figure it out yourself, rookie," Welker said, jokingly.

That was all that it had taken to set Aaron off. "Fuck you, Welker!" Aaron shouted. "I'll fuck you up!"

The incident did not do wonders for Aaron's reputation. "That's kind of what he was like," Ian Rapoport, the sports journalist, remembers. "He was pretty edgy. Guys liked him, but he was edgy and liable to snap on the dime just like that. His temper was so incredibly strong."

But if Aaron had gotten off on the wrong foot, the Patriots' head coach, Bill Belichick, was not the kind of guy who would hold it against him. Belichick's *friends* in Foxborough called him "asshole"—and the coach considered this to be an improvement over other terms of endearment he'd earned: Punk. Jerk. Beli-cheat. When Belichick had worked for Bill Parcells in New York, Parcells had nicknamed him "Doom and Gloom."

Everyone agreed that Bill Belichick knew how to win football games. But not everyone felt that they had to like him.

The coach had gotten off to a bad start with the Patriots. The only losing season Belichick had as their head coach had been his first leading the team, in 2000. He had ended that season 5–11—a dismal showing that he managed to turn around the next year on his way to winning the Patriots their first Super Bowl.

They won it again two years later, and yet again the year after that, racking up three Super Bowl victories in four years.

But in 2007—a year in which they lost the Super Bowl—the Patriots were given the largest fine in NFL history: $500,000 for ignoring a new rule about where cameras could be placed during games, and filming Jets' signals from their own sidelines.

"Spygate" was the first black mark on Belichick's record.

Aaron Hernandez would become the second.

When Aaron Hernandez got to Foxborough, the team that Belichick had built was at the top of the NFL. Tom Brady, who had taken over for Aaron's old hero, Drew Bledsoe, was still one of the NFL's dominant quarterbacks—even though, at thirty-three, he was already old by NFL standards. (By way of contrast, Hernandez had just become the youngest active player in the league.) Belichick pushed his players, who were among the best who had ever played the game, to their limits. He pushed himself just as hard, working twenty-two hour days on occasion. The coach controlled every aspect of his players' performance, right down to the exits they used to leave at the end of their workouts. All of them had to pass by his door, which was always open.

But even a coach as controlling as Belichick was could not control *everything*. And, as Belichick would learn, Aaron Hernandez presented a special set of challenges. Aaron was mercurial, immature, full of himself, but also fragile in ways that made his actions impossible to predict.

"In the locker room, he was sweet and charming," Rapoport says. "Sweet is a weird way to describe a man, but that's what he was—a sweet, endearing guy when he wanted to be. But the other part of it was that, emotionally, he was a wreck. It was not abnormal for him to burst into tears when he made a bad mistake. If he got humiliated in the meeting room, sometimes, he would cry. That's not really normal behavior."

Over time, Rapoport and Hernandez developed a connection. "In the locker room, I would hang out by his locker a lot," the reporter recalls. "He was always accessible. Never a great interview, because he was careful about what he said, but he and I got along. At one point, I shot a video for him— something his cousin was doing. He told me some stuff. We exchanged information, and he said, 'Look, you're my guy in the locker room. If I'm ever going to talk to anyone it's going to be you.' I said, 'Cool, man. I respect you, too.' And he said,

'But I just want to tell you, because I'm big on trust, if you ever fuck me over I'll kill you.'

"I kind of laughed, but he was not joking. I looked at a reporter buddy of mine who was standing there, eavesdropping. He gave me this weird look.

"I said, 'All right, all right. I'll see you later, man.' But later on, when Aaron got picked up, I got a text from that other reporter: 'Remember that day in the locker room? I guess he was serious.'

"I was like, 'Yep. Yes, he was.'"

CHAPTER 30

Aaron was not as massive as the Patriots' other rookie tight end, Rob Gronkowski. Gronk was 6′6″ and weighed twenty pounds more than Hernandez. At first, the big men eyed each other warily. Were they supposed to be competing against each other? Were they supposed to be friends?

Aaron and Gronk "were both humble," Aaron would tell the *New York Times.* They were both "very outgoing," and "a little bit immature."

The tight ends wound up getting along.

Aaron was physical, fast on his feet, and versatile in ways that allowed Coach Belichick to use him as a combination tight end, running back, and wide receiver. And if Gronk's size—his brawn and his arm span—made him tremendously hard to defend, Hernandez's explosive speed made him fiendishly difficult to tackle. Opposing teams could cover one tight end or the other. But seldom were they able to cover both, and double-teaming either was almost impossible.

"Rob takes a lot off me," Aaron told the *Boston Globe*. "He's so dynamic that a lot of people have to worry about him and forget about me. Sometimes they forget about him and have to worry about me, so it's a great combination."

"He's a beast," Gronkowski said. "Great teammate to have, a great tight end. Dude gets out there and gets open. He helps in the running game and everything. It's great to have each other and push each other."

By the end of the 2011 season, Gronkowski had racked up incredible numbers, setting the NFL records for receiving yards and touchdown receptions for a tight end. Playing in his shadow, Hernandez nevertheless made it into the league's top five for tight ends in receptions, yards, and touchdown receptions. Combined, the two tight ends had 169 receptions—shattering a record the Chargers had set in 1984—and an unprecedented 2,237 receiving yards.

With Hernandez as the joker in his deck, Belichick turned the duo into the most effective tight-end pairing in NFL history.

But, like Urban Meyer before him, Belichick was discovering that Aaron Hernandez required careful supervision both on and off of the field. In fact, Meyer had warned Belichick to "keep an eye" on Hernandez.

"What Urban told Bill, as far as I know, was 'You'll have to stay on top of him,'" Albert Breer, the NFL reporter, explains. "Cryptic as it was, that bit of advice was right on: The minute you let him out of your sight, you're in trouble."

CHAPTER 31

On January 14, 2012, the Patriots hosted the Broncos in a divisional playoff game.

The Patriots had won thirteen games in the regular season. The Broncos had won eight. Their quarterback was Aaron's old teammate, Tim Tebow.

In their last game, six days earlier, on January 8, the Broncos had beaten the Steelers—after losing their last three regular-season games by an average of sixteen points. On January 8, Tebow wrote "John 3:16" in his eye black. He ended up throwing for 316 yards, averaging 31.6 yards per completion.

In the first three quarters, he threw 16 passes.

The game's only interception, by the Steelers quarterback, Ben Roethlisberger, had been thrown on 3rd down and 16.

Ratings for CBS's telecast of the game had peaked at 31.6.

It had been exactly three years since Tebow had written "John 3:16" under his eyes for the BCS National Championship Game. Within a few hours, "John 3:16" became the most searched-for term on Google, followed by "Tebow" and "Tim Tebow."

It was a miraculous string of coincidences. But Tebow would need more than a miracle to beat the Patriots.

It was below freezing in Foxborough. The air was dry and clear but the field was rock hard. As the teams faced off, their breath shot toward the ground in billowing puffs of silver smoke. But Aaron Hernandez burst out on the fourth play of the game, running the ball forty-three yards downfield—his longest run of the season. The Patriots scored a touchdown with the next play, then scored four more in the first half.

Hernandez carried the ball five times in the game, giving the best rushing performance a tight end had ever shown in the NFL playoffs. Rob Gronkowski proved his mettle again by making ten catches for a total 145 yards. Early in the fourth quarter, Hernandez was taken out of the game with a head injury—one of several sustained in the course of his football career. But the Patriots' victory was decisive: a 45-10 rout.

"I wish I had [Aaron's] moves," Gronkowski told the *New York Times* after the game. "He can really juke it."

A few weeks later, the boy from Bristol found himself in Indianapolis, playing in his first—and only—Super Bowl.

American Idol winner Kelly Clarkson sang the national anthem, accompanied by a children's choir.

As she came to the "broad stripes and bright stars," NBC's cameras zoomed in on Aaron.

Hernandez looked lost in thought. With his mouth slightly open, he swayed side to side as he took in the moment.

Four years earlier, in Super Bowl XLII, the Patriots had gone into the game with a perfect season under their belts. Beating their opponents, the Giants, in Arizona would have given them the first 19–0 record in NFL history. And the Patriots did hold the Giants at bay—until the very end of the fourth quarter. With 2:37 left on the clock and the ball on their 17-yard line, the Giants began a spectacular eighty-three-yard drive, culminating in David Tyree's astonishing, one-armed catch and Plaxico Burress's game-winning touchdown.

It was a stunning upset, and the game had been thrilling. The Fox telecast broke all previous Super Bowl records. And now, the same teams, same coaches, and same quarterbacks were facing each other again in Indiana.

The Patriots won their coin toss and deferred, giving the Giants first possession. The Giants moved the ball at first. But the Patriots pushed the Giants back for three plays in a row, sacked Eli Manning twice, got the Giants out of field goal range, and forced a punt.

Then, on the Patriots' very first play, Tom Brady found himself in trouble in the end zone, threw the ball away, and got flagged for intentional grounding, resulting in a safety. The penalty gave the Giants a two-point lead.

By the end of the first quarter, the Giants had widened that lead to nine points. A second-quarter field goal by the Patriots brought the score to 9-3. Then, Brady led a spectacular, fourteen-play, ninety-six-yard drive, resulting in a Patriots touchdown.

Heading into halftime, Aaron's team had taken the lead by one point.

Madonna played the halftime show. Then, in the third quarter, Hernandez caught a twelve-yard pass, faked out linebacker Chase Blackburn, and brought home another epic drive, totalling eight plays and seventy-nine yards.

Aaron's touchdown gave the Patriots an eight-point lead.

During the regular season, Aaron's end-zone dance had become an internet meme.

After each touchdown, Hernandez would pretend to toss money into the air—making it rain.

Now, in a revised version of the routine, Aaron pretended to open a safe, remove stacks of bills, and toss them into the air.

"I'm trying to get this money," Aaron had told his childhood friend, Tim Washington. "That's the goal, and I'm going to bust my ass in any possible way to get it."

The goal had been met. Among other things, Aaron's end-zone pantomime conveyed his cockiness—and the sense that, at the age of twenty-two, he had become a bona fide superstar.

At that moment in Indianapolis, Aaron Hernandez stood at the top of the world.

The Giants scored two field goals in the quarter and sacked Brady on a third down, injuring the quarterback's already-tender left shoulder. But the Patriots held the score to 17-15.

In the fourth quarter, Patriots receiver Wes Welker dropped a crucial, game-winning pass.

"It's a play I never drop," Welker would tell the *New York*

Times. "I always make it. And in the most critical situation, I let the team down...It's one I'll have to live with."

Finally, the Giants had an opening. Late in the quarter, Eli Manning took advantage of that opening, with an eighty-eight-yard drive that culminated in one of the most bizarre plays in Super Bowl history.

The Patriots were down to their last time-out. The Giants were on their 6-yard line.

There were sixty-four seconds left on the clock.

The Giants were within twenty-four yards of a field goal. It had been four years since their kicker, Lawrence Tynes, had missed a field goal of less than thirty yards.

All that the Giants had to do now was run the clock down before kicking the field goal and winning the game.

Of course, Bill Belichick understood this. His only hope was to let the Giants score a touchdown, regain possession, and use that last minute to score again.

Eli Manning understood it, too. He passed the ball off to running back Ahmad Bradshaw, who ran hard up the middle, instead of trying to run down the clock.

If the Giants scored now, the Patriots would still have a minute of play.

As he approached the 2-yard line, Bradshaw seemed to realize that no one was trying to stop him. Manning screamed at him to fall down.

The Patriots had parted like the Red Sea.

Right at the goal line, the running back planted his feet, crouched, and spun around. But it was too late—Bradshaw's own momentum continued to carry him over the goal line. As he flopped backward, awkwardly, the Giants scored.

The odd, ugly touchdown gave the Giants a four-point lead, but left the Patriots fifty-seven seconds to work with— and with a quarterback like Tom Brady, fifty-seven seconds could be an eternity.

Brady's first pass, to receiver Deion Branch, was incomplete. Hernandez lost focus and dropped an easy catch. The Giants sacked Brady again on third down, forcing the Patriots to use their final time-out, sixteen yards shy of a first down.

Branch and Hernandez redeemed themselves on the next two plays. Branch ran out of bounds, at the 33-yard line, for first down. An eleven-yard catch by Hernandez moved the Patriots up to the 44. An illegal substitution penalty against the Giants moved the Patriots up another five yards.

Then, with nine seconds left on the clock, Brady threw a perfect Hail Mary to Hernandez in the end zone.

Surrounded on all sides by Giants, Hernandez stretched his hands out and jumped for the ball.

The Giants jumped higher. As Aaron fell backward, two Giants fell on top of him.

The ball went flying. Gronkowski lunged for it, missed.

Once again, the Giants had beaten the Patriots.

Hernandez was heartbroken, he told reporters. At twenty-two, he had many more years to bring home a Super Bowl ring. But in the off-season, Aaron's world began to crumble.

CHAPTER 32

Hernandez had settled in a town house in Plainville, Massachusetts, two hours east of Bristol, Connecticut. Once again, he was within driving distance of his family, and his boys. There were old friends like Carlos Ortiz to hang out with. There was Aaron's cousin Tanya, and TL Singleton—TL and Tanya had recently gotten married. And there were new friends, like Alexander Bradley, who had met Aaron in Bristol while he was still living in Florida.

Bradley was tall and imposing, with a broad chest and broad shoulders. He was soft-spoken. And he was intelligent.

You had to be smart to be as successful as Bradley had gotten to be in his chosen profession.

Bradley sold weed—in "large amounts," by his own estimation. He had a rap sheet: marijuana, cocaine, and battery assault were all on the menu. But Alexander Bradley and Aaron Hernandez got along well. The first time they'd met,

Hernandez had no cash with which to buy marijuana. Bradley had given him an ounce on the house.

"I used to give him credit for weed all the time," Bradley would say. "He didn't have much money before he got drafted. I loaned him money...I wound up getting into it with my girl over hanging out with him so much. I wasn't around as much. She was like, 'If you want to hang out with your boy, hang out with your boy, but this is not going to work out with us.'"

Hernandez and Bradley cemented their friendship by smoking and playing video games for hours on end, and when Hernandez became a Patriot, and moved back to New England, he and Bradley saw each other much more often— three or four times a week, with phone calls and texts on the days in between. They gambled together, driving to Foxwoods Casino or Mohegan Sun. They went to clubs in Boston, Hartford, and Providence. Once, Hernandez took Bradley on a vacation to Miami.

"We were definitely best friends by 2012," Bradley would tell the jury, during his testimony in one of Aaron's subsequent murder trials.

On Sunday nights, he and Aaron went to Cure Lounge, a nightclub in Boston's theater district. Waitresses carried buckets of champagne around its big room, trailing comet tails of dry ice. Sometimes, at the bar, or on the dance floor, patrons would recognize Hernandez and stare.

"He would ask me, 'Why don't people stare at you like that?'" Bradley would say.

"I would respond to him, pretty much, 'Because I'm not you.'"

"He didn't like it when people stared at him," Bradley explained. "He felt like they were trying him. What I usually would say was, 'You're a famous NFL player. That's what's gonna happen. It's not that big of a deal.' In other words, I would try to explain to him that people *weren't* trying him all the time. It's just the situation—the position he was in—and he didn't need to overreact all the time to that type of scenario."

Bradley thought that Hernandez was paranoid. The average person wouldn't be bothered to this extent. But it began to seem as if, every time they went out, Bradley had to step in to stop Hernandez from starting trouble.

"He acted in a manner—like a tough guy all the time. He had a problem with things that most people don't have a problem with."

A few months after the Super Bowl, Hernandez and Bradley were at a Boston nightclub called Rumor.

"What are you looking at?" Hernandez said to a man he'd caught staring.

"I'm looking at you," the man said.

Hernandez got up in the other man's face.

"You lost me a lot of money on the Super Bowl," the man protested.

The room grew tense, but Bradley stepped in, defused the situation, and got Hernandez to walk away.

Of course, Aaron also did things for Alexander Bradley. He supplied Bradley with Patriots tickets. In return, Bradley kept Hernandez supplied with all the weed he could smoke.

According to Bradley, Hernandez went through as much as four ounces a week.

Bradley did other things for his friend, too, acting more like a personal assistant, at times, than a friend. Bradley says that he would drop Aaron off at his cousin Tanya's house on Lake Avenue, where Hernandez would sometimes spend days doing drugs with Tanya, TL Singleton, and their friends.

And, in addition to the weed supply, Bradley serviced Hernandez's cars, did his shopping, and supplied him with firearms.

"He felt like people thought he was soft or something— and he was out to prove something," Bradley explained. "He was fed up with the whole feeling-as-if-people-were-trying-him situation, so he wanted a firearm to protect himself, in the event..."

According to Alexander Bradley, downtown Boston was the place where Hernandez felt he was "tested" most often.

"In the Cure area," Bradley said. "That's where he was on heightened alert all the time."

Jeff London was a promoter for Cure Lounge and other night-clubs in Boston. He met Aaron during his rookie year on the Patriots and, over time, grew to consider him a "good friend." London took care of several Patriots who went out clubbing. From time to time, he'd ask female patrons if they wanted to meet one football player or another.

But, like Alexander Bradley, London noticed that Hernandez could be paranoid and "super-aggressive"—and that he became more paranoid, and more aggressive, as time went by.

"I've seen him punch people," London says. "I've seen him do everything. Five times. Ten times. He'd smack people, punch them in the head, get violent with them."

Because Hernandez was big and intimidating, he tended to get away with it.

"They would just walk away after he hit them," says London.

One day, despite their friendship and the promoter's own size (6'1", 270 pounds), Hernandez picked a fight with London.

The promoter had spotted Hernandez, Bradley, and a third man walking into Cure. He approached to see if there was anything that he could do for the tight end.

"Is everything cool?" London asked. "Do you need anything? You up for a table?"

Hernandez sneered at him: "You're a fed, a snitch. Get the fuck away from me."

"It took me by surprise," London would say, "because, obviously, I'm neither. The bouncers came over 'cause they saw me and I was in shock. His two boys came over to me and I was trying to explain to them: 'What is he talking about?'"

As he so often did, Bradley stepped in to cool the situation. By now, this had become a typical night out with Aaron. Nevertheless, Bradley and Hernandez kept on going to Cure.

CHAPTER 33

Early in the summer of 2012, Hernandez gave Alexander Bradley $350, which Bradley used to buy a .357 Magnum. Silver, with a brown handle, the gun had a couple of rounds in the chamber when Bradley bought it. The next time that Hernandez came down to Bristol, Bradley handed the firearm over.

"It's straight," Aaron said as he inspected the gun, meaning that he thought the firearm looked good.

A few weeks later, on July 15, 2012, Hernandez met Bradley at Bradley's place.

It was a Sunday, their favorite night to go out.

The two friends had a few drinks, a couple of blunts, and talked about where to go: West Hartford, Providence, Boston. They settled on Cure. As they walked to their car, Bradley noticed that Hernandez was holding a silver revolver.

Aaron did not have his club clothes with him, so Bradley had loaned him jeans, a T-shirt, and a Cardinals hat. They walked out to Aaron's Toyota 4Runner, an "endorsement car" that the Jack Fox Toyota dealership in Providence had lent him. Popping the hood, Hernandez stuffed the gun down into the engine block. Then, with Bradley driving, they set out for Boston, pulling into a parking garage on Tremont Street after midnight and walking around the corner to Cure.

Just ahead of them, a group of five friends—all of them Cape Verdean men—were trying to enter the club. One after the next, Daniel de Abreu, Safiro Furtado, Aquilino Freire, Raychides Gomes-Sanches, and Gerson Lopes took out their IDs and paid the entrance fee. At the same time, Aaron and Alex stepped into a special entrance for VIPs, skipping the line and the $20 cover. But Cure had a no-hats policy. There were no exceptions, not even for VIPs. Hernandez and Bradley both had to give their hats up to the bouncers.

Aaron was not happy about it. As he went in, he gave one of the bouncers a hard time.

Then, he and Bradley went straight to the bar.

Daniel de Abreu, who was twenty-nine, and Safiro Furtado, who was twenty-eight, had both been born in Cape Verde, an archipelago off the African coast, but they had met in America.

Furtado, who worked as a tour guide in Cape Verde, had been in the US for less than a year. He'd come to visit his mother and sister, who lived in Dorchester, and earn a bit of money before returning to Africa. In Massachusetts, he worked the overnight shift, cleaning offices with one of his cousins from ten at night until two in the morning. On Sundays, Furtado cleaned a local YMCA, alongside Daniel de Abreu.

De Abreu, who also had family in Dorchester, had arrived in the US in August of 2008. "He served five years as a police officer in Cape Verde and migrated here, looking to better his life and provide for his family," de Abreu's widow, Auriza, would say.

According to family members, neither man had wanted to go out that evening. Both of them had worked long weeks. Both were tired. But Sunday was the one night when de Abreu and Furtado got to see friends. They had changed into their club clothes and rallied, piling into a silver BMW that belonged to de Abreu's sister and driving to Cure Lounge. There, out on the dance floor, Daniel de Abreu bumped into an already agitated Aaron Hernandez.

When Cure was crowded, Hernandez and Bradley would order their drinks two at a time—"a shot of something and another mixed drink," Bradley would say. That's what they did on this night. Then, after downing the shots, they brought the cocktails out onto the dancefloor.

The music was pounding. The dancefloor was packed, and de Abreu had to hold his drink high as he danced his way out from the bar. As he did so, he bumped Hernandez with his hip. Bradley would say that the bump was intentional: "He bumped him in rhythm," as if it was part of the dance. But intentional or not, the jolt caused Aaron to spill his drink. As a few drops splashed onto his borrowed shirt, the Patriot became enraged.

According to Bradley, Hernandez turned and eyeballed de Abreu: "He turned angrily, in a manner in which he was going to make a confrontation out of the issue."

De Abreu, who was not a football fan and did not recognize Hernandez, smiled at the Patriot. That made Aaron even more angry. Playing the peacemaking role he'd grown used to, Bradley "got on top of it, fast." Grabbing Aaron's shirt, he said, "Nah, let's just get out of here."

"I knew something was brewing," Bradley would say. "His temper, the way he was...I just knew what would happen."

"Don't worry about it," he told Hernandez. "It's nothing."

Hernandez allowed himself to be convinced. He and Bradley left the club less than ten minutes after they had entered it. But, outside, Aaron started to vent. "I hate it when people try me, try to play me," he said as they walked back down Tremont Street, toward the garage.

Bradley heard him out, then told him they couldn't get into that type of trouble.

Both of them had too much to lose, Bradley said.

Just then, a promoter who worked at a club called Caprice recognized Aaron and invited him in. He offered the men table service. They declined, but entered the club, walked up to the bar, and ordered drinks. Then, turning around, Hernandez told Bradley that the men they had run into at Cure had followed them into Caprice.

"See, see!" he said. "There they go!"

Hernandez was wrong: Daniel de Abreu, Safiro Furtado, and their friends were still at Cure, where they would stay until closing time. But Aaron was sure that he'd seen what he'd seen. Now, Alexander Bradley would have to convince him to leave the second club they had gone to that night.

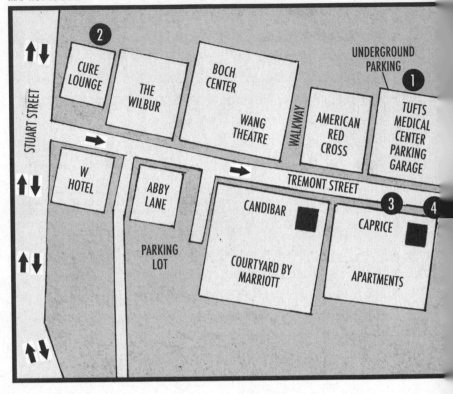

Boston Double Murder, July 16, 2012

1. Hernandez and Bradley park here.

2. Hernandez and Bradley enter CURE LOUNGE just before midnight.

3. Hernandez and Bradley go to CAPRICE around 12:30 a.m.

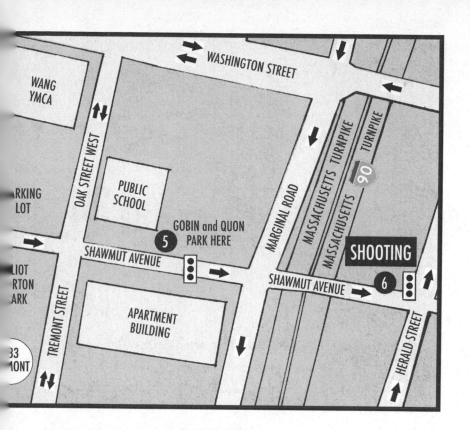

4 Phon sees Hernandez and Bradley here at around 2:15 a.m.

5 Gobin and Quon see Hernandez and Bradley pull up beside them at about 2:30 a.m.

6 Shots fired here as the BMW waits at a red light. Bradley makes a right, heads the wrong way down Herald Street, spins around, and gets onto the Massachusetts Turnpike.

CHAPTER 34

Alexander Bradley would say that, after leaving Caprice, he and Aaron got back into the 4Runner and drove it around the block. They parked on a side street and smoked some more weed. Then, Hernandez popped the hood, removed the gun he had stuffed in the engine block, and put it in the glove compartment. Driving back out to Tremont Street, they parked just beyond the garage they had parked in earlier that evening and waited for the clubs to get out.

Destiny Phon, a drag queen in Boston's theater district, was working that night as the DJ at a club called Underbar. When the club closed, she and a friend decided to run out for Chinese food.

As they were leaving they bumped into Aaron Hernandez, who was "lounging" outside. Destiny was not a sports fan, but her friend followed the Patriots and recognized Hernandez immediately.

"I couldn't really care less, but I looked and thought, 'Oh, he's very handsome,'" Destiny says.

Bradley would say that he and Hernandez were waiting outside to meet women. Instead, they saw Daniel de Abreu and Safiro Furtado exiting Cure.

"There they go, there they go!" Hernandez shouted as he ran back to the 4Runner. Bradley got behind the wheel. Seeing a silver BMW drive past them with de Abreu and Furtado inside, Hernandez said, "Go, go, go!"

For de Abreu and Furtado, the rest of the evening had passed without incident. They had stayed at the club until closing time. Then, at 2:19 in the morning, de Abreu, Furtado, and Aquilino Freire walked toward the garage where they had parked the BMW. The plan, Freire would say, was to circle around and pick up Raychides Gomes-Sanches and Gerson Lopes outside of the nightclub.

A few minutes later, the BMW pulled back around. De Abreu was driving, Furtado sat in the passenger seat, and Freire was in the back. Gomes-Sanches and Lopes joined them there and the five friends pulled off into the night.

Don Gobin and Brian Quon worked security at Underbar. Twenty minutes after closing time, they walked one of the club's promoters to his car, then walked down Tremont to the silver Saturn they had driven up from Rhode Island that day.

"It was a warm night," Gobin says. "But it was very quiet. There were no cars. There were no people. It was like a sci-fi movie, with papers blowing around. Usually folks are out, taxis are waiting. But we went down to our car, started it. I was driving. Brian was in the passenger seat. Out of the blue, in the rearview mirror, I see this car come whizzing up on the passenger side of our vehicle. It comes out of nowhere, pulls up to our car. Two or three feet away from our car it stops. I said to Brian, 'Who is that? Is that someone we know?' We knew a lot of people. We figured, maybe it's somebody playing a joke. But Brian looked up at the driver and said, 'No, I don't think we know him.'"

Leaning over Bradley in the SUV, Hernandez looked down into the car they had pulled alongside. (From the Saturn's passenger seat, it would have looked as if Aaron was driving.) He expected to see de Abreu or Furtado. Instead, he saw Brian Quon.

It was the wrong car. The silver car *they* were looking for was a BMW.

Bradley gunned the 4Runner's engine and ran the red light.

"*He's* in a rush," Gobin said to Quon.

The men watched the 4Runner speed up and overtake the next car.

"The next thing we heard was gunfire," Gobin recalls. "My first reaction was to look in the rearview mirror. I didn't see anything. Then I said to Brian, 'Where is that coming from?'"

Quon pointed straight ahead, at the SUV that had pulled up beside them seconds earlier.

"It's coming from that vehicle up there," Quon said.

*   *   *

As he caught up with the BMW, Bradley would say, he looked over and saw that Hernandez was holding the gun.

"Roll your window down," Hernandez said as he leaned across Bradley's seat.

Bradley reclined, Hernandez braced his left hand on an armrest, and stuck the gun out of the driver's side window.

Inside the BMW, de Abreu and Furtado were both glued to their phones. Hernandez yelled, "Yo!"—but neither man looked up. But when he yelled, "Yo" again, the men turned.

"What's up now, niggas?" Hernandez said. Then he squeezed the trigger and fired.

There were five gunshots, maybe six. Bradley would say that Hernandez emptied the chamber.

Glass exploded. Somebody screamed. Hernandez told Bradley to drive.

Freire, who was sitting in the backseat between Gomes-Sanches and Lopes, remembers stopping at a red light. Then, he would say, an SUV pulled up close—"right next to us."

"What up, niggas?" was the first thing Freire heard.

He heard Furtado say *Pamodi?*—Cape Verdean creole for "why?"

Then he heard gunfire.

"We were still at the red light," says Gobin. "As soon as the red light turned green, we drove toward the car that was sitting there. The SUV had already taken off. And as we pulled up to the car, the first thing we saw was that there was blood all over the side of the car. There was glass in the street. We kind of knew what we were going to find, so we pulled up cautiously. Both the driver and the passenger had been shot. They both had their seat belts on. You could tell that the passenger's chest was not going up and down for air. Both of their heads were on the headrests and the passenger's eyes were closed.

"The driver, his eyes were actually open," Quon adds. "He was still breathing. Labored breathing. At that point, two individuals jumped from the back of the car. One from the left passenger door, one from the right. The first thing they did when they got out was to pat themselves down—probably to see if they got hit by anything. The next thing they did was to start coming toward our vehicle."

"One of them came toward our vehicle, and I had my window down maybe halfway," says Gobin. "He was just saying, 'Can you help us? Help us! Can you help us?'"

Aquilino, Raychides, and Gerson jumped out of the BMW.

"We just went out of the car," Aquilino would say. "I was trying to see if Safiro and Daniel was all right...And then I was all around the car, waving, like for someone to help."

Safiro had been shot in the head. Covered in blood, he was already dead in the passenger seat.

Sitting beside him, Daniel was trying to speak.

"He was dying," Aquilino remembered. "He was trying to say something, but he didn't. I was trying to tell him, 'Just keep strong. We're gonna look for help...'"

Daniel "lasted for two minutes, or maybe a minute" Freire would say.

*   *   *

Destiny Phon and her friend were driving down Tremont when they saw the BMW. "All of the sudden, these guys jumped out of the car and stopped us, asking for help," Destiny says. "One of them had been shot in the arm. Blood was rushing out. We said, 'Put pressure on it!' We didn't want to get out of the car. We didn't know what was happening. We just said, 'Dude, chill, chill, stay away from the car and we'll call 911.'"

"Did you see that?" Hernandez said. "I think I got one in the head and one in the chest."

Aaron took off the T-shirt that Bradley had loaned him and used it to wipe down the gun.

The two friends had no particular destination in mind. According to Bradley, they were "in a state of shock."

They talked about going to Aaron's place in Plainville, but ended up driving to 47 Newbury Street in Hartford. It was the house where Bradley's "baby mama," Brooke Wilcox, lived.

It was five, or just after five in the morning, when Hernandez and Bradley got there.

Wilcox lived on the third floor of a three-floor walk-up, in a small, two-bedroom attic apartment. As soon as she and Bradley were alone in one of the bedrooms, Bradley told her, "This crazy motherfucker just did some stupid shit."

Aaron was hanging out in the living room. At some point, he knocked on the door and asked to use Brooke's laptop. Bradley handed it over, along with a blanket and pillow for Aaron to use. Before doing so, Aaron ran a few searches on Brooke's computer, checking to see if the news outlets were reporting a shooting in Boston.

Brooke woke up at eight and got into the shower.

By the time she got out, Tanya Singleton was standing in her kitchen. She and Aaron were whispering. Brooke had never met Tanya before, but she and Aaron seemed so intimate, Brooke assumed that she was Aaron's fiancée. When Brooke left for work, Tanya was still there.

When she got home, a few hours later, Alexander Bradley was there, but Aaron, Tanya, and the Toyota 4Runner were gone.

CHAPTER 35

Danny was born on Fogo Island, Cape Verde," says Daniel de Abreu's widow, Auriza. "He was infatuated with the law and became a police officer. He was his mother's son, the man of the house, his siblings' provider. My main attraction to him was that, even though he was young, he was responsible, mature, and intelligent. He knew what he wanted and he would do what it took to get there.

"We met at a mutual friend's house in the summer of 2011, exchanged numbers, and started to date right away. I guess you could call it love at first sight. We're from the same country, the same community. We dated for several months and got married.

"That Sunday in July had already been a very sad day. I'd lost a coworker—a nurse—and we had a funeral service that day. Originally, it was the day that we were going to reveal to his family that we were married. He has half brothers and sisters here. He has his father here, who we really didn't see much of. He saw some family, many weren't from the same mother and father. They had their issues. I understood and respect that. But our marriage took place without his family, and on that day, we were going to tell them.

"Daniel worked on the weekends, but on Sundays he worked less. If there's anything he can do for fun or with his friends to enjoy himself—anything to go out, nightlife or something like that—it would be a Sunday night. That day, he said he was tired, but as I was speaking to him, I could hear that somebody else was around. Someone he needed to attend to. Danny calls me 'Iza'—the last three letters of my name. Only people who are dear to me call me that. He said 'Iza, let me call you back.' I went to sleep. If he tried calling me back I don't know.

"I woke up even sadder in the morning. I dropped my girl off at school, right around the corner, but I was feeling so down and depressed—so in need of my mom's presence, of my mom's hug—that I decided to visit her.

"My mom was very happy to see me. As I sat with her I received a phone call from Danny's sister, Patricia. She told me that Danny had been shot.

"I called Tufts. They verified that Danny was not there. Then I called Boston Medical Center. BMC couldn't give me any information because it had been a homicide. They had already determined that Danny had passed, and told me to call the local police. I called the local police not knowing my head from my arm. I tried to be as cool as possible. They questioned me to determine who I was. Then they said to come down to the station.

"Danny's cousins were calling me the whole time. I thought it was something minor. A stray bullet. Maybe he had been shot in the leg. Danny's cousin Americo—named after America—called and told me to come meet him at his house. Danny and Americo grew up together. Danny and I got married in Americo's house. So here I am thinking that Danny and Americo are together—that once I walk into that house, Danny will be there. That he's out of any kind of risk. That he's gone home with his cousin.

"It was a very short distance to Americo's house, but it was horrible. I drove nervously, shaking, like I would never get there. It was something I had never experienced before—the fear of not knowing, the anxiety...But I got to the house and a young man opened the door. I asked, 'Where's Danny?'

"He answered, 'Danny died.'

"Everything went dark. I kept asking, 'Where is Danny?' I wanted to see him. I was not myself. I don't know who I was at that time. The ride to the police station was the longest ride of my life. I was crying, screaming, and cold.

"The detective was very polite. He didn't think my questions were stupid or make me feel that I was aggravating him, not knowing my left from my right. He guided me through and told me that I needed to go somewhere else to identify the body.

"I thought I could see him. I thought I could see his body. I thought I'd actually be looking at him. I wanted so much to touch him and to hold him, but it was only pictures that I looked at. It was the hardest thing of my life. It still is. I'm trying. I'm learning to cope but it's really hard. I've waited so long to try to understand, to see the reasons why.

"So many years have passed. We had plans. He had a future ahead of him. There are so many questions, but I never had closure with him. Never a last word. Never 'hello,' 'goodbye,' or 'I love you.' Never anything."

PART FIVE

CHAPTER 36

On July 27—two weeks after the shooting in Boston—Aaron Hernandez reported to Gillette Stadium, in Foxborough, for the start of the Patriots training camp.

Reporters who'd gathered outside the stadium were joking about Rob Gronkowski's off-season exploits. Among other things, Aaron's teammate had posed for photos with an adult-film actress while wearing his jersey—and nothing else.

"Aaron, was your summer as crazy as Gronk's?" a reporter asked.

Hernandez refused the bait. "Um," he said. "More private. But I still had some fun."

The reporters asked him again about Gronk. They asked what he thought of Tom Brady's off-season cliff-diving. They asked him to be a bit more specific about the "fun" he had had.

"This is a regular job," Hernandez said. "We like to have fun, too. I've been zip-lining and stuff like that, too. They can't really tell you what you can and what you can't do, but you just have to be careful about what you do. If you're out there and being reckless and doing some crazy stuff, then that's your own stupidity."

While Hernandez talked to the reporters, Boston PD continued its investigation into the double homicide outside of Cure. Don Gobin and Brian Quon told the police about a silver SUV with Rhode Island plates—a Nissan Pathfinder, they thought, or a Toyota 4Runner. Both men said that the SUV had been driven by a light-skinned, clean-shaven Hispanic man with short hair. One recalled that the passenger had braided hair.

Then, the witnesses described the shooting's aftermath.

Boston detectives also obtained video footage from Cure Lounge, from a nearby parking garage, and from other locations.

There was no footage of the shooting itself.

An appeal was made to the public: Could anyone help the police locate a silver SUV with Rhode Island plates? Detectives had already looked at various vehicles registered with the neighboring state's DMV, but failed to ID the vehicle in question.

None of their efforts resulted in an arrest, or even a suspect.

CHAPTER 37

The police made no progress in the weeks that followed, but Aaron's life changed drastically all the same.

He found out that his girlfriend, Shayanna Jenkins, was pregnant.

Aaron and Shayanna had known each other since elementary school and dated, on and off, since high school. Shayanna was beautiful, with high cheekbones, a heart-shaped face, and dark hair that fell beneath her shoulders. She was practically family. And now, she and Aaron would be starting a family of their own.

That bit of good news was accompanied by another, delivered by the Patriots owner, Robert Kraft.

On August 27, the Putnam Club at Gillette Stadium was filled with sharply dressed Patriots. It was the night of the team's annual Charitable Foundation gala and Kraft—an avuncular billionaire who had taken Aaron under his arm—worked the room in a gray suit, a blue banker's shirt, and a salmon-colored tie. Cameras flashed. Donors, sponsors, and reporters surrounded the players, paying special attention to Aaron Hernandez, who had just given Myra Kraft's Giving Back Fund a major donation.

"Aaron came into my office a little teary-eyed," Kraft told the reporters, "and presented me with a check for $50,000. I said 'Aaron, you don't have to do this, you've already got your contract.'"

The reporters laughed.

"No," Aaron had said. "It makes me feel good and I want to do it."

"I sensed that he was touched in doing that," Kraft continued. "I didn't request it. It's something that he decided. And to flip the switch from living modestly to all of the sudden having a lot of income, I think we have to work real hard to help our young men adjust to that."

Hernandez could afford to be generous: On that very day, he had signed a five-year, $40 million contract extension with the Patriots. The agreement was heavily structured toward its later years, with a 2018 base salary, of $6 million, that was almost six times larger than what Aaron would get in 2012. But the extension came with a $12.5-million signing bonus—the largest that any NFL team had ever offered a tight end.

Earlier that year, Rob Gronkowski had agreed to a six-year, $53 million contract extension—the biggest contract for a tight end in NFL history. But Gronk's signing bonus of $8 million had been much lower than Hernandez's.

"It's surreal," Hernandez said, when asked about the extension. "Probably when I'm done with this conversation I'll get some tears in my eyes. But it's real, and it's an honor."

Robert Kraft had changed his life, Hernandez told the reporters. And the gesture was all the more meaningful—even extraordinary—because Aaron's original contract was not ending for some time and no other teams were competing for him at that moment.

Hernandez embraced Kraft, and kissed him on the cheek.

"I have a daughter on the way," he said. "I have a family that I love. It's just knowing that they're going to be okay. Because I was happy playing for my $250,000, $400,000. Knowing that my kids and my family will be able to have a good life, go to college, it's just an honor that he did that for me."

Standing a few feet away, Ian Rapoport was struck by the "audible sincerity" in Aaron's voice.

"I have a lot more to give back," Hernandez said. "And all I can do is play my heart out for them, make the right decisions, and live life as a Patriot . . . I just hope I keep going, doing the right things, making the right decisions so I can have a good life, and be there to live a good life with my family."

"I told Aaron on the day of his signing that this was a major accomplishment for him, but also a turning point in his life," Hernandez's agent, Brian Murphy, recalls.

"He wasn't playing for money anymore because he had his contract. Instead, he was playing for his legacy and that was established on and off the field. He had to decide what that legacy would look like as a player, father, and husband. That is why he made the $50,000 donation to the Myra Kraft Foundation when he signed his contract. He was grateful to

Mr. Kraft for drafting him, rewarding him with his new contract, and teaching him the Patriot Way. That was very real.

"Aaron wanted to be the best tight end to ever play. He was constantly studying film, getting work done on his body—massages, soft tissue work—and practiced as hard as anyone. He had a brilliant football mind and honestly felt that he was the best player on the team. Once Aaron got his big contract, he had a lot of demands from an enormous range of people. This is true of many players after getting big contracts, but in Aaron's case, he had some people asking him for some really unusual stuff and there were so many requests.

"Aaron wanted to live life the Patriot Way because it had worked for him. It had gotten him a huge contract and respect throughout the league. Unfortunately, there were powerful forces pulling him in the other direction. That constant pull never stopped and eventually won."

CHAPTER 38

Aaron and Shayanna got engaged that October. A few weeks later, on November 6, Aaron skipped practice. It was the Patriot's twenty-third birthday, but he and Jenkins had something much more important to celebrate: the birth, on that day, of their daughter Avielle Janelle.

DJ Hernandez took to Twitter to express his joy: "I'm an uncle!"

Then, on the very next day, Aaron put on his white jersey and went back to work.

When a reporter asked him—"Why are you wearing your game-day uniform to practice?"—Hernandez replied: "Game time, that's it!"

"I'm engaged now," Aaron explained. "I have a baby. It's just going to make me think of life a lot differently and doing things the right way. Now, another one is looking up to me. I can't just be young and reckless Aaron no more. I'm going to try to do the right things, become a good father and [let Avielle] be raised like I was raised."

Aaron and Shayanna bought a house at 22 Ronald C. Meyer Drive in North Attleboro, just off of Homeward Lane. Located less than ten miles away from Gillette Stadium, the 7,100-square-foot contemporary colonial mansion, which had been built for Patriots defensive tackle Ty Warren, had three stories, five bedrooms, six baths, a three-car garage, an in-ground pool, a movie theater, and a basement sauna and ice bath.

Piece by piece, the young couple were putting together a home to replace the one shattered by Dennis Hernandez's death and Terri Hernandez's marriage to Jeffrey Cummings. Family mattered to them. Aaron was still tight with his cousin Tanya and Shayanna was close to Shaneah, one of her two younger sisters.

Shaneah was more sober-minded than Shayanna, and more serious. She worked long hours, putting herself through Central Connecticut State University, where she was majoring in criminology, with an eye toward becoming a lawyer. Shaneah carried herself so maturely, she looked like the older sibling—although, in fact, Shayanna was two years older. But the two sisters were close, and on weekends, Shaneah would drive out to visit Shayanna in North Attleboro.

On most of the visits, she'd bring along her new boyfriend, a man named Odin Lloyd.

Lloyd had dark skin, a winning smile, an athletic physique. He had been born in Saint Croix, but raised in Dorchester—the same town that Daniel de Abreu and Safiro Furtado had lived in. He had been an excellent football player in high school, good enough to get into Delaware State. But Odin did not have the money for college. When his financial aid fell through, he dropped out and moved home. Still, Odin held on to his dreams: on days off from his job, at a Dorchester lawn fertilizer company, he played defense for a semi-pro team called the Boston Bandits.

Odin and Aaron had met in Foxborough, in August of 2012, when Hernandez had gotten Shaneah a skybox at Gillette Stadium for a birthday present. They had hit it off immediately. Hernandez was a bona fide football star. Lloyd was a stone-cold fan.

Better yet, it turned out that he loved to smoke marijuana.

Aaron himself had not broken the habit. He had not stopped associating with his friend and weed dealer, Alexander Bradley. He was still spending time with Charlie Boy Ortiz, Bo Wallace, and TL Singleton. And, according to Bradley, Hernandez had stuck to his old ways in other respects.

For one thing, he was still paranoid, and still had difficulty trusting people. People were trying to use him, Aaron would say—strangers as well as old friends who were ungrateful for all that he had done for them.

Soon after moving into the house, he installed an extensive surveillance system, with cameras inside and out.

Hernandez also convinced himself that he was being tailed by the feds, that helicopters were following him, and that iPhones could be hacked to record his conversations.

Hernandez warned Bradley not to use his iPhone when he came around. But, before long, Bradley's iPhone became the very thing that came between the two men.

CHAPTER 39

On January 20, 2013, the Patriots hosted the Baltimore Ravens in the AFC Championship Game and lost.

It was the end of Aaron's third season in the NFL.

Three weeks later, Aaron and Alexander Bradley flew to Miami. The Ravens had gone on to win the Super Bowl and Deonte Thompson and Pernell McPhee, who played for Baltimore, were hosting a Super Bowl party in West Palm Beach.

Deonte Thompson and Aaron were tight. They had started for Florida at the same time, and Aaron was close enough to Deonte to call him "D." But when Thompson and some of his friends picked Hernandez and Bradley up at the airport, Bradley realized that he did not know any of them:

A man named "Papoo."

D's nephew, Max "Black" Brown.

Two men, Tyrone Crawford and Je'rrelle Pierre, who had grown up with D in Belle Glade, an hour west of West Palm Beach.

A man who simply said "Soldier" when asked for his name.

They were all strangers to Bradley, who was not sure how he'd be received. More and more, he was uncertain around Aaron, and around Aaron's acquaintances. Just a few weeks earlier, he had been hanging out in Aaron's kitchen when Shaneah and her boyfriend, Odin, had come in. They were there to see Shaneah's sister, and as they passed through the kitchen, Shaneah said "hello."

Odin—who had met Bradley before—did not acknowledge him at all. Even Aaron had said, "That was rude."

Bradley agreed that it was.

Locals called Belle Glade "the muck," or "muck city," because of the dark color of its soil. But the town had another distinction: it produced more NFL athletes than any other place in America.

Papoo's house in Belle Glade was where the pre-party would be.

Papoo's government name was Oscar Hernandez, but he was not related to Aaron. Although he had been D's roommate in Gainesville, he was one of the few men who'd gathered that day who did not play football. But Papoo was in awe of the players, especially Aaron and D. When D asked Papoo if he could borrow a handgun, "for protection," Papoo had handed his own gun over immediately.

Down in Belle Glade, football players tended to get what they wanted—and what Aaron wanted was to get wasted. Before long, *all* of the players were wasted. They stayed that way, too, for several days of partying.

*   *   *

During those days, the men made several trips to Miami. A cavernous Miami Gardens strip club called Tootsie's Cabaret became their favorite after-hours destination. The group caravanned there on February 11, and again on February 12, staying deep into the night on both nights and drinking enough to get sloppy. But the drinking did nothing to dispel Aaron's paranoia.

During their first visit to Tootsie's, Hernandez told Bradley that two customers at the strip club were undercover cops.

According to Bradley, Hernandez thought they were following him.

"If they are," Bradley told him, "it's because of the stupid shit you did in Boston."

On their second night at the strip club, as Bradley sat in a top floor VIP room with Aaron, Je'rrelle, Tyrone, and Soldier, he asked one of the waitresses for a cell phone charger. The waitress said she would look, but never came back. Bradley ended up leaving his phone on the table, and forgot it was there when something else caught his attention: the check. It was for $10,000, or something close to that amount. Hernandez asked Bradley to split it.

"I don't even know these people," Bradley replied.

Why should he have to pay five grand to buy drinks and dances for Hernandez's friends—a bunch of guys he did not even know?

Hernandez was less than thrilled with Bradley's response, but ended up paying the bill himself. Then, Aaron and his friends piled back into the SUV they'd taken to the club.

Bradley recalls riding in the back, beside Soldier. Hernandez was up front, in the passenger seat. Je'rrelle was driving. It was late—almost dawn—and he was tired. But, before they had gone more than a couple of blocks, Bradley realized that he had left his phone in the club.

"Let's go back," he said.

"Nah," said Hernandez.

Hernandez and Bradley argued about it. The car's other occupants took Aaron's side.

"I'll buy you a new phone," Hernandez said.

"I don't want a new phone," said Bradley. "I want *my* phone. It's got my kids' pictures in it."

Hernandez did not want to turn around. Bradley was outraged, and told Aaron so. But Hernandez did not turn around, and Bradley stewed, in the backseat, until he finally fell asleep.

He woke up as soon as he felt the SUV stop moving.

When he opened his eyes, he saw Aaron.

Hernandez was pointing a semiautomatic pistol at Bradley's face. Just as Bradley threw his right hand up to cover it, Aaron pulled the trigger.

The blast was deafening. The bullet tore through Bradley's hand, blew off part of one finger, passed through the bridge of his nose, and exploded his right eye in its socket. Soldier leaned across and started to push Bradley out of the car.

Hernandez got out on the passenger side, grabbed Bradley from the other side, and pulled.

There was light in the sky now. It was 6:30 a.m.

CHAPTER 40

Kevin Riddle bent over his computer, a mug of coffee steaming beside him on the countertop.

At six thirty, it would be time for Riddle to open up his John Deere Landscapes lot.

"Mingle," he said. "You want to go out and get the back gate?"

Mingle Blake, the company truck driver, went out the back door. A moment later, Riddle heard what sounded to him like a gunshot. Worried for Blake, he ran out back. Together, the two men set out to investigate.

"Maybe it was a just a car backfiring," said Riddle.

"I'll unlock the gate," said Blake.

A few minutes later, Blake rushed back toward Riddle. He was out of breath. "There's a body," he said.

Riddle followed him back, sprinting toward a scrubby spot west of the building. When he got there he saw a man, curled up in a fetal position on the far side of a chain-link fence.

The man's hands and face were covered in blood. Both of his eyes were swollen shut.

To Riddle, it looked as if the man had been beaten, shot in the head, maybe the hand, too, and left for dead. But the man was alive.

"Call 911," the man managed to say. "Tell them to hurry— I'm gonna bleed out."

The 911 dispatcher told Riddle to ask the man his name.

"Alex Bradley," the man replied.

"Do you know who shot you?" Riddle asked.

"No."

"Why would somebody do this to you?"

"I don't know," Bradley said. "I'm done talking, it hurts too bad."

The 911 dispatcher told Riddle to make a compress and put pressure on the man's wound. Riddle ran back inside the landscaping shop for a towel. When he came back, a few moments later, the police were already there.

The police asked Bradley the same question Riddle had: "Who did this to you?"

"It hurts," Bradley said. "It hurts too much to talk."

"Paramedics are on the way. What'd they look like?"

"They looked like, uh...big..."

"Big what?"

"Big black males."

"Do you know what they were driving?"

"I have no information for you, sir, with all due respect."

"You don't want us to investigate it, or you just don't know?"

"I don't know...there's very little that I know...but... with all due respect, you do what you got to do. I just ain't got no info for you, man."

Mingle Blake told the police that he had seen an SUV in the area just before hearing the gunshot. Dark green. A Ford Explorer. Maybe a Ford Expedition. Blake said there were cameras trained on the area where Bradley had been, but didn't know if they were set to record.

The police checked and found, to their dismay, that they were not.

CHAPTER 41

Hernandez called Bradley's baby mama, Brooke Wilcox, that morning from the Miami airport.

He wanted to know: Had Brooke seen Alex? They had been in Miami together, Hernandez said, and were supposed to meet at the airport. But now Aaron was at the airport and Alex was not.

Wilcox was alarmed by the news. She called hospitals in the Miami area. She called the Miami police, who told her to file a missing person report at her local precinct in Hartford.

All the while, she kept texting with Aaron: Have you heard from him, she would say.

Have you heard from him yet?

The bullet had ripped apart Bradley's right eye. Miraculously, it had not gone into his brain. The next day—Valentine's Day—Detective Kenny Smith from the Palm Beach Sheriff's Department arrived at St. Mary's Hospital to interview Bradley, who was recovering from surgery, and found him to be conscious and cogent, if not quite cooperative.

"Where were you the night before?" the detective asked.

"Sir, I'm from Connecticut, so that could tell you how much I know."

"Okay," said the detective. "So, what can you give me to try to find the people that did this to you? I mean, it's up to you, you're a big boy, if you won't…"

"He's a fucking asshole, whoever did this to me!"

"Well obviously! You've got a big enough hole in your head!"

"Fuck yeah, I do."

"It's up to you," said the detective. "You can help me. You know where you were, you know what happened, you can tell me, or you can tell me to, just what you said, F-off."

"I'm not saying F-off to you, man, that's the part I'm trying to get you to understand. I'm not disrespecting you by any means. I'm not saying F-off and fuck you, I'm just saying I ain't got the means, I ain't telling on nobody."

"You don't want to cooperate with the investigation. But if I don't have a victim, I don't have a crime. That's up to you…That's your choice, not mine. But you have to understand, next time they may not screw up. They may shoot better, you got it?"

Bradley took the detective's card. He had no intention of calling and sharing what he knew with the Palm Beach police, or with anyone else.

But he did call Hernandez from his hospital bed.

"What's up?" Bradley said when Aaron picked up.

"Who's this?" Aaron said. He sounded surprised.

"You know who this is," Bradley sneered. "It's me, it's your boy."

Aaron hung up on him before he could say anything more.

Bradley called Hernandez back two more times. "I don't know why you keep hanging up," he said when Aaron finally picked up the phone. "I didn't tell the police on you."

Then Bradley said something else: "You know what time it is when I get back."

Hernandez hung up on him once again. Bradley ended up sending a text: I really do love you, my boy, but you won't get away with that.

CHAPTER 42

A week later, Aaron Hernandez flew to the NFL Combine in Indianapolis and surprised Bill Belichick by telling the coach that his life was in danger.

"It's not safe for me to be in New England," Hernandez said, and asked Belichick to trade him—to get him out of the area. The coach told Hernandez that the Patriots would not agree to a trade.

Instead, he offered to help Hernandez with security issues in Boston.

Hernandez was nursing a shoulder injury at the time of this meeting. If he couldn't be traded out of the area, he told Belichick, he would spend the spring rehabilitating in Southern California. That way, Aaron said, he would be closer to Tom Brady, who was spending his off-season on the West Coast with his wife, Gisele Bündchen.

* * *

The Patriots' owner, Robert Kraft, has denied that any such conversation took place. Belichick, who rarely grants interviews and declined requests to be interviewed for this book, has refused any comment. And while the timeline suggests that Hernandez had good reason to be afraid of Alexander Bradley, Aaron's agent, Brian Murphy, has a different read on Aaron's request to be traded.

For Murphy, the request had nothing to do with Bradley and the Florida incident, and everything to do with Aaron's need to put some distance between himself and his friends in Boston and Bristol—with troubles that Aaron had gotten himself into at home.

"From the day I met him, Aaron was constantly trying to get better as a player and as a person," Murphy says. "He was always asking me about what books to read. Always asking what movies to watch. Always asking me, 'How should I handle this? How should I handle that?' He truly wanted to get better. But that's when he was in California, three thousand miles away from Boston. When I would go to visit him in Boston during the season, he wasn't nearly as focused on getting better. He would revert to his immature ways. He had a lot of friends from back home. And, once he got his big deal, that struggle became real for him. He was now a very wealthy NFL player—which is different than just being an NFL player. He was very high profile. He had had a lot of success. He was treated differently, both poorly and better, by his friends back home and by the people he was hanging out with back home, and he found a certain fame off the field that he enjoyed. He enjoyed being Aaron Hernandez from Bristol, Connecticut. That struggle became more real for him. It became harder and harder for him to keep trying to improve. So we sat down and I told him, 'Listen, you have to figure out who you want to be. I can't help you be someone you don't want to be, and I can't tell you who you want to be.'

"At the end of the day—and I wasn't the only one in his life saying this—at the end of the day, he said he wanted to go all in on being a good dad, a good fiancé, a good ball player, a good teammate, and he thought that would be easier and, quite honestly, safer to do away from Foxborough. He didn't think he could make that change in Foxborough. He thought that would be dangerous, in the sense that there's too many old habits to fall back into, along with people would wouldn't be very happy with his decision.

"At that point, he decided to change his life. It was a little late—right?—because he had signed his new contract, they'd paid him all the money, and he had sworn to play on the Patriots. So we said, 'Listen, you have to have an honest conversation. Go in there and talk to Coach Belichick. Tell him how you feel, what you want to do, why you want to do it, and see what he says.' I was going to go to the meeting with him, but Coach Belichick wanted to do it with just Aaron, which made a lot of sense to me. Nothing wrong with that. And when he came out he felt very good about the meeting. They weren't going to trade him, but he had their support. He knew that the Patriots were going to try to help him accomplish those goals as well."

CHAPTER 43

I was at the Combine in 2013," says Albert Breer, the sports reporter. "I went out to dinner with Aaron and asked him, 'What are you doing here?' An obvious question, because it's not common that veteran players are at the Scouting Combine. He told me he was there to meet with Belichick. He was going to tell Belichick that he was planning to spend the off-season rehabbing in California—that he'd got an apartment out there. His story at that point was, 'I'm doing it to be closer to Brady.' That was during a period when Brady was spending a good chunk of his off-season in LA, at the house that he and Gisele had in Brentwood.

"What I found out later was that his reason for staying out of Massachusetts was that he was too close to Connecticut—and the heat was on. But I remember, on that night he had his hood over his head and was nervous and darty."

According to Ian Rapoport, Hernandez "came to Indy to meet with Belichick and ask to be traded. Basically, to tell

Belichick, 'I'm in trouble.' Like he was getting heat back home. At that point, he was dealing with gangs and gangsters and starting to get really paranoid—maybe for a reason. He wanted to get traded. The Patriots ended up saying that the best way to do it was for him to train—to rehab—in California, where Brady was. To do his rehab and get away from Bristol.

"At the Combine, I went out with a bunch of buddies. Aaron's agent, Brian Murphy. Albert Breer. Greg Bedard, who at that point worked at the *Boston Globe*. A couple of other people. We're having drinks. That's what happens at the Combine—everyone has drinks with everyone. Agents, players, personnel people, coaches. Murph says, 'Hey, a friend of mine is going to show up.' It turns out to be Aaron. He hangs out with us, has a bunch of beers."

Afterward, Hernandez went out with Breer, Rapoport, and Bedard. "We went to an Irish bar close by," Breer says. "There was a friend of mine who's a scout for another team and this guy—his team had had Aaron off the draft board. When we bought shots, the scout raised his glass to Aaron and said, 'Man, we were wrong about you.' Think about that stuff in retrospect. It's mind-blowing. We didn't know anything about the double murder in Boston. I lived down the street from where those murders happened and didn't even hear about them—they weren't a big news story in Boston. Someone who was working with Aaron in Florida told me, 'He's the most talented liar I've ever been around.' But the thing about Aaron was, he was a total chameleon. He was just as comfortable walking with executives as he was walking to the corner in Bristol, Connecticut. He could blend into whatever environment you put him in. I think that was why he was able to get away with a lot of this stuff. But on that one night, while we were there, he seemed fidgety."

"We went to one bar," Rapoport says. "We went to another bar. We got fairly drunk and had a good time."

Breer recalls drinking Irish Car Bombs. Rapoport does not remember Aaron being especially fidgety. But as the evening wore on, Rapoport saw Aaron's mood turn.

"He walks outside to get a cab, and we look out there he's peeing on the cab. It's like, 'Jesus Christ, Aaron, what are you doing? You can't do that!' Greg Bedard had to go out there, shake him loose, and say, 'You can't do these kind of things.'

"Aaron got very angry, but sort of didn't understand why he couldn't do that. He was just doing what he wanted. It was interesting."

"The thing with Aaron fit into this mosaic of a guy who thinks he's above the law," Breer says today. "A guy who operates outside the law, or the rules, or whatever they are. That's the way I would look at it. With Aaron, it was just part of a larger picture."

CHAPTER 44

Hernandez may have told Belichick that spending the off-season in California would bring him closer to Brady. Brian Murphy may have thought that Hernandez had moved out west to get away from bad influences in New England. But Hernandez did not see a lot of Tom Brady in the months that followed, and he did not keep himself out of trouble.

The cement house that he and Shayanna rented in March, at the corner of Lyndon and Hermosa Beach Avenue in Hermosa Beach, looked out over the Pacific Ocean. The idea was to spend two months in paradise: he would relax, spending time with Shayanna and their baby daughter. Instead, he found himself flying old friends, like Bo Wallace, out from Bristol—and, eventually, fighting with Shayanna.

On the evening of March 25, a call came in to the 911 dispatcher in Hermosa Beach. Shayanna was calling. Aaron had just hurt his hand.

"I need an ambulance," Shayanna said. "Immediately. He's losing a lot of blood, he cut himself."

"Where did he cut himself?" the dispatcher asked.

"On his wrist."

"Did he do this on purpose?"

"Yes," Shayanna said. "Are you sending someone?"

"Ma'am, I'm making up the call right now. You need to be calm."

The dispatcher asked Shayanna if her fiancé had ever threatened to hurt himself in the past.

"No," Shayanna said. "No, no, no."

She and Aaron had simply gotten into an argument.

Moving down her checklist, the dispatcher asked Jenkins if alcohol or drugs had been involved. "No," Shayanna said, emphatically.

After a bit more prodding, the dispatcher finally got Shayanna to admit that Aaron had put his fist through a window. "You didn't say that before," she told Shayanna. "You made it sound like he cut himself."

"He's bleeding!" Shayanna yelled. "I don't know…"

If the dispatcher couldn't help her, Shayanna said, she should put somebody nice on the line. Then, before the dispatcher could say anything else, Shayanna hung up.

On several occasions, Aaron's neighbors were the ones who called the police.

At around the time of the 911 call, Aaron and Shayanna visited a tattoo parlor in Hermosa Beach and got a set of matching tattoos.

Remind me that we'll always have each other, Aaron's read, referencing a lyric by the band Incubus.

Shayanna's tattoo completed the verse: *When everything else is gone.*

But a few days later, on April 2, the police were called out to Aaron and Shayanna's rental. When they arrived, they heard fighting and saw that furniture had been thrown around the room.

When the police asked Shayanna to file a report she declined.

Nine days later, on April 11, Aaron drove to a Bank of America in Hermosa Beach to make some deposits. One check, from the Patriots, was for $1,835,809.97. Another, from Puma, added $30,000 to Aaron's balance. After depositing the checks, Aaron asked the teller to wire $15,000 to a Florida bank account belonging the parents of Oscar "Papoo" Hernandez.

According to charges prosecutors would file in District Court in Massachusetts, Papoo passed the money along to Bo Wallace and two other men, who used the funds to buy two pistols, a Colt AR-15, a Hungarian-made AK-47, and a used Toyota Camry—which was used to ship the pistols and the AK-47 from Florida to Aaron's home in North Attleboro, where Shayanna Jenkins ended up signing for it.

Aaron liked the tattoos that he and Shayanna had gotten well enough to return to the shop.

This time, he wanted a tattoo that depicted the smoking muzzle of a semiautomatic handgun, like the one that had been used to shoot Alexander Bradley. He asked the artist to ink a spent shell underneath it.

Above his wrist, Aaron got a tattoo of a revolver with five bullets in its chamber, and had the phrase "God Forgives," written backward so that it could be easily read in the mirror, tattooed beside it.

Subsequently, prosecutors would argue that chambered bullets symbolized the five shots that were fired on the night of the double murder in Boston.

All the while, Aaron was receiving a steady barrage of text messages from Alexander Bradley—who had not forgiven Hernandez at all.

If anything, Bradley seemed to believe that Hernandez owed him recompense for his injuries.

u did that bullshit for no reason n me being the real friend I was to u I didn't try to ruin u even after u tried to kill me, Bradley had written in one text message. think about how real that is . . . the tears should be in my eyes after the way u betrayed me I never crossed u n no way . . .

I luve u and u r not gonna frame me for some bread, Aaron replied.

I would never try to frame u u left me with one eye and a lot of head trauma u owe for what u did n its too bad u don't know me enuff to know that this convo is private between us this ain't for no lawyer or cop too see we both know what happened the truth is the truth if I dealt with police my boy this woulda been over n done with that's whats crazy about this situation we know each other so well u know i aint on no bs u too paranoid that's what made u do this shit u did N last but not least i always wanted the best for u remember that you obviously didn't feel the same.

I will always be there for u till the day u die, Aaron texted, but not in the state of mind ur in nd been in and I don't kno wat gotten into u after all the yrs we were inseparable but everything aside ur always on my mind and I love u and always will no homo.

Whats crazy is I believe that part is true, Bradley replied. u prolly do think about how real of a nigga I am n how u even flipped on me but what sickens me is the fact that u r deny-ing this shit like its for the lawyer or cops yo u must really not know me but i guess i didn't know u either cause i woulda never thought, ud try to end me...

At around this time, Aaron updated his contacts in his phone. From now on, Alexander Bradley would come up as "Lies."

On April 11, the day that Aaron wired $15,000 to Papoo Hernandez's parents, he and Bradley had yet another exchange.

do u have trust worthy niggaz like me around doubt it dog, Bradley texted. 6 strong wit a lot of weapontry so hey u turned this convo into this...

Once again, Aaron denied having done anything wrong.

if u ever got me in trouble or ruin my life for suttin I didn't do I don't even wanna get back at you but u will pay!!!, he texted. I'll be back around the way in a couple months too and I can't wait to see u cuz I see u still be at ur baby mothers crib a bunch! Love u cuz can't stop loving someone that was the only person that I fucked wit and was like a brother to me but dam u are trying to sue me for suttin I didn't do and don't even kno about!!! If u could win that then God is on ur side but I doubt something can be proved that isn't true!!!

Here u go threaten again u know that dont scare me tho if u knew how g eed up i am u wouldnt even say that, Bradley told Hernandez. Then he told Aaron how exactly how "G'd up" he'd gotten, with AK-47s, MAC-11s, MAC-90s at the ready, four bulletproof vests, and Oh, almost 4 got da right niggaz 2 use the weopontry . . .

if you think them wolves ain't on deck then try what u gotta try, Bradley wrote.

The two men went back and forth, mixing threats, veiled and unveiled, with endearments:

What makes u think I wanna kill u u da one who tried 2 kill me n oh I promis ull pay 4 that n u r so boxed in ull be number one suspect . . . (Bradley)

I swear to God either you know you're trying to ruin my life and kill me when all I did was be there for you I still love you no homo I will always love you. (Hernandez)

Now if it aint gonna be this way say fuck it u aint gettn shit from me i file civil suit u loose it al n we hold court n da street u think im scared 2 die . . . (Bradley)

I MISS U AND LOVE YOU and still watch videos of us having fun every single day and can't believe this and will keep saying I can't believe all of this cuz I truly can't believe all of this shit is goin on!! . . . if I would really try and kill u when we were that close!! I wouldn't and never would wanna hurt u and u kno that . . . Love u good nite. (Hernandez)

Not to bother u but feel me on this, Bradley wrote back, sounding like a scorned lover. When u did that . . . its like u coming home 2 yr crib n catching ur broad in bed with another . . . U stole my trust n tore my ego.

CHAPTER 45

At around this time, Hernandez had Bo Wallace contact a company called International Armored Group and place a $120,000 order for a used armored Ford Expedition.

Then, on April 19, Aaron showed up at the Chelsea Pub & Lounge, a few blocks north of his Hermosa Beach house. There, he began to drink—hard: double shots of Patrón Silver, alternating with the bar's "Adios Motherfuckers" cocktail, which blended vodka, rum, tequila, and gin. This had become Aaron's preferred way to drink: a shot of something stiff, followed by some sort of cocktail. On this night, the alcohol went to his head.

Twice, Aaron tried to take his cocktail out onto the sidewalk in front of the pub. Twice, a bouncer had to come out onto the sidewalk to ask him to come back inside.

It was a cool night in Hermosa Beach. Aaron could hear the sea pulling out, the cries of birds. The bar's music blared from inside as he drank. He tried to ignore the bouncer, but the man was persistent:

"Sir," he said. "You can't take drinks outside the bar."

Hernandez sighed as went back inside. He finished his drink, went to the bar, ordered another round, and headed toward the door for a third time.

The bouncer stopped him before he could reach the sidewalk. This time, the bouncer asked him to leave. Hernandez refused, and sat down at a table to finish his drink. He did not seem to understand why he could not take it outside.

As he sat there, fuming, Aaron began to curse at the staff. A few more bouncers approached, and he cursed them, too.

It was the kind of conflict that Alexander Bradley had gotten used to defusing. But Hernandez had pushed Bradley out of his life. By shooting his friend in the head, he had tried to make it a permanent arrangement.

Now, Bradley was one more thing that Aaron Hernandez felt paranoid about.

Sitting there at the table, with the bar's bouncers and staff all around him, Aaron hesitated for a moment. He'd already had run-ins with the cops in Hermosa Beach. If Shayanna had been less loyal, two weeks earlier, he would have gotten arrested.

Aaron did not want to get arrested. Scowling at the staff, he paid his bar tab and left.

CHAPTER 46

That same week, in Florida, Bo Wallace walked into a True Value hardware store—a family-run shop located at the back of a parking lot used by parishioners of the First Baptist Church of Belle Glade.

He passed a display of Wolverine boots and a rack that held silver machetes and cane knives, stopping at the "Guns and Ammo" counter, and asked the clerk for a .22-caliber pistol.

According to Massachusetts State Trooper Jeremiah Donovan, Wallace liked small guns. "He likes having a little gun on him because it doesn't stick out and it does the job," Donovan explains.

According to Carlos Ortiz, Wallace's name for a .22 was a "deuce deuce."

The clerk had just the gun Wallace wanted. He pulled out a small silver-and-black Jimenez, and Wallace bought it, paying with cash that Papoo had given him, and left.

Wallace knew Belle Glade well. He had grown up sixty miles south, in Miramar—another small, dying American town. His mother, Angella, still lived in Miramar and he would visit her often, swimming in the pool behind Angella's house.

It was a welcome break from the kind of trouble Wallace got into up north, in the company of his old friend Aaron Hernandez.

A month later, on May 18, Hernandez and Wallace were drinking at Viva, a bar one block away from Brown University in Providence, Rhode Island. It was two o'clock on a Saturday afternoon, and Viva was packed with football fans. But the Patriots had lost the championship game that year, and not all of them were happy to see Hernandez. When Aaron and Wallace exited the bar, a large group followed them out to the street.

"Fuck the Patriots," one man said. "I'm a Jets fan!"

Once again, Hernandez decided to walk away. There were too many hecklers to deal with. Splitting from Wallace, he walked north, passing the Avon Cinema's old, historic marquee. But the crowd from Viva followed him, heckling loudly.

For once, Aaron was glad to see the police, who arrived quickly to break up the crowd. The cops were concerned that Hernandez was going to be assaulted—and a few men from the crowd did manage to break away and follow Aaron as he walked toward his car. But the police scrambled and detained them, too.

As they did so, a Brown University police officer patrolling a few blocks away saw a man toss a small handgun under a parked car. The campus cop yelled after the man, who ran up the block, crossed the street, and disappeared from sight.

The cop never got close enough to identify the man, with any certainty, as Ernest Wallace. But he did retrieve the handgun.

It was the Jimenez .22 that Wallace had purchased down in Belle Glade.

The gun was fully loaded.

PART SIX

Terri Hernandez, yearbook photo, 1977

TERRI A. VALENTINE
Sophisticated Lady

Dennis Hernandez, yearbook photo, 1975

Dennis Hernandez
The King

Aaron Hernandez's childhood home on Greystone Avenue *(Getty Images)*

Hernandez in
2005 (*AP*)

Playing in the Battle for the Bell (*Mike Orazzi*)

Aaron and DJ Hernandez
(*Mike Orazzi*)

Tim Tebow (*Mark Seliger*)

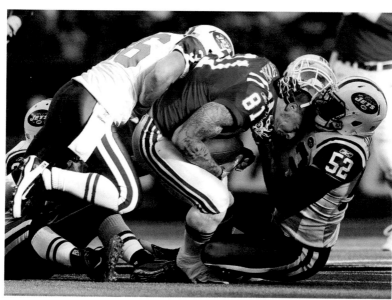

Hernandez playing against the New York Jets, 2011 (*Getty Images*)

Hernandez in 2012 (*Getty Images*)

Odin Lloyd (*Getty Images*)

The clearing where Odin Lloyd's body was discovered (*Bristol County Clerk's Office*)

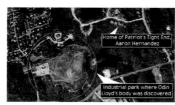

Aerial photograph of the crime scene, introduced into evidence in the Odin Lloyd murder trial (*Bristol County Clerk's Office*)

Hernandez's home in North Attleboro (*AP Photo* / Attleboro Sun Chronicle, *Mark Stockwell*)

Surveillance footage of Hernandez holding a gun *(Bristol County Clerk's Office)*

Surveillance video of Shayanna Jenkins removing a box from her home *(Bristol County Clerk's Office)*

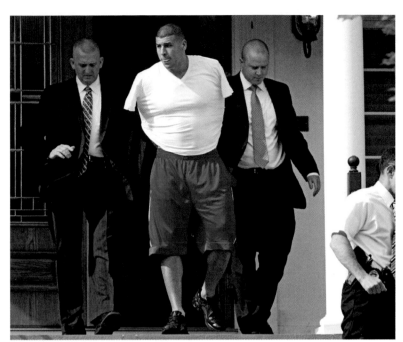

Hernandez placed under arrest (*George Rizer*/Boston Globe)

Prosecutor William McCauley questions Detective Mike Elliott during the Odin Lloyd murder trial. (*AP Photo/Dominick Reuter, Pool*)

Carlos Ortiz (*AP*)

Ernest Wallace (*Bristol County Clerk's Office*)

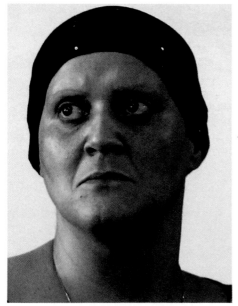

Tanya Singleton (*AP*)

Defense attorney James Sultan during the Odin Lloyd murder trial *(AP Photo*/Boston Globe, *John Tlumacki, Pool)*

William McCauley questions Patriots owner Robert Kraft. *(AP/*Boston Globe, *John Tlumacki, Pool)*

Shayanna Jenkins testifies. *(CJ Gunther/AP)*

Jennifer Fortier takes the stand. *(AP)*

Terri Hernandez and Shayanna Jenkins break down as the verdict is read. *(Trial footage)*

Shaneah Jenkins consoles Ursula Ward. (*Dominick Reuter/AP*)

Souza-Baranowski Correctional Center (*Sandy Hill/AP*)

Hernandez and Jose Baez (*Chris Christo/AP*)

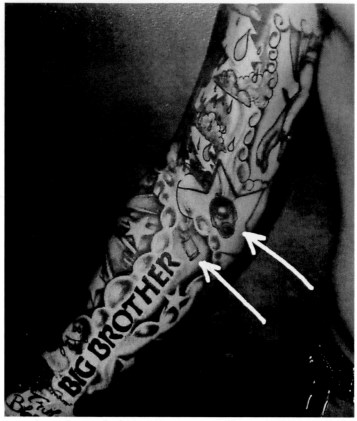

An evidence photograph of Hernandez's tattoos, including a smoking muzzle and a spent shell (*AP*)

Hernandez's "Lifetime Loyalty" prison tattoo (*AP*)

Alexander Bradley testifies. *(Steven Senne/AP)*

Shayanna Jenkins and Avielle Hernandez in court *(Keith Bedford/Boston Globe via AP)*

Hernandez blows kisses to his daughter, Avielle. *(AP)*

Kyle Kennedy *(AP)*

Hernandez cries as the jury delivers its verdict in his second trial. (*AP*)

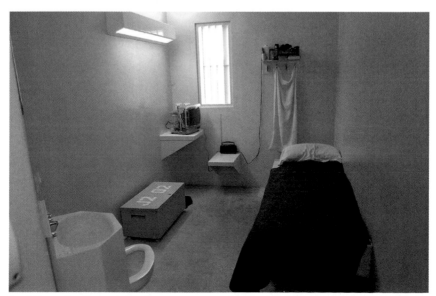

A cell identical to Hernandez's cell at Souza-Baranowski (*David L. Ryan*/Boston Globe *via Getty Images*)

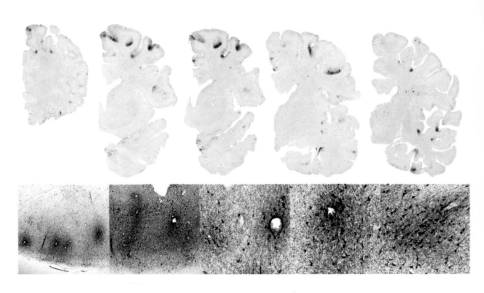

Cross sections of Hernandez's brain *(Anne McKee, MD/CTE Center, Boston University)*

CHAPTER 47

Aaron had been manning the grill all day. Three days earlier, on May 29, Shayanna had turned twenty-four.

Now that the weekend had come, she and Aaron were going to party all the way through to Sunday.

If Aaron had spent the past few weeks arming himself, preparing for an all-out war with Alexander Bradley, he'd done an excellent job of concealing his fears from his friends.

Dozens of friends and family members had spent the afternoon at his place, jumping in and out of the swimming pool, drinking, eating off the grill. Shayanna's sister Shaneah was there, along with her boyfriend, Odin.

Once again, his mask was firmly in place.

DJ Hernandez was at the house, too, along with Shayanna's uncle, Azia "Littleman" Jenkins, and Aaron's friend and henchman, Bo Wallace. Slowly, as the day progressed, people left, until only a dozen remained. Now, with nighttime approaching, that dozen piled into a party bus Aaron and Shayanna had booked for the occasion.

They were headed to Rumor, a nightclub in Boston. The trip would take an hour each way, but inside the party bus the music was blasting and booze was flowing freely.

When they arrived, Aaron and his friends found that Rumor was packed.

This was no surprise—the club was one of Boston's most popular nightspots. But Aaron Hernandez was a VIP, and the staff at Rumor made sure that he and his friends got a good spot to continue their party.

The club closed at two. Aaron's bus made its way back to North Attleboro. Odin Lloyd split off for home.

Lloyd lived just a few miles away, in Dorchester. Unlike Aaron, who only played football, Odin played football *and* worked for a living. Like his girlfriend, Shaneah, Odin had dreams, and was willing to do whatever it took to realize them.

But, Odin had to admit, hanging with Aaron Hernandez was fun.

A week later, he, Aaron, Shaneah, and Shayanna were partying again, at South Street Café in North Providence. Odin and Aaron went outside, several times, to smoke marijuana. Hernandez's nickname for Lloyd was "Blunt Master"—Odin was just that quick, rolling his blunts. Aaron went through blunts almost as quickly as Odin could roll them. And when a waitress stepped outside to ask Aaron and Odin to smoke somewhere else, Aaron laughed her off.

The truth was that marijuana had never been a big deal for Aaron. The promises he had made before signing with the

Patriots had all been forgotten. As time went on, an acquaintance recalls, Hernandez became brazen about it.

"First of all," the acquaintance says, "Aaron was always into drugs. Obviously, he had failed drug tests. But the crazy thing was, he became so flamboyant about what he was doing with drugs. I know for a fact that there was a player's phone that he would take and do drug deals on. A phone right there, in the Patriots' locker room."

It was as if Aaron was making the point, yet again, that everyday rules did not apply to an Aaron Hernandez.

Another work week went by and then, on June 14, Odin was back at Rumor, along with Aaron Hernandez and Aaron's barber and friend, Robby Olivares. A friend of Odin's—a man named Kwami Nicholas—was also at the club that night.

Along with other witnesses, Nicholas would later say that it looked as if Aaron and Odin were not getting along. Outside of the club, Nicholas said, Aaron and Odin got into an argument. Surveillance videos taken that night back Nicholas up: It shows Hernandez waving his arms angrily. Afterward, he and Odin gravitated toward different groups in the club. They remained apart for the rest of the evening.

Some witnesses would say that Aaron was angry at Odin for talking to people, inside of the club, that Aaron had not wanted Odin to talk to.

Some said that those people were friends of Daniel de Abreu and Safiro Furtado—the Cape Verdean men who had been gunned down outside of another Boston nightclub, a year previously.

It's also possible that Lloyd was talking to West Indian

cousins of his at the club, and that Hernandez took those men to be Cape Verdean.

Whatever the conflict had been, Aaron and Odin seemed to have resolved it by the time the club closed. They left together, with Aaron picking up a couple of women on their way home.

One of those women, Jennifer Fortier, was the on-again-off-again nanny for Aaron's daughter, Avielle.

CHAPTER 48

Like many NFL wives and girlfriends, Shayanna had come to accept the fact that Aaron would not—or could not—be faithful to her.

A few years earlier, Shayanna had caught Aaron cheating and moved out for several weeks. When they reconciled, it had been on Aaron's terms. "I made a decision that if I was going to move back with Aaron, I would have to kind of compromise on his behavior—and that included infidelity and everything that came along with it," Jenkins would say on the witness stand.

But Aaron did not go out of the way to flaunt his indiscretions. That was one of the reasons he'd gotten himself an apartment in Franklin.

Located ten miles away from Gillette Stadium, the apartment was a crash pad for Aaron and his friends (Bo Wallace stayed there on several occasions), as well as a place to smoke weed. The Patriots' director of player development, Kevin Anderson, had helped him to rent it in May.

It was Aaron's destination on the night that he and Odin Lloyd argued, and Aaron took Odin, Jennifer Fortier, and Fortier's friend, Amanda DeVito, along for the ride.

Jennifer Fortier was young and attractive. With her dark hair and high cheekbones, she looked a bit like a lighter-skinned Shayanna Jenkins. On the witness stand, she would say that she and Amanda had just left the club when they spotted Hernandez, who was sitting in an SUV with Odin Lloyd and Robby Olivares, the barber.

"I just looked over and there he was," she explained. "I walked by and I saw him, and I looked in and he saw me and said, 'hello'—and then he said, 'get in.'"

Fortier says that she had asked Hernandez for a ride to her car, parked a few blocks away. Aaron said yes. She and Amanda climbed in the back, where Robby was sitting, and Aaron drove off in the opposite direction.

Surprised, Fortier asked Hernandez to turn around. "I kept telling him I needed to leave, because I was the babysitter and I wasn't comfortable."

Several times, Fortier asked Hernandez to bring her back to her car. But Aaron was already out on the highway. "There's a rest area," he told Fortier. "Do you want me to drop you off here?"

The nanny refused. She had no idea where they were, it was the middle of the night, and the battery on her cell phone had died.

According to Jennifer, Aaron, Odin, and Robby were high.

"The three guys were smoking," she would say. "And they were smoking what I would think was marijuana."

Ignoring the nanny's objections, Hernandez drove "all the way back to North Attleboro to drop the kid that was sitting to the right of me off," Fortier recalled. According to her, Hernandez told Olivares that he did not want Shayanna to see his car. The barber could walk to his own car, which he had parked close to Aaron's house.

Once he had let Robby out, Aaron drove Jennifer, Amanda, and Odin to the apartment in Franklin.

CHAPTER 49

Carol Bailey is a retired biology professor who still lives next door to Aaron's old apartment in Franklin. On warm days, she sits out in the courtyard, minding her two cats and getting to know her neighbors.

"It's an apartment complex," she explains. "I was in number 11. He was in number 12. We shared a common wall in the living room, kitchen, bathroom, and one of the bedrooms. Because the wall is made out of cement blocks, and extremely insulated, I wasn't able to hear anything. But the hallway doors are not soundproofed at all. I had to pass his unit on the way out of the building. When I did, I could hear and smell anything from inside.

"Number 12 had been empty for a while. Then it was bought by a local real estate agent. I would see him coming and going. A certain amount of work went into the place. I knew they were getting ready to rent it. Somebody mentioned that someone connected to the New England Patriots would be moving in.

"Well, this is a not the high-rent district. This is an affordable area. I pictured a statistician moving in, or a groundskeeper. Goodness knows, I didn't picture a football player! But one day, I went out into a courtyard and an SUV—a big one—drove in. I didn't recognize it and thought, 'Oh, this is someone who doesn't live here.' Then that person parked the car and got out. I said, 'Hi! Are you moving in?' He said, 'Yes,' and I said, 'Oh, you must be my new neighbor!' He said, 'I'm moving in with my cousin, Aaron,' but it didn't register with me. He might as well have said 'Alan,' or 'Adrian.' But he was very pleasant, we had a very nice chat, and then he went in."

Bailey's new neighbor told her that his name was "George." Then, a day or two later, another vehicle that Bailey did not recognize drove into the courtyard. "This was a great, big, black Hummer," Bailey says. "The guy who got out was tall. He's got gray sweatpants and a gray hoodie. I said, 'Hi! You must be my other new neighbor. You must be George's cousin!'

"He looked at me and grunted. That was it. I could see his face very clearly, and a little later I went online, looked up Patriots players, and saw one named Aaron Hernandez who looked exactly like the man I had seen."

Sometimes "George" and Aaron would come in together. Sometimes they came and went separately.

"Whenever I would see George," Bailey says, "he would give me a great big smile and wave and say pleasant things: 'Nice day' or 'How're you doing.' Every time Aaron came or went and I said anything to him, he either ignored me or grunted. I didn't see him very often. He probably came in later in the evening, when I had come in from the courtyard. But then I'd be sitting here, getting my supper, and all of a sudden, a strange smell would come in under my door from the hallway.

"At first, I didn't know what it was. It smelled like a skunk, and I'm a wildlife biologist, so I thought, 'Oh my gosh! There's a skunk in the neighborhood!' But when I went out on my balcony and sniffed, there was no skunk smell outside, and as I got closer to my living room door, the smell got stronger. When I opened the door into the hallway, it was considerably stronger. I thought, 'That's funny. That skunky smell is coming from the hallway. Then, I began to notice that the smell would happen late in the afternoon, early in the evening, or later in the evening.

"At some point, I asked a young couple who were neighbors in the complex: 'There's a strange smell in the hallway and it seems to be coming from my new next-door neighbors. It smells sort of like skunk.' They looked at each other and made funny faces. One said, 'That's pot.' The other one said simultaneously, 'That's weed.' I thought, 'My gosh, that's strange because that's not what it smelled like when I was in college.'

"One thing I neglected to mention is that, from that very first day that he walked by and grunted, wearing the hoodie and all, it occurred to me that my neighbor didn't want it to be known who he was or that he was living here. I thought, 'I will respect his privacy. I won't say anything.' If people asked I would say, 'I don't know.' But no one asked. No one said anything. I got the feeling that other people didn't know—or that, if they did know, they did like I'd done. They wanted to respect his privacy, too.

"Then I found out that he had a mansion in North Attleboro and realized this was his getaway. He didn't want to smoke pot at home with his baby and his girlfriend, so he came here to hang out and do guy things. There wasn't so much smoke that it bothered me, and George was always very pleasant. I live on the third floor. If I was carrying heavy groceries, he was happy to help. One day he knocked on my door. He had a plug-in air-freshener in his hand and two little glass vases with liquid and sticks in them. He said, 'Do you mind if I put these in the hallway? Because sometimes it smells out here and these might help. He put the plug-in at one end of the hallway, and the vials with the liquid and sticks coming out at the other end. One of those vials is still out there."

A few weeks later, Bailey recalls, "I was coming home and two reporters came out of their car. They said, 'We have a video clip to show you from Florida.' They opened up their laptop, or whatever the heck it was. They didn't say anything else—they just showed me the video. It was someone being arraigned in front of a judge. The judge was saying, 'Give us your full name please.' He was talking to a black man with salt-and-pepper hair, like George had. The man looked to be about the same age as George. When the man said, 'My name is Ernest George Wallace,' I thought: 'By golly, that's George!'"

CHAPTER 50

Up on the third floor of the apartment complex, Aaron took out a key and opened the door to number 12.

Turning to Jennifer Fortier, he explained that this was his uncle's apartment.

"There was a kitchen, a living room, two bedrooms, and a bathroom," Fortier would say. "We got there and Aaron had got some wine out of the fridge. I didn't have any because I don't drink. We just sat. The boys were smoking, Aaron and Odin."

A half hour later, Fortier says, Hernandez left the living room, disappeared into one of the bedrooms, and started to call her name. Fortier walked over. Aaron was sitting on the bed. The two of them talked for about ten minutes. Then, Fortier says, Aaron leaned in kissed her.

"He kissed me and I pushed him away and told him, 'No. I'm your nanny. I can't do this,'" Jennifer recalled. "He said he understood, that it was okay and he wasn't mad at me."

Aaron ended up falling asleep. Out in the living room, Odin was also sleeping. Jennifer borrowed her friend Amanda's phone. "I called every cab place that I could to get one as soon as possible," she would say.

Fortier and DeVito left together, taking the cab that had finally arrived to the W Hotel in Boston, where their car was parked. Then, DeVito drove Fortier to Salem, New Hampshire, where Fortier's mother was waiting to meet her for breakfast.

All in all, Fortier's ordeal had lasted for five or six hours.

When he woke up on Saturday and found her gone, Aaron sent a text, on Odin's phone, to Shayanna.

I fucked up again, he wrote, at 8:57 in the morning, and fuck, I didn't mean to but got drunk and too fucked up and O took care of me an somehow tol him about my other spot and I just woke up buggin I'm sorry and on way home.

In the weeks and months that followed, police officers in and around North Attleboro would take it for granted that Jennifer Fortier had made up her story. As far as they were concerned, it was obvious that "Hernandez had been banging the babysitter."

If Fortier's cell phone was dead, why did she wait until the very end of the night to use DeVito's? And what was DeVito herself doing, during the duration of this ordeal?

Whatever the answers were, the cops reasoned, Fortier's trip to Franklin gave Aaron Hernandez a reason to be suspicious of Odin Lloyd, and anything Odin might have said to Shayanna's sister.

In truth, any number of things could have caused Aaron and Odin to argue, earlier that evening or afterward. Aaron could have told Odin about the double murder, then had second thoughts. Odin might have overheard something about the shooting of Alexander Bradley. Or, Aaron might have seen Odin speaking to friends of Safiro Furtado and Daniel de Abreu, and grown suspicious.

Law enforcement officers would also come to believe that (despite his supposed affair with the nanny) Aaron was bisexual. If so, the possibilities shifted: The police wondered if Aaron had made a pass at Odin. If Aaron *was* bisexual, their reasoning went, he had gone to great lengths to conceal it. If Odin had rebuffed him, there was no telling what Aaron would have done.

Of course, there were other possibilities: Aaron and Odin had gotten drunk, gotten stoned, and had some stupid, drug-induced misunderstanding. Or, Aaron was so paranoid that he had picked an argument over nothing. In the past, Alexander Bradley had reined Aaron in, to an extent. But now, Alex Bradley was gone—or, not quite gone.

If anything, Bradley's refusal to quite go away might have set the stage for Odin Lloyd's murder.

The fact of the matter is, no one knows. What we do know is that, within twenty-four hours, Odin Lloyd was dead.

CHAPTER 51

That Sunday—Father's Day, June 16, 2013—Aaron Hernandez texted Brian Murphy. He caught the agent just as Murphy was sitting down in church.

Murphy knew about the threatening texts from Alexander Bradley. He had advised Aaron not to reply. He'd been in the room for a phone call between Mark Humenik, general counsel for Athletes First, and Bradley's lawyer.

Murphy and Humenik had discussed the possibility of a monetary settlement—Bradley was asking for $1.3 million—with the lawyer. But the phone call had failed to produce an agreement.

Aaron's agent had also directed him to Ropes & Gray, a law firm with offices in Boston.

Murphy had been a lawyer himself. After graduating from Harvard Law, in 1995, he'd spent a few years working at Ropes & Gray. He knew the firm's lawyers in Boston well, and had flown there, after the texts from Bradley be-

gan to come in, to discuss the matter with them and with
Aaron.

Despite their best efforts, the texts kept on coming.

*Don't understand why if you was man enough to shoot me you
ain't man enough to compensate me,* Bradley had written.

And: *I guess I'm a bitch cuz when I think about what you
did I cry.*

And: *How I felt when you did me like that in front of them niggas was heartbroken and ego-torn. Dog, niggas in my hood was
saying 'this nigga let this Bristol ass nigga smoke him.' Thought I
was retarded till I started coming through and hitting niggas up
for spreading rumors about me or my kids.*

And: *I'm not going to allow you to go on living this high life
without compensating me for that bum sucker shit.*

Despite Murphy's advice, Aaron couldn't help but engage.
Time and again, Hernandez told Bradley he loved him. That
there was no one else he could trust. And, at times, Bradley
adopted the same affectionate tone: *If you really loved me and
then you'd want to settle this. And whatever is in store for us is in
store. If we're going to be cool again that's what it'll be but it gotta
start with resolving this incident that went down.*

Listen, Bradley told Hernandez, *again, I hate that it comes to
this but you can't go through life consequence free when you do
certain shit. You should want to do this if you really miss and love
me. It's crazy enough in itself that I really don't even feel a way toward you, in the sense that I don't even think about trying to hurt
you or anyone you love. It's really like I have forgiven you, but you
gotta do what you gotta do, meaning you know this conversation
thing is inevitable. I hate the fact that I even gotta handle this like*

this. You shoulda been offering this to me. But just like it was real when it happened to me, it's real. It's going to happen to you if we can't resolve this. And I know you know that I don't lie about this shit. You were my brother, best friend, and a lot of things to me . . .

But, for all of Bradley's pleading, Aaron had not offered to compensate him. If Bradley was trying to game him for evidence, Aaron would simply deny having shot him. But, of course, Bradley *knew* who had shot him. He knew that *Aaron* knew. This made Aaron's denials all the more infuriating. And so, Bradley finally took action.

For months, Bradley had been threatening to file a civil lawsuit against his former friend.

"You're the closest thing to the police without being the police," Hernandez had told him.

("The matter of me trying to sue him, he was trying to equate that to me being a snitch," Bradley would say.)

Nevertheless, on June 13, Bradley had finally filed the lawsuit.

Now, with Bradley backing him into a corner, Hernandez was texting his agent.

Maybe the lawyers could get him out of this jam.

CHAPTER 52

The sun was sinking slowly in Boston. Odin Lloyd's football team, the Boston Bandits, had just arrived at a high school football field for a Father's Day scrimmage against the Eastern Mass Seminoles.

Lloyd's coach, Mike Branch, was unloading gear in the parking lot when he saw a brand-new black Chevy Suburban roll in.

"Nice car," the players said. But it wasn't the SUV that had the coach's attention. It was the driver.

"*Odin?*" Branch said.

The coach knew that Odin did not own a car. If anything, Odin was known for his habit of showing up to football games on a BMX bike.

"Whose car is this? You ain't got no goddamn car!"

Lloyd told Branch that he shouldn't worry, but Branch did not let the matter drop.

"I'm just going to go to the glove box and see whose car it is," he told Odin. "Odin was like, 'You know whose car it is!' That's all that he had to say."

"How's it hanging with that dude?" Branch asked.

"He's all right," Lloyd said. "He's cool. He dropped some money at the bar the other night."

Lloyd had played for the Bandits since 2007—the year that Aaron began playing for Florida. Since then, Coach Branch had seen Odin lose his job as an electrician and go to work as a day laborer for a landscaping firm. The coach knew that the work was hard. "He was busting his ass with the landscaping," Branch remembers. He would ride Odin's ass about getting onto a better career path: "I know he didn't want to be a police officer," Branch says. "I'm like, 'Why not go into firefighting? You're big. You're strong. You care about people.'"

Branch worked as Chief Probation Officer at the district court in Brockton. He took his coaching role seriously. His players thought of him as a big brother, and he took an interest in their off-field lives. When Odin fell in love with Shaneah Jenkins, he took notice.

"He was out in Connecticut, working for the electric company," the coach recalls. "They put him up at a hotel, she worked at the hotel, and he liked her, so he kept working and working. He kept going down to her shift and talking to her. I knew that he was getting hooked because I'd be like, 'Yo, we've got a game. We need you. I need you this week.' But he would tell me that he couldn't make it."

Now, in Jamaica Plain, Branch watched Lloyd greet his friend Darryl Hodge—a running back who ran like a track star and treated Odin like a brother. The two of them had planned on hanging out after the scrimmage and watching game five of the NBA finals. But Odin's boss had called to say that he would be needed early in the morning. They got barbecue with the rest of the Bandits instead, with Odin dropping Darryl off afterward in the SUV, which Aaron Hernandez had rented and loaned to him.

Just as he was pulling up in front of Darryl's home, at around nine in the evening, Lloyd received a text from Hernandez.

Earlier that day, Aaron had gotten a text from Brian Murphy: They are voluntarily withdrawing lawsuit so we can engage in settlement talks without this getting to the media, the agent had written. Huge win for us. Call me.

Murphy had informed Bradley's lawyer that, if he *did* file the lawsuit, Hernandez would have no incentive to settle. Aaron "had clearly not done what was being claimed," the agent says, "but the negative publicity was not welcome. We may have been willing to pay a small price to avoid that."

According to Murphy, the lawyer wanted to settle, and agreed to withdraw the suit. It's also possible that the lawsuit was withdrawn due to a filing error. Whatever the case was, Murphy was happy to pass along the news.

But if Aaron had managed to escape at least one of the traps that Bradley had laid for him, he was about to get himself into far more trouble over Odin Lloyd.

I'm coming to grab that tonight, Aaron told Odin. u gon b around I need dat and we could step for a little again.

Odin looked at the text and told Darryl that they'd catch up soon.

But the next time that Darryl would see Odin's face, it would be on the news.

CHAPTER 53

Two minutes after texting Odin Lloyd, Hernandez texted Bo Wallace: Please make it back CuZ, I'm Def trying to step for alittle.

Then Aaron texted Odin again: Whaddup.

Aite where, Odin replied.

Idk it don't matter but imam hit you when I'm dat way like Las time if my phone dies imma hit u when I charge it which will be in a lil.

One minute later, Aaron texted Wallace again: Get ur ass up here, he wrote.

Wallace and Carlos Ortiz were at Tanya Singleton's house in Bristol, a hundred miles southwest of North Attleboro. Aaron told them to hurry, but they were still driving at midnight, when Lloyd texted Hernandez again.

We still on? Odin asked.

Surveillance footage from the security system at Aaron's house shows Wallace and Ortiz arriving at Hernandez's house eight minutes later. Aaron's nanny, Jennifer, lets them in and they go down to the basement to wait for Aaron's arrival.

Twenty minutes later, Shayanna's Audi Q7 pulls up and Aaron and Shayanna get out. Bo and Carlos walk outside to greet them, then the four of them go back inside. In the living room, surveillance cameras capture Hernandez passing a gun from one hand to the other before he accompanies Wallace and Ortiz back to the basement. A little while later, they head back upstairs, go outside, and climb into a Nissan Altima Aaron had rented.

Over the course of the next hour, Lloyd got five calls from Wallace's cell phone. Then, at two thirty in the morning, Hernandez picked Odin up at the Dorchester home he shared with his mother and sisters.

One of those sisters—Shaquilla—was sitting in a car down the street when Hernandez pulled up. She watched Odin get into the Altima. A half hour later, he sent her a text: U saw who I'm with, Odin had written.

A law enforcement official familiar with the case says that, after picking Odin up, Aaron blew through tolls on the Massachusetts Turnpike and fired a Glock .45 at road signs they passed.

The official also believes that Hernandez hit a traffic cone on the turnpike, broke off his driver's side mirror, and kept driving.

Inside the Altima, Odin kept checking his cell phone. It had been ten minutes since he'd texted Shaquilla. Ten minutes and no response.

Odin sent another text: hello.

Eight minutes later, Shaquilla finally replied: my phone was dead who was that?

Lloyd responded: Nfl.

Lol you're aggy, Shaquilla wrote back—cell-phone shorthand for "aggravated." But inside the Altima, the mood had turned.

One minute later, Odin sent Shaquilla one more text: just so you know, he wrote.

After that, there were no more messages.

CHAPTER 54

Odin Lloyd's mother, Ursula Ward, had gone to church—
the Episcopal Church of the Holy Spirit, in Mattapan—
on Sunday morning. Afterward, Odin pulled up at the
house to wish her a happy Father's Day.

"Mom," he said. "You look so beautiful today. I love those
colors on you."

Ursula was wearing earth colors: A dirt-brown top along
with a brown skirt that had yellow, green, and gold "en-
twined into the whole."

"I wore the same outfit at his funeral," Ursula says. "I know
he loved to see me in it."

Ursula had raised Odin by herself, in Saint Croix and
Massachusetts, where she worked as an aide in a senior cit-
izens' home. "He was one of *those* kids," she says now. "His
smile alone would brighten your life."

In 2011, Ursula Ward lost her job. By the summer of
2013, she had used up her unemployment and was paying

her mortgage by dipping into her 401K. "It was a struggle," she says. "A really right struggle." But Ursula was a strong woman. She had gone back to school. Her church and her children gave her life meaning. Odin—Ursula's only son—was her pride and joy.

Ever since Odin had met Shaneah Jenkins, he had been happy and full of purpose.

"Mom," Odin would tell her. "She's the one, Mom. I'm really serious with her. She's going to be my future wife."

Afterward, Ursula says, she grew to love Shaneah "like she's my child."

On his way out of the house that Sunday, Odin had told his mother that he was on his way to a scrimmage. "Mom, you know I love you," he said.

At nine thirty on Monday evening, a call from Trooper Eric Benson came through.

"Ms. Ward," Benson said.

"Yes?"

"Do you know Odin Lloyd?"

"Yeah. That's my son."

"Okay, ma'am. I'm sending two detectives, and probably two detectives from Boston Police, to your house."

Ursula did not allow herself think, immediately, that anything had happened to Odin. But then her daughter Olivia started to cry.

"Why are you crying?" Ursula said.

"Mom, they don't just send the police to your house for nothing," Olivia said.

"What do you mean?"

"Mom," Olivia said. "I watch enough *CSI*."

"She kept saying these things," Ursula recalls. "Well, I am not going to think anything bad. Maybe my son is in a hospital. Maybe he needs blood. That's why they're coming over here. She's like, 'No, mom.' I say, 'Take the negative thing and get out of my room, please.' She walked out of the room, and went into her room, and started crying. I was already in my pajamas, so I got up and put on some clothes. At about ten thirty, they arrive at the house.

"I don't remember who answered the door. But I remember it was four officers that came up the stairs. One asked me a bunch of questions. I said, 'Listen. I am not answering any more questions until you all tell me what is going on with my son.' One said to me, 'I'm sorry, ma'am, but your son was shot and killed.'

"I fell to the floor. I said, 'Someone just took my heart out.' Then I jumped right up and said, 'First of all, why you are coming here talking foolishness to me? How do you know that was my son?' He said to me, 'Ma'am, he had his wallet in his pocket with his driver's license.' And I just fell right back down again.

"You know throughout this whole thing—it taught me so many lessons about life. How people pretend to be one kind of person, but you find a monstrous person underneath. I never met the young man before. I can't tell you he was a nice guy coming into the house. I can't tell who he was. But I know who my son is, and I know that if my son knew anything negative about this individual, he would not have stayed around him."

CHAPTER 55

Shaneah Jenkins's first thought had been, "Odin's calling." It was late: just past one in the morning on Tuesday, June 18. Shaneah had tried Odin several times on Monday, without hearing back. She didn't know where her boyfriend was. But, now, as she looked at the phone, she realized she did not know the incoming number.

Trooper Benson was on the other end of the line.

Benson had been out at the clearing where Odin's body had been discovered. He had seen the storm roll in, watched the detectives as they scoured the crime scene for evidence. Back at the station, he had called Enterprise Rent-A-Car, and traced the keys Odin had had in his pocket to Aaron Hernandez. Then, he had placed the call to Odin Lloyd's mother.

A few hours later, the task of calling Shaneah had also fallen to him.

Jenkins cried when Benson told her that Odin was dead. She recalled meeting him, at the Comfort Suites hotel she'd worked at in Southington. That front desk job (which Shaneah had gotten through Shayanna, who had worked at the Comfort Suites herself) was one of three jobs Shaneah had held down at the time, while putting herself through college.

Shaneah was smart and ambitious, as well as hard-working. She'd planned ahead for her future with Odin.

Now, she was alone in Dorchester and Odin would never be coming home. The only place Shaneah could think to go was her sister's house. She arrived, along with her uncle Littleman and one of her nieces, just before six in the morning, entering through the garage and walking up into the living room.

Shayanna greeted her there with a long, strong hug. Shaneah sobbed and Shayanna listened, sympathetically. Finally, Shaneah lay down on her sister's sofa and fell into a deep, dreamless sleep, from which she woke crying. She checked on her niece, who was sleeping beside her.

Then, at around eight in the morning, she watched Aaron come through the front door.

"I've been through this death thing before," Hernandez told Shayanna's sister. "It will get better in time."

PART SEVEN

CHAPTER 56

While Shaneah slept, Shayanna ran all over the house. First, she took a large, black garbage bag down to the basement, out of view of the home's surveillance cameras. Moments later she came back up with the same black bag and left the house, taking her sister's car.

Inside of the bag, there was a box that Aaron had told her to get rid of.

It was still morning and Shayanna drove around "aimlessly," as she would put it, until she found a dumpster that called out to her. She tossed the garbage bag inside, along with the box that Aaron had given her.

"I'd learned not to ask questions," she would say.

Aaron Hernandez had also been busy. Upon waking, he'd called for a cleaning crew to come to his house. Before long, three women had arrived and gone straight to work. (Prosecutors would later accuse Shayanna of threatening the women with deportation if they talked about anything they had seen.)

That afternoon, Hernandez, Wallace, and Ortiz left the house. With storm clouds looming on the horizon, they drove to an Enterprise rental location to return the Altima he had used the night before. As they were driving, Matthew Kent, the high school student, jogged through Corliss Landing and stumbled upon Odin Lloyd's body.

At the Enterprise, Aaron told the location's branch manager, Keelia Smyth, that the Altima had been damaged: A broken mirror, the dent in the driver's side door.

Aaron was polite—he offered Smyth a piece of chewing gum.

What's a twenty-three-year-old man doing with a pack of Bub-blicious, Smyth thought. *Aren't you a little old for that?*

"I'm good," she told Aaron.

Hernandez told Smyth that he didn't know how the car had been damaged.

"I could tell he was lying," Smyth says, today. "But he had full coverage on our vehicle."

The manager offered Hernandez a Kia Soul.

Hernandez wouldn't be caught dead in a Kia, he said.

"I know, I know," Smyth replied. "I'm just kidding you."

She gave Hernandez a Chrysler 300 instead, and Hernandez, Wallace, and Ortiz drove back to North Attleboro. It was just past five in the afternoon. Before the hour was up, North Attleboro police would be at the clearing.

At five fifteen, Wallace climbed into the driver's seat of the Chrysler, Ortiz climbed into the passenger seat, and the two men headed up to the apartment Hernandez had rented in

Franklin. While they drove, police secured the crime scene, setting up the tent and tarps they would use to keep the rain from washing evidence away.

Down at the station, North Attleboro PD traced the rental car keys that they had found in Odin Lloyd's pocket back to Aaron Hernandez. They searched Odin's cell phone and saw the last batch of texts that Odin had received and sent.

But "at that point," an officer involved with the investigation remembers, "we didn't know any more. We thought that Aaron might be dead, too."

That evening, at twenty minutes to ten, Massachusetts State Trooper Michael Cherven and Detective Daniel Arrighi took their unmarked Ford Escape down to Aaron's house and parked in the driveway. Lights were on all over the house—downstairs, upstairs. From the front porch, Cherven could see into Aaron's living room. The large, flat-screen TV was on. There were half-full glasses on the coffee table. A bottle lay on its side on the couch. But when Cherven knocked on the door, and rang the bell several times, no one answered.

Cherven ended up walking over to the garage, where Arrighi gave him a boost so that he could peek through the windows, which were high off the ground.

There was a car inside. It was the Toyota Camry that Papoo Hernandez had used to ship guns up from Florida. But the police did not know that, and nothing about the car looked suspicious.

Then Cherven and Arrighi went around to the backyard. Taking out their flashlights, they looked for signs of forced entry.

"We progressed to the side of the home," Detective Arrighi would say. "Then we walked towards the back area...There's a large pool. A cabana. We looked inside the back quarters. There were windows in that location. We looked through."

They were no signs of a break-in.

Aaron's next-door neighbor happened to be the Patriots special teams coach, Joe Judge.

When Detective Arrighi and Trooper Cherven knocked on his door, the coach told them he hadn't seen Aaron since June 13, at a practice. He confirmed that Hernandez played for the Patriots, but said he did not have contact information. Judge had no idea when Aaron would be home, but offered to call the team's head of security.

Once he had done so, leaving a message on the security director's voicemail, Cherven and Arrighi went back to their SUV, pulled it out of the driveway and into the street, parked across from the house, and waited.

CHAPTER 57

Inside the house, Hernandez called Brian Murphy.

"Hey, Murph," he said. "There's a cop car outside of my house, just kind of sitting there?"

"Okay, Aaron," Murphy said. "Let me ask you a question. Did you do anything wrong?"

"No. I didn't do anything wrong."

"Okay, then. Why is there a cop car out there?"

"Well, I don't know. You just never know what's going to happen."

"I don't understand," Murphy said. "If you haven't done anything wrong, why would you be concerned?"

"Well, I don't want them thinking—I think they're waiting to get a search warrant."

"Listen, dude," Murphy said. "Why don't you just go up there and ask him what he wants, you know?"

"Just walk up to the car?"

"Yeah. Walk up to the car, ask him what he wants."

*　　*　　*

Half an hour after pulling out of the driveway, Trooper Cherven and Detective Arrighi saw Aaron walking toward them.

Arrighi, who'd been sitting in the passenger seat, walked up and met him halfway, identified himself, and shook Aaron's hand.

"Did you rent a black Chevy Suburban?" the cops asked Hernandez.

"Yeah," Aaron said. "I rented it for my friend O."

"Who's O?"

"Odin."

"How do you know Odin?"

"My girlfriend's sister dates him."

"When was the last time you saw Odin?"

"I was up his way yesterday."

Cherven asked Hernandez where Odin's way was.

"Boston," Aaron said. He could not provide the exact address, but had it in his GPS. Then Aaron said, "I saw you out here on my security monitors. What's with all the questions? I'm gonna have to speak to my attorney."

Hernandez walked back up the drive and went inside the house, locking the front door behind him. Cherven and Arrighi followed. A moment later, Aaron opened the door and handed Cherven a business card.

"Ropes & Gray," it read. A law firm in Boston.

"We're investigating a death," the detective said.

Instead of asking, "Whose death?" Hernandez slammed the door in the cops' faces and locked it again.

CHAPTER 58

Slamming that door was a mistake on Aaron's part.

It wasn't how innocent people acted.

"If somebody says, 'We're here about a death investigation,' I don't even know if it's possible not to say, 'Who died?'" Lieutenant King, of the state police, says today. "But he doesn't. At that point, we don't jump to conclusions, but we *do* have to see it through. Clearly, it's a lead we have to follow. At that point, he became a person of interest."

At the time, Trooper Cherven became suspicious enough to place a call to Assistant DA Patrick Bomberg.

Bomberg was close friends with a Ropes & Gray lawyer named Robert Jones. The two men had known each other for twenty years. Now the DA called Jones and told him that he was at the North Attleboro Police Station. Bomberg was there in connection with a homicide, he said, and the police were interested in speaking with a Ropes & Gray client—Aaron Hernandez.

In the meanwhile, Trooper Cherven and Detective Arrighi had returned to their vehicle. They waited there for Hernandez to come back outside.

A little while later, he did. "I'll follow you to the police station," he said, "to talk."

Aaron left the house with Shayanna, who was carrying their daughter, Avielle. Shayanna put the girl in the back of their white Nissan Juke (the car's vanity plates read HERNANDZ) and climbed in the driver's seat. Aaron rode shotgun, with the officers following in their own car as they made their way toward the North Attleboro police station. When they arrived, Shayanna let Aaron out at the entrance and started to pull away. Trooper Cherven followed and flashed his blue police lights. Shayanna stopped. Cherven and Arrighi walked up to her car.

Did Shayanna know that Odin Lloyd had been murdered? When Cherven told her that Lloyd was dead, she started to cry.

Shayanna told the officers that she didn't know Lloyd all that well, but knew that he dated her sister. She said that he smoked and probably dealt marijuana, and that the last time she'd seen him was Saturday morning. She gave the officers Aaron's cell phone number, and said that she and Aaron had been home all day Sunday, she said. But Aaron was not there when she'd gone to bed, and had not come home at all that evening.

Just then, Shayanna's phone rang. It was Aaron. He told her that his agent, Murph, had said not to talk to the cops anymore.

*   *   *

"She dropped him off," an official close to the investigation remembers. "The baby was in the backseat. She was questioned in the parking lot—that's when she said, 'Odin's a drug dealer.' This must have been around eleven. Why would she leave Aaron at the station? She had the baby with her. But she left, and went home, and then she left again.

"The reason, I'm sure, is that on the way to the station, Aaron had said, 'Go home, get the guns.' So she went home to get the guns. After that, triangulation—cell phone towers— prove that she drove to Franklin, and then to the state line between Connecticut and Rhode Island."

On her way to the state line, Shayanna drove to an ATM in Plainville, where she and Aaron had once lived. She withdrew the maximum—$500—then drove to an ATM in Coventry, Rhode Island, and made another $500 withdrawal.

Having done so, Shayanna met up with Bo Wallace and Carlos Ortiz at a McDonald's in Rhode Island.

"You okay?" Wallace asked as she gave him the stack of bills. "Everything's gonna be okay," he said.

Jenkins told Wallace, "Be safe," before driving back to North Attleboro.

CHAPTER 59

Inside the police station, Hernandez was led to a second-floor interview room. He asked detectives for a phone charger. Then he asked if the lights could be turned off, and if he could lie on the floor—Aaron's back was bothering him, he explained.

Outside of the room, detectives dialed the cell phone number Shayanna had given them. It was the same as a number that Odin Lloyd had in his cell phone, marked on the dead man's contact list as "Nigga Dis."

Inside the room, Hernandez's cell phone rang.

Half an hour later, Hernandez's lawyers, Michael Fee and Robert Jones, arrived at the station.

Patrick Bomberg met Jones and Fee down in the lobby. He told them that Hernandez was alone in an interview room, and said that the police wanted to question him in connection with a homicide in North Attleboro.

Bomberg also told the lawyers that his wife was a partner at Ropes & Gray, and that the lawyers should be sure to disclose this to their client, along with the fact that Bomberg and Jones were old friends.

Fee, who seemed to have assumed the role of Aaron's primary spokesperson, assured the DA that they would.

Aaron had not been placed under arrest. He had not been questioned yet. When his lawyers arrived, he was allowed to leave the station.

Hernandez, Jones, and Fee walked outside and conferred for forty-five minutes.

As they did so, Detective Mike Elliott made his way to the dispatcher's room, where the controls for the police station's security camera were located. Elliott had twenty-five years on the force. Back when the station was built, he had served as a tech and helped to install the security system. Now, in the dispatcher's room, he picked Aaron and the lawyers up on an exterior camera.

They had walked to a car in the station's parking lot. One of the lawyers opened the driver's side door. Luckily for the detective, he left it open. With the car's interior light on, Elliott could see Hernandez climb into the passenger seat, take out his cell phone, and remove the battery. Then the lawyer removed another cell phone from a briefcase in the backseat and passed it to Aaron.

At one in the morning, the lawyers walked back into the station. In a conference room, with two police officers present, Assistant DA Bomberg provided them with more information: a Dorchester man named Odin Lloyd had been found dead that evening.

Lloyd's girlfriend was the sister of Aaron Hernandez's girlfriend.

A set of rental cars keys found in Lloyd's pocket had been traced to a car that had been rented in Hernandez's name— the Suburban, which had already been found near Lloyd's apartment in Dorchester.

Michael Fee told Bomberg that his client had no objections to the DA's friendship with Robert Jones. But, Fee said, Hernandez did not want to be interviewed that night. He was tired. He was not dressed appropriately for a video interview. And Fee himself wanted more time to consult with Hernandez.

When the police asked to see Aaron's cell phone, Fee declined.

CHAPTER 60

The police didn't know what to make of the case. North Attleboro was Patriots Country. Aaron Hernandez was a local celebrity. What's more, in every passing encounter they'd had with him, over the years, Aaron had shown himself to be polite, deferential, and outgoing.

Every encounter, that is, that led up to the point of Detective Arrighi and Trooper Cherven showing up on his front door.

"Hey," a local cop said, at the start of the investigation. "I have a helmet that Hernandez signed!"

"Lose your fandom," the cop's partner replied. "You realize we might have to shoot this guy, right?"

Despite all the evidence they had collected—despite the rental car keys they had found in Odin Lloyd's pocket—there were still cops in town who looked up to Hernandez.

*   *   *

Detective Elliott had stayed at the station until well past three. Monday night had turned into Tuesday long before he went home.

After a few hours of sleep, he'd woken up, put on his sport coat and tie, and headed back in to work. In the parking lot, he ran into State Police Lieutenant Michael King.

King had stayed at the station until five or six in the morning, left for two hours, and returned at eight.

No one else was due in to the station at that hour. But the local Enterprise Rent-A-Car office was already open. King and Elliott drove down, and discovered that Aaron had returned an Altima the day before and checked a Chrysler 300 out of the lot.

They found that the Altima had already been cleaned—and that it had been damaged: the driver's side mirror was gone and there were scratches down the car's side.

King and Elliott secured the Altima, inspecting it and taking photographs. Then, Elliott drove down to Corliss Landing, where Odin Lloyd's body had been found.

First, he went to Metalor—a gold refinery with barbed wire around it, and 24/7 security, that stood at the entrance to the park. Detective Elliott knew the company well: North Attleboro PD kept a close watch on the premises. If there was video of an Altima going into the park, Metalor would have it.

It turned out that Metalor did. So did the North Attleboro Electric Department, on the far side of the clearing. Paul Belham, who owned Bell's Powder Coating, was a selectman in town. His daughter was a dispatcher for North Attleboro PD. He was happy to cooperate.

Belham told the investigators that Bell's had video, too, in high resolution.

All in all, there were seven videos of a Nissan Altima pulling in, and then out of, the clearing.

Piece by piece, the case against Aaron Hernandez was starting to come into focus.

CHAPTER 61

On Tuesday afternoon, a few hours after Detective Elliott's visit to the industrial park, Trooper Michael Cherven, Sergeant Paul Baker, Assistant DA Patrick Bomberg, and several other police officers drove down to Aaron and Shayanna's house.

Shayanna answered the door. Aaron was inside, on the couch. He did not bother to get up when the police entered.

This time, they had brought a search warrant with them.

Rumors about the murder had already gotten around. "The Patriots tight end isn't believed to be a suspect in a murder investigation near his home in North Attleboro," CBS Sports had announced. For the moment, other media outlets were playing the news the same way.

Now, while the police were searching his house, Hernandez went down to the basement—the "man cave" as Shayanna called it—and started to play pool with Shayanna's uncle, Littleman. The television was on. Game six of the NBA finals was about to start. During a commercial break in the pregame, Aaron turned to Littleman and said, "My endorsements are gone."

When they left the house, the police took several evidence bags with them. Those bags contained a white iPhone 5 with a bedazzled case, one BlackBerry, one iPad tablet, two iPad Minis, a DVR with surveillance footage from fourteen cameras Aaron had installed around the house, and a one-terabyte hard drive.

On Wednesday morning, Hernandez drove to Gillette Stadium. There were news trucks parked in the parking lot. News helicopters hovered overhead. But Aaron made his way to the weight room, where he stayed until Robert Kraft came down to meet with him.

In an office adjoining the weight room, the Patriots' owner voiced his concern and asked if Aaron was involved in any way with the murder. Hernandez gave Kraft a hug and a kiss and said he'd had nothing to do with it.

Aaron also met with Mike Briggs, the team's director of security, who wanted to hear from Hernandez himself that he was not involved in the murder.

Hernandez assured Briggs that he was not, swearing on Avielle's life he was telling the truth.

Hours later, a car drove up toward Aaron's house and parked next to the news vans that had started to gather. The man who got out spoke to a state trooper, then made his way to the front door. He'd come from a law firm, and carried a manila envelope. A reporter called out to him: "Who's it for?"

"Mr. Hernandez himself," the man said. Inside the envelope there was a summons: "A lawsuit has been filed against you."

The summons was from Waks and Barnett, a Miami firm known for representing passengers injured in cruise ship accidents.

Waks and Barnett was the law firm that Alexander Bradley had retained.

Bradley had not cooperated with the police investigation. Hours before Odin Lloyd's murder, he had agreed to withdraw the civil lawsuit he'd been threatening. But in the wake of Odin Lloyd's murder, he had gone ahead and filed it.

That same evening, the results of Odin Lloyd's autopsy were released. The death had officially been ruled a homicide, and reporters were telling their editors that Hernandez had "ties" to Lloyd.

Now, the media outlets began to report that Hernandez "'hasn't been ruled out as a suspect." *TMZ* broke the news of Alexander Bradley's civil suit. Several reporters dug up Hernandez's 2010 NFL Scouting Report and wrote articles with headlines like "Aaron Hernandez's NFL entry: What did scouts know back then?"

As the day drew to a close, Ted Daniel of Boston's Fox affiliate took to Twitter with a series of breaking announcements:

> 9:26 PM: LAW SOURCE places Hernandez and victim in two locations.

10:12 PM: LAW SOURCE: Aaron Hernandez was driver of a vehicle Odin Lloyd and 2 others in. Lloyd found dead one mile from Hernandez home.

10:15 PM: 2 LAW SOURCES: Homicide victim Odin Lloyd sent text to a friend that included a reference to Aaron Hernandez.

10:18 PM: LAW SOURCE: 4 men together in vehicle. Only 3 return to Aaron Hernandez's home. Odin Lloyd NOT one of them.

CHAPTER 62

By daybreak on Thursday, the streets around 22 Ronald C. Meyer Drive were packed with news vans from Boston, Providence, and Hartford. National media outlets were present, along with ESPN, which had its headquarters in Aaron's hometown of Bristol.

Camped out across the street with cameras, large reflectors on C-stands, umbrellas, and coolers, the reporters looked like they were having themselves a tailgate party.

By now, the news stations were saying that Aaron was directly tied to the homicide.

The police had their own questions for Aaron. They wanted to know why his security system looked like it had been destroyed intentionally. They wanted to know why Aaron's cell phone had been "in pieces" when his attorneys had finally given it to investigators. They wanted to know why cleaners had been called out on June 17 to scrub the house down.

None of Aaron's actions seemed to be those that an innocent man would have taken.

But, for the moment, Aaron was still a free man. Climbing into Shayanna's SUV, he drove past the reporters and headed out to Gillette Stadium. From the air, a news helicopter traced his movements, reminding viewers of OJ Simpson in his white Bronco.

Upon his arrival at the stadium, at 11:23 in the morning, Aaron ran into Mark Briggs.

The director of security told him to leave, immediately. Aaron's being there was "bad for business," Briggs said.

Hernandez took the news well enough. He finished up the phone call he was making, shook Briggs's hand, and headed for the door.

That afternoon, media outlets began to report that the Patriots had barred Aaron from their stadium. Then, on Saturday, state troopers and North Attleboro PD returned, with yet another search warrant and several police dogs.

"During the search, he just sat there and talked to us like he was talking to any other person," an officer recalls. "He had no expression on his face. He knew we were there for a murder. But he didn't show any nervousness. He'd lay on the couch watching TV, playing with his daughter, smiling, laughing. He didn't care. He thought he was above the law."

That day, after a four-hour search of the house, the police left with a dozen evidence bags, a 7.62x39mm caliber semi-automatic Hungarian-made AK-47, and a Sentry Safe that contained a box of .22-caliber ammo.

CHAPTER 63

Keelia Smyth hadn't thought much about the shell casing she'd found in the Altima that Aaron Hernandez had rented. The days that followed had been so busy, she'd simply forgotten.

"Honestly," Smyth says, "people leave some of the strangest, weirdest, most ridiculous things in rental cars. I've found things that I've called the cops about. One town I worked in, I found needles in the car. I know there's a protocol for the disposing of needles. But when I called the cops, they said, 'What do you want us to do? Drive it to the state line? Take it and toss it in a dumpster yourself.'

"I've lived in Attleboro for a long time. I know there's a gun range in North Attleboro. At the time that I found the bullet, I didn't know about a crime. There's no issue. I'm not going to call the cops for every little thing that I find.

"The only reason I had even noticed it was, there was a chunk of gum on my rug. I was annoyed by that. You can't get gum out of the carpet. There was a child's picture back there, too. I didn't want to touch the gum with my hands, so I used the child's picture. I moved the seat forwards. I saw what I thought was a bullet. I took all that together—the gum, the child's picture, the bullet, and tossed it into a dumpster. But a few days later, I thought, 'Oh, my god. What if this is important? What if it's not there anymore? I don't arrange when the dumpster gets dumped. That's when I called the police.'"

"You're gonna kill me," Smyth said when Detective Elliott picked up the phone.

"What's the matter?" the detective asked.

It was Thursday. Aaron Hernandez had just been barred from Gillette Stadium.

"I forgot to tell you: I found a bullet."

"Say that again?"

"I found a bullet in the car! I put it in this piece of paper with all this coloring on it. It looked like it had been done by a kid."

"Where is it now?"

"I threw it in the dumpster."

"Is the dumpster emptied yet?"

"No. I checked and there's not much in there at all."

The police had already seized guns and ammunition from Aaron's house, along with surveillance tapes that showed Hernandez holding a gun on the morning of Odin Lloyd's murder.

The police believed that Aaron had destroyed several hours of surveillance footage taken by his own security cameras, and had their own surveillance footage of Aaron taking the battery out of his cell phone. They had shell casings recovered from the murder scene. But a shell casing recovered from the Altima would tie the whole case together.

"Hang up," Detective Elliott told Smyth, "and go to the police station now. Someone will meet you out front."

It was the sort of break detectives live for. With his police lights flashing, Elliott rushed to Enterprise to secure the evidence.

Chief Reilly and Captain DiRenzo, of the North Attleboro Police Department, and Lieutenant King and Sgt. Paul Baker of the state police, met Elliott on the scene.

Baker jumped into the dumpster and started to root around. Within a few minutes, he'd emerged—not with a bullet—but with a shell casing stuck in a wad of Bubblicious that had been wrapped in the child's drawing that Keelia Smyth had mentioned.

The drawing looked a lot like a child's drawing detectives had seen in Aaron's kitchen—a drawing by Tanya's young son, Jano, who called Hernandez "Daddy Aaron."

The shell casing looked *exactly* like ones that detectives had found at the scene of Odin Lloyd's murder.

PART EIGHT

CHAPTER 64

On Monday, June 24, police officers in wet suits searched a stream in the woods by Aaron's house. They did not find any weapons. But that same day, acting on a tip, detectives drove to 114 Lake Avenue in Bristol to interview TL Singleton, who had married Aaron's cousin Tanya.

Singleton was not at home. But the police returned to Bristol the following day to meet with members of Bristol PD, and discovered that Detective Pete Dauphinais's wife, Jodie, was Carlos Ortiz's probation officer.

A few weeks earlier, Ortiz had admitted to the officer that he was a daily user of PCP, alcohol, cocaine, and marijuana. She had put him in a drug program. Ortiz had failed to show up. But Ortiz had bigger problems to worry about: The probation officer knew about his relationship with Aaron Hernandez, the New England Patriot who had just become the leading suspect in a murder investigation. Now, detectives knew about the relationship, too.

Ortiz was due to check in with the Jodie Dauphinais on that very same day. He ended up meeting, instead, with the police.

In a basement conference room, Detective Elliott and Sergeant John Moran of the Massachusetts State Police told Ortiz that they wanted to speak with him about what had happened on the night of Odin Lloyd's murder.

"First," Elliott said, "it's just your Miranda rights. You've heard them before?"

"Huh?" said Ortiz.

"You've heard Miranda before, your rights? You've never been arrested or anything?"

"Yeah."

"Okay. It's just basically that's all I'm doing. You're not under arrest or anything. I've just got to read them to you."

Ortiz consented, but denied any knowledge of the shooting.

"I didn't do anything," he said.

Sergeant Moran took his turn. He told Ortiz that they were investigating a homicide that Aaron Hernandez and Ernest Wallace seemed to be connected to. He said that the police had text messages and surveillance footage. They knew that Ortiz had gone to Hernandez's house on Sunday night.

"Hernandez's like family," Ortiz explained. Once again, he denied any wrongdoing.

"We know you weren't the shooter, right?" Moran said. "But you got roped into this fucking thing."

"That's bullshit, though," Ortiz said.

"Someone else is the shooter," Moran agreed. "And guess who's going to be left without a chair?"

"I'm the only one in the bullshit."

"They think you're going to be the patsy," Moran said. "That's what they think. You got eight million for an attorney? [Hernandez has] got eight million. They love him. You're the throwaway guy, you know. You realize this. I've been doing this for twenty years... You're the guy and you know why—because you're all fucked up... So you're in a bad spot here. You're in a bad spot because they're going to blame you. We can go to court if we want. Jesus Christ, we've got everything."

Ortiz protested. He didn't know where Lloyd lived. He didn't know where the industrial park was located.

"I'm not even a violent person," he said.

"I know that," said Moran. "Why do you think I'm talking to you?"

Ortiz told the police, "I never went to the frigging scene."

What about the towel, the police wanted to know. What about the shell casings?

"I don't know why you guys didn't clean the car before you brought it back. There was a shell casing in the car."

"That's what I'm trying to tell you," Ortiz said. "I don't got no intention of harming nobody."

Ortiz said that he had been drunk on the night in question. The plan had been to go to a club, but Ortiz had crashed at Aaron's Franklin apartment instead.

"That's a lie," Moran told him. "I'm not disrespecting you. That's an absolute lie."

"Honest," Ortiz finally said. "I don't want to be involved in this bullshit."

"We don't want you to be involved in this, but you are," Moran told him.

Ortiz became agitated. He had so much on his plate, he said. He had four children to take care of.

"And that's how upset you got when you figured out what was going on," Elliott told him. "We understand that."

The police showed Ortiz the surveillance footage they had. There he was—Ortiz could see himself clearly—with Wallace and Hernandez at the gas station that they had stopped at before picking Lloyd up in Boston.

"I know you want out of this," Moran said. "I know you want to get out of it, but you can't. But you know something. We don't think you did it...You're a good person...You want to get help. You want to do better...But why the fuck did [Hernandez] do this? Why did he drag you in? *Why did he drag you in?*"

"Why is he leaving you out to dry?" Elliott added.

"Probably because I'm the only one with a good heart."

"Exactly," said Elliott.

The interrogation started at two in the afternoon. It went straight through into the evening.

"You know what I'm scared of?" Moran asked Ortiz. "I'm scared of this guy TL, because guess what?...I was scared that they would put one in you and dump you someplace. That's what my fear was. So you're out of the way, you're shot, and it's like, 'Yeah, it must have been that kid. He's gone. He disappeared.' And you're lying in some fucking swamp."

"All this is a fucking joke," Ortiz said.

"You know it's a joke," said Moran. "Except for this poor bastard who was killed five times."

Finally, Elliott and Moran got Ortiz to admit that he was in the Altima—asleep, he said. Then, he had heard shots. Ortiz was "shocked," he explained. "Hypnotized."

Ortiz said that he'd never gotten out of the car.

The cops had not given Ortiz anything to eat. Mentally and physically, he was exhausted. But the interrogation was not over yet. Elliott and Moran pressed for a polygraph test.

"How about you do *them* a polygraph?" Ortiz asked, referring to Hernandez and Wallace.

"What them?" said Moran. "We don't care about them. I mean, I don't care what they say."

CHAPTER 65

Nine hours into the interrogation, Carlos Ortiz submitted to the polygraph test.

When it was done, the test administrator asked Ortiz how he felt about it.

"I think I did good," Ortiz said.

"You think you did good?"

"Yup."

"Excellent," the administrator said.

"How do you think I did?"

"I already know how you did. I already know. It's pretty clear: you lied."

"What?" Ortiz sputtered.

"You lied."

"Oh."

"You lied," the administrator said. "Right now, you've got a small window of opportunity to help yourself out. It's as simple as that, okay? You know you lied, okay? I'm here to help you out. I want to do what I can, okay? I really do. But I'm not into playing games and doing all this stuff. I'm just straight up with you. You know you lied. Tell me the real story and let's go from there."

"Hmmm?" Ortiz said.

"There is no 'hmmm.'"

"I didn't get out of the car. I opened the door. I didn't get out of the car."

The administrator was not buying any of it.

"Carlos, you can say that all you want...You are lying."

"What you want me to tell you?"

"I want you to tell me the truth because that's not the truth, all right? We can help each other out here. You can be honest about this whole thing. Carlos, tell me what really happened that night, 'cause you are not. You are trying to be a little..."

"Listen, listen, I mean, I didn't see what happened. I mean, I seen when everybody got out, you know. I never got out. I was about opening the door and that's when I heard the gunshot."

"Okay. What did you see?"

"Aaron was, like, towards, like, the car, like, towards behind, like. They took a little walk. I didn't hear no arguing. Nothing. And it just happened like this, like, you know. So that's what I really seen. But I remember Aaron—as soon I went like this, I see Aaron run in the car, okay, and Bo slam the door."

"All right. Here is the problem, okay, because that's very similar to what you've told me before. You failed the exam as far as being out of the car. You failed the exam, okay? You failed the exam all around. You failed it. All right."

"Yeah, but I was nervous. I'm nervous right now."

"You're nervous now, because now I know that you know more."

"No, I was nervous right there, too."

"No, Carlos. Right before all this, we sat here, and we talked, and we said if you had done something, if you were there..."

"I never—I never—I've been doing good—I've been telling you, I never—I didn't get out of the car. I never got out of the car 'cause I remember I never got out of the car. Bo was still right there. He and Aaron took a walk, whatever."

"So maybe what the problem is...here is what the problem is..."

"I never got out of the car."

"I'm trying to give you a chance to give some truth to this, okay? If you didn't get out of the car, the only real possibility of you failing this exam—"

"Nervous."

"Listen to me, nervousness has nothing to do with it, nothing, all right?"

"I'm scared. I'm scared."

"Look at me, Carlos. Here is what happened: You saw Aaron shoot him."

Ortiz said, "No." But he was inching his way toward a more believable story.

"I'm willing to do—like, help, anything, like," he said. "I want to cooperate, like, work with you. Like, I'm—like this is—call me a snitch. Call me what the fuck you want. I'm willing to tell you what I know."

"Carlos, you have been put into an awful, awful situation."

* * *

Ortiz had agreed to a DNA swab. During the polygraph test he had also been asked: "Did you shoot O?" "Did you shoot O that day?" and "Did you get out of the car when O was shot?"

His answers had been categorized as "deception indicated."

Then, Ortiz had changed his story: he *had* opened the door, he explained, but he had not stepped out of the car.

It was too dark to *see* Hernandez shoot Lloyd.

But right after hearing the gunshots, Ortiz said, he had watched Aaron run back to the car, cradling the gun in his hand.

CHAPTER 66

I t was so stupid," says an officer who took part in the investigation. "If Hernandez had shot Lloyd in Dorchester, or even in Plainville. If he'd done it in the club's parking garage, he would have gotten away with it. Think about it: Hernandez left the shell casings there, by the body, for us to collect. A few days later, we were collecting evidence from a dumpster. The casing that came out of his car was a perfect match. Same firing pin and everything. People would say, 'How did that shell casing get in the car? He must have shot Lloyd in the car.' Well, he didn't shoot Lloyd in the car. Hernandez was so freaking crazy, he pulled out of the clearing and drove down the street shooting at street signs. He was so stoned, so drunk. Just out of his mind."

Hernandez was also famous, and rich, with access to excellent lawyers. The case against him needed to be bulletproof.

By Wednesday morning, the police were convinced that it was.

*　　*　　*

Wesley Lowery was checking Twitter in his third-floor walk-up apartment in Allston when he saw the news: Jenny Wilson, a *Hartford Courant* reporter, had been on an overnight stakeout of Hernandez's house. She was reporting that the Patriot had just been arrested.

The police had marched Aaron out of the house in handcuffs. The Patriot's arms were hidden inside a white V-neck T-shirt that stretched over his hulking torso like a giant straitjacket.

Lowery, a twenty-three-year-old reporter for the *Boston Globe,* jumped up, got dressed, and ran to his car—a Pontiac Grand Prix with a power-steering problem.

As he did, he checked in with his editor.

The *Globe* had only just hired Lowery, who'd interned at the paper previously and been a reporting fellow at the *Los Angeles Times.* For the most part, he'd covered local politics, along with general assignments from the metro desk. But, young as he was, Lowery had proven himself to be smart and tenacious. In 2014, the National Association of Black Journalists would name him "Emerging Journalist of the Year." Two years later, he would win a Pulitzer Prize.

Lowery had staked Aaron's house out already that week, and interviewed Odin Lloyd's mother.

He did not want to miss out on Aaron's arraignment.

"It's going to be in North Attleboro," the editor said. "File from inside the courthouse."

*　　*　　*

Lowery had been inside the Attleboro District Court building before. He knew that it was a dead zone, as far as communications went. Nothing went in or out of the building. But his editor wanted up-to-the-minute reporting: iPhone video, live tweets.

Less than two hours after Aaron's arrest, another news bulletin had come in: the Patriots had cut Hernandez.

"A young man was murdered this week and we extend our sympathies to the family and friends who mourn his loss," the team said in its statement. "Words cannot express the disappointment we feel knowing that one of our players was arrested as a result of this investigation."

Now, as he made his way out to Attleboro, the reporter tried to think of the best way to file.

"I pulled up and parked, and there was already a massive stakeout in front of the courthouse," Lowery recalls. "There were people and cameras everywhere. Fox is there. ESPN. Everyone wants the shot, the video, or still image of Hernandez being driven up and led in. Sitting out there for a moment I thought, this is actually a pretty small courthouse. It's not equipped for the massive amount of camera equipment, for all the reporters, all the technology. There might not be enough outlets in there."

The first order of business was avoiding the scrum of reporters who would be caught in the hallway while Aaron was being arraigned inside one of the courtrooms.

Approaching a clerk, Lowery asked for a best guess: Which courtroom would Hernandez be brought to?

"Finally," Lowery says, "Hernandez arrives. You can feel it, even inside the courthouse. You see all the media members rushing around the building to get the shot of him being driven in. Then, there's a massive rush back inside."

The clerk's best guess turned out to be a good one. By staying inside of the building, Lowery had gotten ahead of the pack. He was in the room when the doors were thrown open and Aaron Hernandez was led inside.

"It was a complete mess," Lowery says. "It was standing room only. It was the biggest news story of the moment, and I didn't know if they could get video out of the courtroom."

Lowery had a front-row seat for the proceedings.

Hernandez was still dressed in the red shorts and white T-shirt he had been arrested in. He betrayed no emotion while charges against him were read.

There were six in all. Five for firearms violations. One for murder.

"Everyone was like, 'Wait? *What!?*'" Lowery remembers. "'They're actually trying Hernandez for *murder?*' The disbelief was palatable."

Then, the prosecutors began to lay out the evidence: The last text from Odin Lloyd, sent at 3:23 a.m. Surveillance footage of the Nissan Altima leaving the clearing four minutes later.

"They had pictures of Hernandez holding what they believe is the gun moments after the murder," Lowery recalls. "They walked through a series of text messages between Lloyd and Hernandez."

Lowery had set his phone up to send tweets out via text. For a moment—"an eternity at a time like this"—he was the only reporter there who could communicate with the outside world.

He did so until the arraignment ended, with Hernandez pleading "not guilty" to all of the charges.

"What just happened?" a sports reporter asked Lowery.

"They just charged him," Lowery said. "That's what happened."

According to Lowery, the feeling in the air was, "There was *no way* that Aaron Hernandez had murdered someone. He might have *been* there. He might have been in the wrong place hanging out with the wrong guys. He didn't *kill* this guy."

Lowery was not so sure. He had seen other defendants arraigned. He had seen the full range of emotions, running all the way from defiance to despair. He had never seen a reaction like Aaron's.

Hernandez "was relatively stone-faced," Lowery recalls. "He looked in so many ways normal. It was almost as if he was supposed to be there."

CHAPTER 67

That evening, a white-and-gold van belonging to the Bristol County Sheriff's Office passed a press gaggle stationed outside of the Bristol County House of Correction in Dartmouth, paused at an outer gate, and went inside the facility. (Bristol County, Massachusetts, is about 120 miles east of Bristol, Connecticut, where Aaron Hernandez grew up.) A black Ford Explorer and a K-9 unit pulled in behind the van.

There was a second gate on the far side of the first. For security purposes, it only opened when the first gate closed. (Prison officials called this space "the trap.") When the van had passed through both gates, corrections officers opened the back doors, helped Aaron Hernandez step down, and led him into the jail.

In the processing room, Aaron's wrist and ankle restraints were removed. He was told to stand with his back to the wall. Then he was ordered to sit in a metal-detecting "boss check" chair.

If Hernandez had anything stuffed up his rectum, the chair would sound an alert.

Then, Hernandez was led to a body scanner. He was told to stand sideways on a short conveyer belt, keeping his arms and his head up.

The belt moved him through in three seconds.

Up to this point, everything Hernandez experienced was standard operating procedure at the jail. What came next—an interview with the warden himself—was a departure.

"I told my staff to notify me when he's on his way," says Sheriff Thomas Hodgson. "When he came in, I pulled him aside and introduced myself: 'I'm the sheriff here. There's a couple of things I want you to know. First of all, you're not going to be treated any better or any worse than anybody else. Number two, we have rules here. You are to follow the rules. If somebody's in the area where you are that does not belong in the area, you need to notify the staff or the supervisor on duty.'"

Given Hernandez's stature, the sheriff says, "we wanted to make sure our staff wasn't tempted to hang out with him, because of his notoriety and his wealth, and that he was not using his popularity to try to manipulate the staff."

The sheriff let Hernandez know that he was going to be held by "special management" in the jail's medical unit for a week or two.

"He was coming from a seven-thousand-square-foot home to a seventy-square-foot cell, and that in itself was a huge transition, never mind his popularity. He was going from a place where people revered him to a place where he was just another number—and that, in a nutshell, speaks to the drastic difference that he was going to be stepping into."

Following his conference with Hodgson, Hernandez was asked a series of standard questions. He was sent down the hall for a mental health interview, which showed nothing abnormal. Then, he was put into a one-man holding cell. This was standard operating procedure for famous prisoners, as well as for sex offenders—seclusion from the prison's general population.

After a while, Aaron heard his name called. The cell door opened and he was brought to a property room, where he was ordered to strip. Aaron's red shorts, underwear, shoes, socks, and XXL white T-shirt were put in a mesh garment bag (prison officials called it "the strap") and his prison outfit was issued: two pairs of socks and underwear, a T-shirt, a jumpsuit, and a set of shoes, along with a "care kit" that contained one sample-size deodorant, a toothbrush, a tube of toothpaste, and a bottle of three-in-one wash.

Finally, Aaron was led down Medical Hallway to Cell #1 in Sector C: Health Services. A metal bed welded to the floor in the center of the room took up all but a two- or three-foot ring of floor space. The bedframe had holds for restraints. A thin blue mattress sat on top of it. In the upper left corner, a camera surveyed everything in the room. A safety light hummed from the ceiling, fluorescent, encased in stainless steel, impossible to tear down. In the corner by the door there was a sink–toilet unit that had not been flushed since the cell's previous resident had used it.

CHAPTER **68**

At two in the afternoon on Thursday, June 27—the day after his arraignment—Aaron Hernandez was driven to the Bristol County Courthouse, in Fall River, for his bail hearing.

Bristol County Assistant DA Bill McCauley described the argument Hernandez had had with Odin Lloyd. He admitted that the police had not recovered a murder weapon, which they believed to be a .45 Glock. Hernandez seemed to be holding a Glock in surveillance footage taken from his house, the police had recovered a clip of .45 ammunition from a Humvee that Hernandez owned, they had found .45 bullets in Hernandez's apartment in Franklin, and, McCauley said, a photograph had emerged of Hernandez holding a Glock .45.

James Sultan, who was one of Aaron's lawyers, pointed out that Aaron had no criminal record. But Hernandez did have a home, a fiancée (who was there at the hearing), and an infant daughter. Aaron's celebrity status would make it hard for him to flee justice, Sultan argued. Moreover, the Commonwealth's case against his client was weak: There were no eyewitnesses to the murder. The evidence was entirely circumstantial.

"Mr. Hernandez is not just a football player but he is one of the best football players in the United States of America," Sultan said. "He's a young man who is extremely accomplished in his chosen profession."

Aaron would post a large cash bail, and agree to house arrest and a GPS tracking bracelet. "He wants to clear his name," Sultan assured the court.

Judge Renee Dupuis was skeptical. She pointed out that it was rare for bail to be granted in first-degree-murder cases and called the circumstantial evidence against Hernandez "very, very strong."

"This gentleman, either by himself or with two other individuals that he requested come to the Commonwealth, basically, in a cold-blooded fashion, killed a person because that person disrespected him," Dupuis said. "If that's true, and based upon presentation it seems to be, I'm not confident that type of individual would—he obviously doesn't adhere to societal rules. The idea that I can release him on a bracelet and he would comply with court rules is not something that I am willing to accept."

Shayanna burst into tears when bail was denied.

Once again, Aaron betrayed no emotion.

CHAPTER 69

That evening, Massachusetts police issued a wanted poster for Ernest Wallace.

Aaron's friend was "wanted for accessory after the fact for the murder of Odin Lloyd in North Attleboro," the poster read. "Wallace is considered armed and dangerous and was last seen operating a silver/gray Chrysler 300 R.I. Registration Number 451-375."

It had been several days since Wallace had seen the Chrysler, which had been abandoned outside of a housing complex in Bristol. And it had been several days since anyone in Massachusetts had seen Wallace, who was holed up at his mother Angella's house in Miramar, Florida.

To get to there, Wallace had hitched a ride with TL Singleton's aunt, Euna Ritchon.

Ritchon lived with her mother in Bristol but had seven grandchildren of her own down in Georgia. She had already been planning to see them when TL's wife—Aaron's cousin,

Tanya Singleton—convinced her to move the visit up by a week, taking herself and Wallace along.

The three of them had driven through the night, using back roads. In North Carolina, Ritchon's car broke down. Euna's daughter drove eight hours to get them and bring them to Georgia, where Ritchon watched Tanya give Wallace a new cell phone and use her credit card to buy him a bus ticket to Florida.

In Florida, neighbors had seen Wallace swimming in his mother's pool.

And on Friday, Wallace walked the half mile from Angella's house to the local police station and told the cops that he wanted to talk, even though his attorney had advised him not to.

Two days later, on Sunday, June 30, Tanya's husband, TL, drove his Nissan Maxima off of a road in Farmington, Connecticut. After flying through the air for one hundred feet, the car crashed into the side of the Farmington Country Club, where it lodged, six feet up in the air. Miraculously, Tabitha Perry—Singleton's twenty-seven-year-old ex-girlfriend, and the mother of one of his children, who was riding in the passenger seat—survived the crash, only to die of an accidental overdose later that year.

TL Singleton died on the scene. According to the toxicology report, he had cocaine, PCP, oxycodone, and alcohol in his system at the time of his death.

On Saturday, July 6, the Patriots announced that fans who had bought Hernandez jerseys could swap them out.

By five o'clock in the afternoon, the team's Pro Shop had processed 1,200 exchanges.

The Hernandez jerseys would all be burned. Aaron's sponsors, Puma and CytoSport (the makers of Muscle Milk), had already dropped him. And in the weeks and months that followed, the former Patriot's reputation would suffer other indignities: EA Sports would remove him from their video games; Panini America, a trading card company, would take him out of their sticker books and replace his trading cards with ones that featured Tim Tebow; and the University of Florida would remove his name from the stadium in which he had played—a task that required the use of power tools.

CHAPTER 70

On Tuesday, July 16, three weeks after Aaron's arrival at the Bristol County jail, Sheriff Thomas Hodgson held a press conference to discuss his famous new inmate.

"Hernandez is locked in a seven-by-ten-foot cell for twenty-one hours a day," Hodgson told the assembled reporters. "The rest of his time is spent in the exercise yard, making collect phone calls, or taking a hot shower. He doesn't have any physical contact with other inmates, but that's mostly for his own safety."

Reporters were given a tour of the Special Management unit, where Hernandez was being held in near-solitary confinement.

"We're assessing how the inmates are reacting to him right now in this smaller unit," Hodgson said as he ushered the reporters into a gray cell.

General population inmates were allowed outside, the sheriff explained. They could see trees and grass, and interact with other inmates. But for his own safety, Hernandez had been denied these privileges. He was allowed outside for just one hour a day, and during that hour he was alone, in a cement yard that contained three chain-link cages topped with tin roofs and razor wire. He worked out in one of the cages, running extremely short laps and doing push-ups, squats, and sit-ups as a corrections officer watched.

The reporters wanted to know: How did Aaron Hernandez like this arrangement?

"I think he'd like to be out in general population playing basketball," Hodgson admitted.

One of the several reasons that Aaron had *not* been put into general population was that Sheriff Hodgson was trying to determine whether rumors about his gang ties were true.

"My gang investigators went in and interviewed him," Hodgson says. "When they came out, they said, 'We think he probably is tied into the Bloods. But we can't be absolutely positive.'"

Hodgson, who prided himself on his skills as an interrogator, decided that he would investigate the matter himself. On Saturday, his day off, he arrived at the jail in shorts and a golf shirt and sat down to speak with Hernandez.

"I started talking casually to him," the sheriff recalls. "About life and his family. Then I said, 'I want to talk to you about those tattoos.'"

"Oh, no, it's not the Bloods," Aaron said. According to Hernandez, the tattoos advertised a local gang from Bristol, Connecticut.

Then Aaron said, "Hey, can I ask you a question?"

"Sure," the sheriff replied.

"Did you wear those shorts in here to get me to relax?"

"What are you, an idiot?" Hodgson said. "I'm on my day off. You think I'm going to get dressed up in a suit and tie to come and talk to you? You've got to be shitting me."

Hernandez laughed, the sheriff remembers.

"Let me tell you something," Aaron said. "I pay attention to what goes on. And I'm the best at reading people."

"I bet you are, but you're not the best," Hodgson said. "You're not better than I am."

"Oh, yeah, I am."

"Really? Do you know about the key motivations in people?"

"What do you mean?"

"There are three different types of motivations in people: kinesthetic, auditory, and visual."

Hernandez looked perplexed. "I don't know what you mean," he said.

"You're a visual type."

"How do you know that?"

"Because every time I talk to you, you'll say, 'That looks good.' If you were an auditory type, you'd say, 'That rings a bell.' If you were kinesthetic you'd talk about your feelings: 'That feels good to me,' you would say."

Aaron was impressed. He said "Wow," and Sheriff Hodgson felt encouraged to continue.

"You know how to overcome your behaviors?" he asked.

"No," said Aaron.

"Let's say that you're overweight, and go by a Burger King. You've already lost ten pounds, but now you're thinking about hamburgers. You haven't had one in a while. And now your body's reacting to what you're thinking. You argue with yourself, but you lose. So you get your hamburger and some French fries, and you're driving down the road eating them, thinking 'Son of a bitch. I should not be eating these.'"

Aaron appeared to be paying close attention to the story.

"The way you overcome that," Hodgson said, "is to shatter the picture you have and create a new one. Take a picture of yourself, from when you were twenty pounds lighter. Stick it up on your visor. And whenever you think about breaking your diet, pull the visor down and look at that picture. It will reframe you, and teach you to refrain from the things you want to refrain from."

Aaron nodded. He said "wow" again. The sheriff may not have established the matter of whether he had ties to the Bloods, but Hodgson *had* taught Hernandez something about impulse control. And, of course, Aaron's issues with impulse control were the very thing that had landed him in jail in the first place.

CHAPTER 71

As the summer wore on, and the days and nights he spent alone in his cell bled into one another, Aaron wrote letters, worked out, and read, requesting books from the jail library: Michael Connelly, Dan Brown, James Patterson.

Hernandez was especially fond of Patterson's Alex Cross novels.

Aaron also made phone calls, and some of his friends made calls of their own. Taken together those calls told a story:

July 12, 2013:

Aaron Hernandez: Hey, [watch] what you say. The phone is recorded. What you up to?

Tanya Singleton: I know, I know, I know. Hi, honey.

Hernandez: You got my letter?

Singleton: Yeah, I did. I—of course I did. I got you one. I got you a card and a letter.

Hernandez: Watch what you write. They read that shit.

Singleton: I—no, no, like I don't know that.

Hernandez: Well, I got to get going. I will probably call you, um, probably like once a week or something like that.

Singleton: Yeah, that's perfect.

Hernandez: Yeah, and—I'll also help you out with that, too. Obviously don't say nothing, but I love you.

Singleton: I know. I'm not saying nothing. I love you so much.

July 28, 2013:

Tanya Singleton: Um, I'm going back up there Thursday.

Ernest Wallace: What, to go visit?

Singleton: No. I have to be up there to be in front of the grand jury whatever 'cause they're fucking dumb, but I got a good lawyer.

Wallace: Wait up, wait up, wait up. You gotta go to court for what?

Singleton: They subpoenaed me to go in front of the grand jury and I got a lawyer. That's why I got, uh, a real nice lawyer, a good lawyer from over there.

Wallace: Yeah, my nigga.

Singleton: Yup.

Wallace: My nigga got you with that?

Singleton: You already know.

Wallace: All right. Say no more.

August 1, 2013:

Shayanna Jenkins: Um, Tanya's in jail.

Aaron Hernandez: Tanya?

Jenkins: Yeah.

Hernandez: For what?

Jenkins: I don't know. Yup. So she's in jail. She got arrested today.

Hernandez: They picked her up by her house?

Jenkins: No, she went for—she was—I don't know. You probably should talk to your lawyer about it.

Hernandez: Oh.

Jenkins: But she told me to tell you that she's gonna be just fine and to keep your head up and to know that she love you.

Hernandez: Oh, my God. Let me call you right back.

[15 minutes later.]

Hernandez: Hey.

Jenkins: Yeah.

Hernandez: I knew about . . .

Jenkins: Huh?

Hernandez: I knew about that. I thought it was [inaudible]

Jenkins: I'm just letting you know.

Hernandez: Yes, they just being asses about it, but they get—they got to go out of their way to be assholes and, like, the longest she'll do is, like, probably less than a month or a month until the grand jury is done, investigation, do you know what I mean? The only good thing about Tanya being locked up is she's gonna lose weight.

August 7, 2013:

Ernest Wallace: Trust me, man, if I was in here for

something that I know I did wrong...But this just came right out of the blue, out of nowhere. This is the last thing I thought was going to be happening to me.

Angella Wallace: Oh, my God.

Ernest: [He] had a fucking career. Forty-million-dollar football career.

Angella: Everything's gone.

Ernest: Why would he jeopardize his life to go kill somebody a mile from his house?

"You have a big mouth," Aaron told his mother, in the course of one call. "There's so many things I'd like—I would love to talk to you so that you can know me as a person, but I never could tell you and you're going to die without even knowing your son."

"Well, if you feel like you can't talk to me..." Terri Hernandez said.

"How could I? How could I? You are not trustworthy at all...It's so sad...I wish I could be closer to you but it can't and it kills me, but I can't."

"You would always tell me the bad things," Terri said. "Oh, my God, such bad things. Why would you tell me these things?"

Hernandez bristled.

"Don't even talk on the phone like that," he said. "It is what it is. Why do you think me and Tanya are so close?"

CHAPTER 72

Everyone involved with Aaron Hernandez had had a bad year. But Tanya Singleton's year had been especially rough. Her husband, TL, had died a month earlier. A cancer that doctors had found in her breast was spreading to her other organs. And now, she had been held in contempt, and incarcerated, for refusing to testify before Aaron's grand jury.

Prosecutors knew that Tanya had driven Ernest Wallace to Georgia and bought him a bus ticket to Florida. They also believed that she had offered to fly Carlos Ortiz to Puerto Rico to get him away from law enforcement officials investigating Odin Lloyd's murder.

They had offered her immunity in exchange for her testimony. But Tanya was dying. She didn't care about immunity. And Aaron had offered her something more valuable.

In yet another jailhouse phone call, Hernandez had told her that he had already set up a trust fund that Jano (her son with Jeffrey Cummings) and Eddie (the child she had had with TL) could access when they turned eighteen.

"It already started off at $100,000 for them, do you know what I'm saying?" Aaron had told Tanya. "I think about seventy-five apiece or something like that and every seven years it doubles."

Assistant DA Patrick Bomberg would claim that Hernandez was lying: "He says, 'I set up an account,' and lo and behold he didn't."

But Aaron's word had been good enough for Tanya, who stood by her refusal to testify. In a series of phone calls, placed before her appearance before Aaron's grand jury, she had told Ernest Wallace that she would do whatever she had to do for her children.

"It's by my choice," Tanya said. "We didn't fucking do nothing wrong, so they can kiss my ass. We don't know nothing. I don't know nothing. What the fuck they want me to say?"

"Fuck them," she said, referring to the grand jury.

CHAPTER 73

On several occasions, Aaron answered the letters he received from fans.

Sometimes, over his objections ("Please, keep this private is all I ask!" he wrote to one correspondent), Aaron's responses were leaked to the press or purchased by tabloids.

Everything happened for a reason, Aaron told a fan, in a letter that *TMZ* published on August 1, 2013—the day that Tanya Singleton was jailed for refusing to testify in front of Aaron's grand jury.

"I know 'GOD' has a plan for me and something good will come out of this."

The accusations against him were false, Aaron said. "I've always been an amazing person," he wrote, "known for having an amazing heart."

Aaron was strong, he said. Nothing would break him.

"I fell off especially after making all that money but when it's all said and done 'GOD' put me in this situation for a reason! I'm humbled by this ALREADY and it will change me for ever."

A few weeks later, on August 19, *Radar Online* published another letter, which Aaron had sent in July: "Stay away from all negative people so your always there for your little boy cuz I miss by little girl terribly an my biggest fear of all is she wont know daddy!" he had written. "She said daddy first time or should I say 'DaDa' and had to hear it from jail."

"Im a great dude don't believe all the neg. publicity please!" Hernandez had added, in the postscript. "Media is the Negative of the fame!"

Three days later, on August 22, Hernandez was formally indicted for murder.

On August 27, he submitted a urine test that turned up positive for Neurontin, a prescription drug known to cause aggressive behavior and suicidal thoughts.

On August 28—one day before the NFL reached a tentative $765 million brain-injury settlement with 18,000 retired players—*Rolling Stone* published a story suggesting that Hernandez was a habitual user of PCP, one of the drugs that had appeared in TL Singleton's toxicology report. Among other things, PCP was known to cause hallucinations, paranoia, hyper-aggression, feelings of invulnerability, and violent behavior.

"Friends, who insisted they not be named, say Hernandez was using the maniacal drug angel dust, had fallen in with a crew of gangsters, and convinced himself that his life was in danger, carrying a gun wherever he went," the story in *Rolling Stone* claimed.

But Aaron had bigger things to worry about than negative press.

All summer long, Boston Police, who had stalled in their investigation of the 2012 double homicide, had been looking more deeply into the case.

If not for Odin Lloyd's murder, the murders of Daniel de Abreu and Safiro Furtado might have been forgotten: just two more cold cases in a city with a notoriously low clearance rate for homicides.

But bad luck—and a nineteen-year-old woman named Jailene Diaz-Ramos—also played a part in this parallel investigation.

Like the media, good fortune had finally turned its back on Aaron Hernandez.

CHAPTER 74

Two months earlier, on June 21, Jailene Diaz-Ramos had been involved in a four-car collision on I-91 in Springfield, Massachusetts.

Jailene was taken to a hospital nearby. But when her car was searched, as was customary when cars were towed from accident scenes, the police recovered a Smith & Wesson revolver—a .38 Special—from its trunk.

Jailene was from Bristol, Connecticut. She had been busted several times, for assault, disorderly conduct, forgery, criminal impersonation, larceny, failure to appear in court (twice), and driving with a suspended license.

Now, the police were charging her with possession of a firearm without a license.

As she was being booked, Diaz-Ramos told the police that the gun belonged to a friend—a football player named "Chicago." A few days earlier, she said, she had given Chicago and a few other football players a ride, and they had left all of their stuff in the trunk.

Chicago's government name was John Alcorn. Like his girl-friend, he had been arrested before, for disturbing the peace and failing to appear in court.

He turned out to be a cousin of TL Singleton.

The next day, June 22, an anonymous caller had contacted North Attleboro PD.

The caller—who was later identified as Sharif Hashem, a bouncer at Rumor, the nightclub in Boston—said that he had information about a double murder. He gave specifics re-garding the time and location.

He mentioned an SUV with Rhode Island plates.

And he said that the murder was connected to the Odin Lloyd investigation.

When the dispatcher asked the man how knew all of this, the man said, "someone accidentally spilled the beans in front of me."

On June 26, several cars full of police officers had arrived at Tanya Singleton's house on Lake Avenue.

"From the surveillance video, we identified Wallace and Ortiz," Trooper Jeremiah Donovan remembers. "We knew there were ties to Bristol. And when we got to the house, Wednesday evening, they were actually having a house party."

The little blue house was full of people. Out in the yard, more people had gathered around the grill.

Aaron's Uncle Tito stood in the doorway, watching the police arrive, with a tumbler of vodka in his hand. Detective Peter Dauphinais knew Tito. He walked up and said, "Hey, Tito, we have a search."

"Any search is antagonistic," Trooper Donovan says. "It's not like police show up at your house and you make them coffee. But we didn't show up with a SWAT team or anything like that, and the party was winding down anyway. I wouldn't say people were running away. It wasn't like a bunch of gang members sitting there, drinking forties on the porch. It was more like a family cookout.

"While searching the house, we saw a picture that someone ended up selling to *TMZ*—a selfie Aaron had taken, where he's holding a Glock up in front of a mirror. So we knew there was a connection to Aaron. But more importantly, there was a garage. The windows were painted over, but somebody had done a crappy job so we could see inside, and we saw a Toyota 4Runner. The garage was part of our search warrant, so we asked Gina whose car it was."

Hernandez had left the car there a year earlier, Gina said. No one had driven it since. That much seemed true: The SUV had been detailed, but it was covered in dust and cobwebs. Its battery was dead. But the license plate number—635035—matched the number on a 4Runner that could be seen on surveillance footage taken from Cure, the nightclub in Boston, on the night of the double murder.

"We wrote the license plate down," Donovan says. "A Rhode Island registration. We had no idea what it meant. And we were there in Bristol all night.

"The next day, we had a meeting. No matter where you were, you either called in to the meeting or tried to get to it. Mike Elliott was there. Eric Benson was there. Bill McCauley, the Bristol County DA, was there. McCauley had spoken with Patrick Haggen, the Suffolk County DA, and Pat had told him, 'Hey, Hernandez was at a club last summer where there was a shooting, and we're looking for a silver SUV with this license plate.' It wasn't even official—it was casual, Pat had just happened to mention it. But when Bill mentioned this, I looked at my notes and thought, *Ah, what do you know? This is the car that we found in Bristol.*"

In the course of their search of the house on Lake Avenue, police recovered a DOC intake sheet for Ernest Wallace, a Connecticut Prison ID card for Carlos Ortiz, a Kel-Tec gun box, a box of Speer Lawman brand .38-caliber cartridges (containing forty-seven shells), a box of Punta Hueca brand .38-caliber cartridges, four child's drawings—and a bag full of clothes that matched the ones Aaron had been wearing that night.

But the police had more than the car Aaron had been driving on the night of that murder, and more than the clothes he had worn.

As soon as ballistics came in on the .38 Special, they also had a murder weapon: the gun recovered from Jailene's car was the same one that had been used to kill Daniel de Abreu and Safiro Furtado. By June 27, the day of Hernandez's bail hearing for the Odin Lloyd murder, the results of the parallel investigation into the 2012 mur-

282 • JAMES PATTERSON

ders had leaked, with Boston's Fox affiliate breaking the story.

"Hernandez being looked at in connection to double homicide in Boston," the headline read.

PART NINE

CHAPTER 75

I t was a little past nine in the morning, on February 25, 2014, and Aaron was in his cell in the Special Management unit.

On a previous occasion, as corrections officers were locking him in for the night, Hernandez had beaten his chest like King Kong. "I'm like that truck," he had said. "Tough. I'm built for this shit."

Now, Aaron set out to prove how tough he was.

Exiting his cell, which was unlocked at that hour, he approached Corrections Officer Kevin Sousa, who was escorting a shackled inmate down a set of stairs.

According to Sousa, Hernandez "had a smile on his face."

Still, Sousa was suspicious. He ordered Hernandez to back up and return to his cell. But Hernandez refused the order, and punched the shackled inmate in the face.

Another corrections officer called a Code Blue. Two COs restrained Hernandez, who turned to the inmate he had punched and said, "Go ahead, run your mouth now!"

When the scuffle was over, the inmate Hernandez had punched explained that, on a previous occasion, Hernandez had passed by his cell and said, "Why you looking at me?"

"I'm a Patriots fan," the inmate had said.

According to him, the beef was just "typical jail shit."

"I don't want to press charges against Hernandez and you will never get me in court to testify," the inmate told the COs. He had a bruised elbow and a bump on his head. ("I could give two shits about a bump and a bruise," the inmate said.) But he was proud of getting in the last word.

"You're a bitch," he'd told Hernandez, as they were being separated. "I still look good enough to fuck your girl."

Afterward, Hernandez was charged with assault and battery and given two weeks of straight-up solitary confinement. Publicly, Sheriff Hodgson voiced his surprise over the incident. "We were so worried about protecting him," he said, "we never thought that he would be the aggressor..."

Privately, Hodgson had already gotten to know Hernandez well enough to see just how troublesome he could be.

Within a few weeks of arriving at the jail, Hernandez had been led out into the hall for a routine search of his cell. Watching the officers going through his correspondence, he had gotten upset.

"You're not allowed to read my legal mail," Aaron yelled.

Three times, Hernandez had to be told to back away.

When the search ended, the officers asked Hernandez about a piece of paper he was holding in his hand. They had seen what Aaron had written on it: "MOB."

Hernandez told them that the acronym meant "Money Over Bitches."

The officers told him that, in prison, "MOB" meant "Member Of Bloods."

Hernandez became enraged. "What if I don't give this back to you?" he asked. "What the fuck you all gonna do about it?"

The officers told Hernandez that he would be given a disciplinary report.

"I don't give a fuck about no disciplinary report," he replied. "I'll eat the motherfucker."

In the end, Aaron did get the report—and, to the officers' amazement, he did eat it.

When Sheriff Hodgson found out, he went to see Hernandez in his cell.

"I walked through the door," Hodgson would say, "and I looked at him and just went, 'I am so disappointed in you. I can't believe that you acted the way you acted.'"

"Well that's bullshit," Aaron replied, testily. "They was going through my stuff!"

"Excuse me," the sheriff said. "Why are you yelling at me? Am *I* yelling at *you?* What I'm seeing right now, that's not the Aaron Hernandez I know."

Aaron calmed down. He had grown to respect the sheriff, even to trust him to an extent. On several occasions, the men talked about their lives, their faith, and lessons imparted by their fathers. But while Hodgson administered pep talks, it fell to his staff to discipline Hernandez.

Once, after Aaron had been placed on disciplinary detention status, he managed to have a care package delivered from the jail's commissary: cakes, breakfast bars, and two dozen honey buns.

"I'm smart, dude," Aaron told Major James Lancaster, the following day, when corrections officers asked him about the delivery. "I knew you were going to be coming this morning for this stuff."

When Lancaster told Hernandez he was not allowed to order food in detention, Hernandez said, "I know. That's why I ate as much of the food as I could before you came in."

Major Lancaster ended up confiscating four honey buns. True to his word, Hernandez had eaten the other twenty and kept the wrappers to show the officers, in case they accused him of passing honey buns out to other inmates.

"Could I eat the last four honey buns?" Aaron asked.

"No."

"Why?" Hernandez said. "I am *so hungry!*"

Other infractions were far more serious. One month after testing positive for Neurontin, Hernandez was cited for possessing paraphernalia signaling his allegiance to the Bloods. Five weeks later, when a corrections officer denied him an extra meal, Aaron called the officer "a scared bitch" and said that, when he got out, he would kill the officer and shoot his family.

"After stating this, inmate Hernandez appeared to make a noise that sounded like a machine gun," the officer wrote in his report.

"I did not say I was going to kill him or his family," Hernandez said, in his own defense. "I said if I see COs that act tough in jail, out of jail, I'm going to slap the shit out of them."

Several disciplinary reports describe fights that Aaron got

into with other inmates, and occasions when he was found with improvised tattoo guns, or "fishing lines" that were made from torn sheets and tubes of toothpaste, and used by prisoners to pass notes.

"He is constantly kicking his cell door and screaming at the top of his lungs," corrections officer Joshua Pacheco wrote in one report, "utilizing profanity at times when he wants something, regardless of how minuscule it is. It is not uncommon for Hernandez to kick his cell door constantly until an officer approaches his cell merely to ask the officer for the current time, this to him is comical, causing a disruption in normal operation within the unit."

All in all, in the course of ten months that he spent in the Bristol County jail's segregated unit, Hernandez racked up 120 days in solitary confinement.

He seemed to hold Officer Pacheco in special contempt. Once, while Aaron was in the middle of one of his workouts, he told the officer that he had a peculiar dream:

Thanks to a disciplinary report that Pacheco had given him, Aaron had dreamed that an upcoming visitation with his daughter had been canceled.

"But," Aaron told the officer, "the dream changed locations. You and your family were on vacation and *I* was chasing *you*."

Hernandez was glaring hard at Pacheco as he said this. The only weapon at Pacheco's disposal was a canister of Mace. He was thinking of reaching for it when Aaron said, "then the dream ended," and turned back to his workout.

Pacheco reported the incident as a threat to his family.

Aaron denied this: "It was just a dream," he explained. "Was not meant to be threatening and was taken out of context."

Hernandez got off with a verbal warning. But a month later, in July, he had another run-in with Pacheco.

Lunch for the Special Management inmates arrived in Styrofoam containers. The stench of the gray food inside crept into every corner of the unit. On July 5, it was Officer Pacheco's turn to deliver it. As Hernandez saw the officer approach, he yelled: "I need to be your father figure and show you how to be a man! Show you how to have your balls drop! I didn't know the Army created little boys and not men!"

When Pacheco left the unit, Hernandez called out again: "I haven't had any more dreams about you," he hollered.

CHAPTER 76

Fatherhood, and father figures, came up often in Hernandez's conversations with Sheriff Hodgson.

"There's a saying my father used to always use with my twelve brothers and sisters," the sheriff recalls telling Aaron. "He used to say, 'Always remember, God writes straight with crooked lines.'"

"What does that mean?" Hernandez had asked.

"That there are certain things that are going to happen, you're not going to know why or how, but they're going to happen. Do you read the Bible?"

"I used to. My coach in Florida used to get me into the Bible stuff."

"Did you find it useful?"

"Yeah, I did."

"Well, you've got a Bible in your cell. When you get back there, I want you to read it, and talk to your father, and think about what I told you about crooked lines."

"I can't talk to my father," Hernandez said.

"If you don't, then you won't be able to access all of the things that he taught you."

"I've only gone to my father's grave once."

"That's something you're going to have to do," the sheriff said. "You put an emotional wall up because you were so hurt by the loss of your father. All of the lessons he taught you are on the other side of that wall. The only way you're going to pull the wall down is to talk to him."

"I don't know if I can do that."

"Okay," said the sheriff, and left it at that. But when he saw Aaron again, he brought the matter back up.

"I didn't talk to my father," Aaron said. "But I did read the Bible. The weirdest thing happened: I opened it, randomly, and it was all about me."

"You remember what I told you about crooked lines?" said the sheriff. "Opening that book randomly, and finding something about yourself, is what I was talking about."

On yet another occasion, Hernandez told Hodgson that reading the Bible had caused him to cry.

"My father told me never to cry in front of another man," Aaron said.

"Really? Why would he tell you that?"

"I don't know. My father cried about everything. And he had an ugly cry."

"When would your father cry?"

"At my football games."

"Because you lost?"

"No. Even when we won."

"You know why that is?"

"No."

"It's because your father was sitting there watching you, feeling so proud about what a great player you had become."

"Aaron's father was thirteen when *his* father died," Hodgson explains. "I said to him, 'Your father is sitting there, thinking, not only how proud he is, but how sad it is that *his* father couldn't be there to see you play. *That's* what your father was crying about. He wasn't telling you not to cry in real life. He was telling you not to cry out on the football field.'"

Aaron seemed to take it all in. He told the sheriff that he felt himself changing. Even Shayanna had remarked, during a phone call, upon how calm he seemed, and how nice he was being to her. Maybe, Aaron said, the sheriff had had something to do with it.

CHAPTER 77

By the start of 2014, the police had effectively wrapped up their investigations into the murder in North Attleboro. "We had learned about the incident in Providence," Trooper Donovan says. "We had learned about the incident in California. We had tracked the guns from Hermosa Beach to Massachusetts. We were tracking down the armored car in New York. With every rock we turned over, more rocks appeared—2014 was shoring up the evidence we had, combing through it, and preparing witnesses for the prosecution. Witnesses like Bill Belichick, who never got called, as well as all of the witnesses who did."

"If they had people in Bristol they wanted to interview or anywhere in Connecticut through the prisons, they would come down, we'd facilitate," says a law enforcement official in Bristol. "Just background knowledge because we knew all these people. They'd come down, we'd hook up with them, find the people, bring them in and they would use our interview room. There's probably a couple hundred interviews they did that don't really have relevancy at the end of the day. They were ruling things in, ruling things out, seeing if there was anything out there that they were missing. It was very thorough—as thorough as anything I've ever seen, the distance they went to in order to loop in Hernandez. The distance was incredible. And they had other things going on elsewhere, Florida and California."

If the DAs were unusually thorough, it was because the police in Bristol, North Attleboro, and Boston had gone to unusual lengths in their own investigations.

Eric Benson, Michael Cherven, Michael Elliott, and Special Agent Michael Grasso of the Bureau of Alcohol, Tobacco, Firearms, and Explosives had made several trips to Florida to trace guns that were shipped up to Aaron. They had zeroed in on Oscar "Papoo" Hernandez in Belle Glade—Papoo was subsequently indicted—and traced a pipeline that TL Singleton had used to send drugs, as well as guns, up from Georgia to Bristol and North Attleboro.

According to a source close to the investigation, Singleton had been "famous" among drug dealers in Central Connecticut. "Virtually never been caught. A couple of nickel and dime things but nothing of substance. He'd never held a straight job in his life but always had money."

It turned out that the police in South Carolina had had better luck than the cops up in Bristol: On February 12, 2013— the day before Aaron Hernandez shot Alexander Bradley, down in Miami—Singleton and another man, named Johnny Booze, had been pulled over for driving 80 on a 70 miles per hour stretch of I-95.

When the police searched the car, they found large quantities of cash, cocaine, and heroin.

Both men had been charged with trafficking, though charges against Booze would later be dropped.

"TL would bring pills and weed up," a person close to the investigation recalls. "He'd bring stuff up for himself and Aaron would get that stuff. Aaron was throwing money at him."

"The path for the guns? TL is sort of that path," another law enforcement official explains.

CHAPTER 78

But TL Singleton was dead. Tanya Singleton had been charged with conspiracy to commit murder after the fact. And Carlos Ortiz and Ernest Wallace had already been indicted as accessories after the fact to the murder of Odin Lloyd. (Prosecutors subsequently upped the charges to murder.) Their trials would not start until well after Aaron's was over.

Shayanna Jenkins had been charged with a single count of perjury—prosecutors alleged that she had lied, twenty-nine times, to Aaron's grand jury. Among other things, prosecutors would say, Jenkins had lied about: conversations she and Hernandez had had about Odin Lloyd's murder; a conversation she had had with Wallace after the murder; the number of guns she had seen in her home; the removal of items from her home; and whether she had threatened the women who had cleaned her home, after the murder, with deportation.

(The prosecutors ended up dropping these charges in light of Shayanna's testimony during Aaron's trial.)

Oscar "Papoo" Hernandez had also been indicted for lying to Aaron's grand jury.

Odin Lloyd's family had filed a wrongful death lawsuit against Aaron Hernandez.

The families of Daniel de Abreu and Safiro Furtado had done the same.

Alexander Bradley, who was still pursuing his civil suit against Aaron, had gotten into an altercation at a Hartford nightclub called the Vevo Lounge Bar & Grill.

Shots had been fired outside of the club. Bradley was hit three times in the leg but managed to get to his car, grab his own gun, and fire ten or twelve rounds into the club.

On May 15, 2014, Aaron Hernandez himself had been indicted for two counts of first degree murder, three counts of armed assault with intent to murder, and one count of assault and battery with a dangerous weapon—charges resulting from the investigation into the double murders in Boston.

One month later, on Friday, June 20, Hernandez's lawyers filed a motion to have Aaron moved to a jail that was closer to Boston.

"In order for Hernandez to receive constitutionally guaranteed effective access to and assistance of counsel, in both cases, he needs to be held in a facility that does not require his counsel to drive up from two, up to three to four hours round-trip each time they need to meet with him," the lawyers argued. But there was more to the motion than that.

The motion also contained several e-mails between Sheriff Hodgson and prosecutors. According the lawyers, they suggested an unprecedented degree of cooperation between DAs and the sheriff.

Hodgson had "abandoned his role as a professional jailer and energetically embraced his role as a full-time agent of the District Attorney," the lawyers claimed, taking every opportunity to speak, publicly, about his most famous inmate, and engaging in "self-promotion and virtually non-stop publicity of every imaginable kind." (Sheriff Hodgson denied all of these charges, and said that speaking, publicly, about Hernandez provided Aaron's fans with a valuable object lesson.)

According to the lawyers, Hodgson's actions had poisoned the potential jury pool.

Moreover, they argued, Aaron's life was in danger in Bristol County. Because corrections officers at the prison were under the impression that Aaron had threatened CO Joshua Pacheco's life, his safety could no longer be guaranteed. (This impression was false, the lawyers claimed. Four days earlier, Aaron had been arraigned on charges of assaulting an inmate and threatening Pacheco.)

Sheriff Hodgson scoffed at the idea that anyone in his jail would retaliate against Hernandez. "I have a staff that is very professional," he told *TMZ*. "They understand they're dealing with a high-profile person and go the extra mile to ensure his safety, and other inmates' safety."

Nevertheless, on July 7, the lawyers' motion was granted.

Two days later, Hernandez was moved to Boston's Suffolk

County Jail, where he would spend an uneventful and incident-free six months.

Then, on January 8, 2015, Hernandez was sent back to Bristol County Jail, where he would remain for the duration of his trial for the murder of Odin Lloyd.

PART TEN

CHAPTER 79

Bristol County's Superior Courthouse stood like a sentry at the corner of Main and Borden in Fall River, Massachusetts.

It was January 29, 2015. A cold, clear day in the decaying industrial city. Aaron Hernandez's murder trial, presided over by Judge Susan Garsh, had already been postponed, several times, because of blizzards.

Today, the trial would finally be starting.

Outside, it was the usual media circus, with TV reporters huddling in their news vans for warmth as they waited for Aaron to arrive at the courthouse.

Inside, Hernandez was brought to Courtroom 7 on the building's fifth floor. Through the windows, he had a view of Braga Bridge and beneath it, the Quequechan River. But Aaron did not look around the courtroom as Assistant DA Patrick Bomberg—one of four prosecutors assigned to the case—laid out the Commonwealth's position.

Aaron did not glance at Shayanna, who was sitting with Terri and DJ, as Bomberg did so.

Shaneah Jenkins, who had graduated from college and enrolled in law school, was also there in the courtroom, sitting far away from her sister and next Odin Lloyd's mother, Ursula.

It was an obvious sign of the rift that Odin's death had caused between the sisters.

Ursula was wearing purple, Odin's favorite color.

Aaron was dressed in the same dark suit he had worn to his indictment, seventeen months earlier. As he had on that occasion, Aaron kept his composure and showed no emotion.

Everyone in attendance knew that the trial would be long, complex, and sensational. The British did not play American football, but British tabloids would cover the case closely. So would the *New York Times, Fox News, CNN,* and faraway media outlets in Hawaii, Alaska—even Fiji.

At *Sports Illustrated,* the in-house legal analyst, Michael McCann, geared up to file long, daily dispatches.

For the prosecutors, the stakes were remarkably high: Bristol County District Attorney Sam Sutter had signed up to prosecute the case himself. But just before Christmas, Sutter had been elected mayor of Fall River. Now, First Assistant District Attorney William McCauley would be leading the prosecution.

McCauley and Susan Garsh had clashed in the courtroom before.

In 2010, the assistant DA had prosecuted George Duarte, a

New Bedford man who had shot and killed a fifteen-year-old boy. McCauley had won that case, but criticized Garsh for exhibiting "unnecessary, discourteous, and demeaning" words, tone, and behavior during the trial. But if there was no love lost between the judge and the DA, Garsh was bent on presiding over Aaron's high-profile trial. When McCauley asked for another judge, citing the "well-known and publicly documented history of antagonism" between them, Garsh denied the motion.

She would also allow the case to be taped for broadcast, guaranteeing it an even more permanent place in the twenty-four-hour news cycle.

For Aaron Hernandez, the stakes could not be any higher: McCauley had charged him with murder in the first degree. If his lawyers, Michael Fee, James Sultan, and Charles Rankin, lost the case, Hernandez would be imprisoned for life automatically, without the possibility of parole.

But Hernandez was not the only person on trial.

The law enforcement officials who had investigated Odin Lloyd's murder would find themselves under blinding public scrutiny. Whatever mistakes they had made would be held up for the whole world to see.

The NFL itself had entered a prolonged period of public scrutiny: accusations relating to armed robbery, kidnapping, forced imprisonment, and sexual assault (Keith Wright), dog-fighting (Michael Vick), child abuse (Adrian Peterson), domestic violence (Ray Rice, Lawrence Phillips, Greg Hardy), drug trafficking (Travis Henry), DUI manslaughter (Josh Brent), conspiracy to commit murder (Rae Carruth), and murder-suicide (Jovan Belcher), were hitting the league on a regular basis.

In 2011, Dave Duerson, who had played for the Bears, Giants, and Cardinals, committed suicide by shooting himself in the chest. His suicide note read, PLEASE, SEE THAT MY BRAIN IS GIVEN TO THE NFL'S BRAIN BANK.

In 2012, Junior Seau, who had played for the Patriots as recently as 2009, committed suicide in the same manner.

Seau, Duerson, and Belcher were all found to have been suffering from CTE—chronic traumatic encephalopathy—a degenerative brain disease caused by multiple blows to the head.

Other scandals had hit close to home in New England: Spygate. Deflategate was just over the horizon. If Bill Belichick had shown himself to be a coach who won, at any cost, it seemed fair to ask: What had the Patriots known about Aaron's past when they drafted him? Had they turned a blind eye to the violent acts he'd committed while playing for the team?

The families of Daniel de Abreu and Safiro Furtado had already expanded their wrongful-death lawsuit against Aaron Hernandez to include the Patriots and the team's owner, Robert Kraft Enterprises. What would a guilty verdict mean for that lawsuit? And if Aaron Hernandez was found to be not guilty, how would the verdict affect the millions of dollars still left on his contract, at the time of his termination from the team?

*   *   *

Aaron's trial would fuel the feeling that the NFL was its own world, with its own rules—rules that had long since gone out of alignment with core American values.

Hernandez believed he could get away with anything, up to and including murder. He'd gotten away with so much, for so long. He'd been rewarded with fame and riches. A verdict of not guilty would also prove that his sense of impunity had been justified all along.

In effect, it would prove that organized football had encouraged a monster—or even created one.

CHAPTER 80

Because the DA's office had decided to try Hernandez for first-degree murder, which called for premeditation, Assistant DA Bomberg would have to make the jury believe that Aaron had *planned* to kill Odin Lloyd before murdering him.

Putting Hernandez at the scene of the crime would not be enough.

But the prosecution had a mountain of circumstantial evidence, including the text messages that Odin Lloyd had exchanged with Hernandez before he was murdered. Those went a long way toward establishing premeditation, while surveillance footage that seemed to show Aaron holding a gun indicated that he was the shooter.

It took Bomberg fifty minutes to lay out his case.

In his own opening statement, Michael Fee dismissed that case out of hand: "You just heard quite a story," the lawyer said. "A dramatic story. An exciting story...It's just a story. And it's not true.

"We are here," Fee continued, "because the police, and the prosecutors, *targeted* Aaron from the very beginning. As soon as they found out that Aaron Hernandez, the celebrity football player, the New England Patriot, was a friend of Odin Lloyd's, Aaron never had a chance. It was over. They set out on an investigation, ladies and gentlemen, collected evidence, in order to support the story they just told you, even when that evidence they collected should have led them in another direction. They locked on Aaron, and they targeted him, even when they developed evidence that two other men—who, unlike Aaron, were not friends with Odin—were with Aaron and Odin that night. The evidence will show that the investigation was sloppy and unprofessional."

In a sense, Aaron's defense strategy was akin to the one OJ Simpson's lawyers had used: A famous football player, framed. A botched investigation.

But OJ Simpson's lawyers had had Detective Mark Fuhrman's history of racist outbursts to work with, while Aaron's investigators—Michael Cherven, Michael Elliott, Eric Benson, Daniel Arrighi, and several other officers, all appeared to be solid, even exemplary, cops.

Aaron's defense would depend on his lawyers' ability to convince the jury, and the judge, otherwise.

CHAPTER 81

On February 1, 2015—three days after the start of the trial—the Patriots won Super Bowl XLIX.

Hernandez, who had no TV privileges, missed a good game, dominated by his former teammates Brady and Gronk. Soon, the Patriots would be going to the White House to meet with Barack Obama. But on that day, and most other weekdays, Aaron would be woken at six and asked to put his feet and hands through openings in his cell door. Then, he would be cuffed and loaded into the van that carried him to and away from the courthouse in Fall River.

This was Aaron's life now: off to the courthouse, then back to Special Management—a small, triangular unit, which prison officials had painted blue, yellow, and white. There were only eight cells in the place. Each one could hold two men, but Aaron was always imprisoned alone, bunking by himself and moving, at the whim of prison officials, between Cell 1 and Cell 2 on the unit's ground floor.

Both cells had tight, vertical windows, offering a view of the space corrections officers called no man's land—a panorama of razor wire, tarmac, and glass, which could not compare with the view from the courtroom. Once a day, Aaron was allowed to work out in the 8'x12' cage in the jail's recreation area. There were always more books to request from the jail's library. And going to court had become a daily diversion.

On February 5, the sixth day of the trial, prosecutors called the first of several law enforcement officers to the stand. Captain Joseph DiRenzo was an imposing man, with close-cropped hair and wide shoulders. He had spent twenty-six years on the force in North Attleboro. Second in command in the department, he ran the patrol division, supervised the chief of detectives, as well as internal affairs, and handled the department's day-to-day duties.

DiRenzo described his arrival at Corliss Landing, where he had knelt down by Odin Lloyd's left flank to inspect the body.

He described the bullet wounds: "A hole, with some ripped shirt, blood around it. There were flies around it. There were flies around his nose, also."

Step by step, he walked the jury through the measures that he and his officers had taken to protect the crime scene as a strong storm blew in. He described how State Trooper Michael Cherven had gone, methodically, through the dead man's pockets: "He would go through the pocket and announce what he was doing to the other troopers and officers that were there, so that they could mark it down. He went through one pocket, inventoried what was there. Went through the other pocket, emptied it, inventoried what was there, and announced it."

DiRenzo himself was methodical and calm as Aaron's lawyer James Sultan tried, aggressively, to convince the jury that he and his men had somehow contaminated the crime scene, rushing their investigation because of the storm that was coming, even though that storm was still far away.

Sultan did not succeed. But he had another opportunity six days later, when North Attleboro police officer Edward Zimmer took the stand. Zimmer, a nine-year veteran on the force, had also worked the crime scene, setting up a perimeter, and logging arrivals.

Zimmer had stayed on the scene for hours, carefully documenting the movement of evidence.

Within three minutes of his cross-examination, James Sultan succeeded in getting Zimmer to admit to an error in his logbook.

"Is that log accurate?" Sultan asked.

"Yes," Zimmer said. "There is one typo."

"There's a mistake on the log. Correct?"

"Yes. There's one."

Within a few minutes, Sultan had scored one more point: Why did Zimmer's logbook describe the shell casings and the towel, but not the baseball cap and the blunt?

Zimmer had only recorded what was reported to him, he said.

These small points may have opened a modicum of doubt about notes that the North Attleboro police had taken from the scene. On the one hand, they seemed to point to the fact that, if the police had made errors in their investigation, those errors were inadvertent and small.

On the other hand, they were still errors.

CHAPTER 82

This was how murder cases progressed in real life: point by minuscule point until a picture began to emerge, like a pointillist painting.

The prosecution scored body blows with video evidence, a steady parade of expert witnesses, and pained testimony delivered by Shaneah Jenkins and Ursula Ward, who choked up when she was shown a photograph of her son's corpse.

"I understand that this is very emotional for you," Judge Garsh told Ward. "But it's very important that you manage during this time you are testifying to retain control of your emotions, and not to cry while you are looking at any photo that may be shown to you."

Shayanna's sister told the court about going to her sister's house after Odin's death, and about Aaron's attempt to comfort her by telling her, "I've been through this death thing before."

When the DA pulled up video surveillance that showed Shaneah coming into the house and giving her sister a long, strong hug, Shaneah began to cry, took a tissue out of her purse, and dried her tears.

Shaneah also said that Aaron had not visited Odin's family after the death. Aaron and Odin had been friendly, she said, but not especially close.

Given Aaron's defense—based, in part, on the idea that Lloyd and Hernandez were far too friendly for Aaron to have had anything to do with the murder—this information was less than damning. Still, it was enough to cast doubts on the relationship Aaron's lawyers had set out to describe.

The defense scored smaller points, like the ones they had scored with Officer Zimmer.

But on February 12, Detective Daniel Arrighi took the stand.

The prosecution was already at a disadvantage, insofar as Arrighi went. During the lead-up to the trial, Judge Garsh had ruled that the text messages that Odin had sent to his sister, immediately before his death, would not be admissible.

The texts were hearsay, Garsh had said, because they were statements, made out of court, by someone who could not be called to testify.

This was a heavy blow for the prosecution. But Garsh had *also* ruled that evidence seized in the course of one of the searches at Aaron's home in North Attleboro would be inadmissible.

A state trooper named Michael Bates had deprived the prosecution of that evidence by filling his paperwork out sloppily, and failing to properly transfer a few details from the affidavit to the search warrant.

The judge didn't think that there was anything malicious in the mistake. According to testimony Trooper Mike Cherven had given on June 18, 2014, the omissions shouldn't have mattered at all because he had carried both documents into Aaron's home at the time of the search, and had made them "available at all times" for the duration of the search itself.

In fact, Cherven had said, the documents were attached to each other with a paper clip.

But after reviewing evidence that indicated that Cherven had entered the house empty-handed, and left again, seven minutes later, to conduct an interview at the North Attleboro police station, Garsh ruled against admitting the cell phones and iPads that the police had seized in their search.

"The court credits none of this testimony," Garsh had written, in a sharply worded ruling. "Even if Cherven had brought the affidavit in a folder along with the search warrant to the residence, and the court finds that he did not, indisputably he was not present 'at all times' during the search."

Given the harshness of the judge's ruling, the DAs had good reason to leave Mike Cherven off of their witness list.

But the downside of the DA's decision was that Detective Arrighi, who had worked closely with Cherven during the investigation, would have to work twice as hard during James Sultan's relentless cross-examination.

On the stand, Arrighi appeared to be a bit nervous. Maybe it was just his manner. But Sultan seemed to smell blood.

The lawyer came out swinging.

Sultan interrupted Arrighi several times, badgered him, questioned his training. Time and again, he allowed a note of contempt to creep into his voice.

"You peeked into the windows?" Sultan asked.

"Correct," said Arrighi.

"You peeked into the garage?... You gave Trooper Cherven a boost so that *he* could peek into the garage? And then the two of you went *into* Aaron Hernandez's backyard?"

"Yes, sir. Correct."

"Were you invited to go into his backyard?"

"No, we were not."

"And then you peeked through the windows in the back-yard, right?"

Sultan kept emphasizing the word: "Peeked...peeked... peeked..." implying that Arrighi and Michael Cherven had acted like trespassers and Peeping Toms. Moreover, Arrighi and Cherven were both dressed in street clothes. Their SUV was unmarked. How was Aaron to know they were cops? And what made Arrighi and Cherven think that Aaron was under any obligation to come to the door when they knocked?

Next, Sultan attacked Arrighi for stopping Shayanna's car, after she had dropped Aaron off at the North Attleboro Police Station.

"Miss Jenkins and their baby started driving away?" the lawyer asked. "Right?"

"Yes, sir. Correct."

"Driving home? Is that a fair assumption?"

"Yes. Fair assumption, yes."

"It was eleven o'clock at night by then, right?"

"Correct."

"And you and Trooper Cherven—or, Trooper Cherven— activated his blue lights and pulled her over, right?"

"Correct."

"Now, when the two of you pulled Shayanna Jenkins, *and her baby,* over—*at eleven o'clock at night*—was she committing any traffic infraction?"

"No, he just activated the blue lights—"

"Will you answer my question," the lawyer interrupted. "Was she committing any traffic infraction?"

"No, sir."

Sultan gave the cop a long, questioning stare—as if to say, *"Really?"*

"The baby was in the car, asleep. Right?"

"Yes."

The implication, here, was that Detective Arrighi and Trooper Cherven had acted like creeps.

CHAPTER 83

The jurors had already visited Shayanna's home in North Attleboro, as well as the clearing where Odin's body had been found. They had heard testimony by Matthew Kent, the high school student who had found the body, along with testimony given by crime scene investigators, ballistics experts, forensic geologists, swabbing experts, and pathologists. A DNA expert who had worked on OJ Simpson's case confirmed that the blunt found next to Odin's body contained Aaron's DNA, as well as Odin's.

There were dozens and dozens of witnesses.

An employee of the Glock firearm company had told the jury that the black object they had seen Aaron holding, in surveillance footage taken from his house just after the murder, was, in fact, a Glock .45.

The jurors had also seen the surveillance footage of Aaron taking the battery out of his cell phone, in the North Attleboro police station's parking lot. It was the footage that

Detective Mike Elliott had watched on the system that he had helped to install.

A few days later, the jurors heard from Detective Elliott himself.

Following a discussion of the surveillance footage, the lawyers turned their attention to the shell casing Elliott had found in the Enterprise dumpster, wrapped in a wad of Blue Cotton Candy Bubblicious chewing gum.

James Sultan questioned Elliott's methods: Why had the police placed items they had retrieved from the dumpster in the bed of a pickup truck, instead of waiting for Crime Scene Services to arrive? *No one* from Crime Scene Services was on site when the items were removed from the dumpster?

"Was it raining *that* night, sir?" the lawyer asked.

"I don't believe so," Elliott answered.

"Were there dark rain clouds moving in?"

"I don't believe so."

"And do you recall that Sgt. Baker pulled his pickup truck next to the dumpster?"

"Correct."

"You identified some photographs yesterday, about what happened at Enterprise that evening. Who took those photographs?"

"Crime Scene Services."

"Well, those photographs were taken while the items were being recovered, right?"

"Correct, sir."

"And Crime Scene Services didn't show up until *after* the items were being recovered. Isn't that correct, Detective?"

"It is correct."

"So, *who took the photographs?*"

"I believe I did."

"You *believe* you did?!"

As he had with Detective Arrighi, Sultan kept hammering away: "You're an experienced detective, right?"

"Correct."

"You're trained in the collection of evidence?"

"Yes."

"Has anyone ever taught you to collect evidence *that* way, sir?"

"No."

But, if Detective Arrighi had been nervous on the stand, Detective Elliott remained unflappable—and the evidence that he had gathered spoke for itself.

The Enterprise branch manager, Keelia Smyth, had already told the jury about the piece of Bubblicious bubble gum Aaron had offered her on the day after the murder.

Prosecutors had already established that, on the evening of the murder itself, Aaron, Ernest Wallace, and Carlos Ortiz had stopped at a gas station, filled up their car, and bought a cigar and a pack of Blue Cotton Candy Bubblicious. Video surveillance from the gas station's security cameras had shown Carlos Ortiz stepping out of the Nissan Altima with a white towel, similar to the one found at the murder scene, draped over his neck.

And there was another detail stuck in the jury's minds: the same video footage had shown Aaron dancing, like a man without a care in the world.

CHAPTER 84

On Thursday, March 26, a bomb threat was called in to the courthouse.

The evacuation was orderly, if tense.

"There is absolutely no reason to believe that the interruption was in any way related to this case," Judge Garsh assured the jury, after the building had been swept for explosives and cleared.

The call was a hoax, it turned out. But the bomb threat set the stage for a sensational turn in the case: After months of speculation, in the media as well as the courtroom, about whether Shayanna would be called to the stand, it was revealed that same day that Jenkins would be testifying on Friday.

The trial had gone on for two months already. But, as yet, there was no smoking gun.

In fact, there was no gun at all.

According to Assistant DA Bomberg, this was because Shayanna had disposed of the murder weapon. As a result, circumstantial evidence was all that Assistant DA Bomberg had to work with. But as that evidence kept piling up, it seemed, more and more, to point to Aaron.

Shayanna had been there for most of the trial—though she was conspicuously absent when the nanny, Jennifer Fortier, testified. Shayanna wore the big engagement ring that Aaron had gotten her. She and Aaron smiled at each other whenever the opportunity arose. They blew kisses. They mouthed the words "I love you." And when Shayanna did take the stand, she proved herself to be utterly loyal to Aaron.

The prosecution had a problem: Lawyers are not allowed to call a witness whose testimony they know to be false—and, following her testimony before the grand jury, Shayanna had been indicted for perjury. As a result, Aaron's lawyers argued, the DAs could not call Jenkins to the stand—unless the DA had reason to believe that her testimony would be substantively different on matters that she had been charged with lying about. Judge Garsh agreed, and ruled that the prosecution would only be allowed to question Shayanna about matters that were *not* elements of the perjury charges. Because Shayanna had been accused of lying about twenty-nine specific matters, this restriction put the prosecution at a distinct disadvantage. But Jenkins was at a disadvantage as well. Weeks earlier, at the prosecution's request, she had been granted immunity from prosecution as an accessory to murder. But this also meant that she could no longer plead the Fifth Amendment to avoid incriminating herself. As a result, both sides had to tread carefully. Nevertheless, Jenkins's testimony was more dramatic than anything that the jury had heard.

The DA began by asking Shayanna about the night after Odin Lloyd's murder.

Shayanna described driving Aaron to the police station. Afterward, "when he got home from the police station," she said, "when I had found out that Odin was murdered, I asked him if he did it. He said, 'No.' And that was the extent of our conversation."

She also recalled a text message Aaron had sent her, asking her to get rid of a black box that they had in the basement.

She described a black gun she had found in a junk drawer, and the "stern look" she gave Aaron afterward.

When she went back to the junk drawer, she said, the gun was no longer there. But when the DA showed her a still from a video of Hernandez holding a similar gun, she said the image was too vague to make out—"only a black blob it looks like"—and when he showed her an actual Glock, she recoiled.

"It's a secured firearm?" she asked, as the gun was placed in front of her.

When the DA asked Shayanna if she and Shaneah were "close, as sisters," Shayanna winced and did not answer.

"Have you been in the past, ma'am?" the DA persisted.

Shayanna grimaced. "I, I mean we're...estranged, kind of," she said.

When the DA played the video surveillance footage of

Shayanna and Shaneah embracing, Shaneah ran out of the courtroom in tears.

When Shayanna resumed her testimony, on Monday, Shaneah was not in the courtroom. Whatever bond the two sisters still shared had been shattered, once and for all.

The DA dove right in, asking Shayanna about her role in disposing of evidence that was crucial to the prosecution's case against Hernandez.

Specifically, the DA had in mind a black box that, he believed, contained the Glock .45 that Aaron had shot Odin Lloyd with.

"I was instructed to take it out of the home," Jenkins said.

"Was it important to him for you to get rid of it?" the DA asked.

"Yes."

"You were also asked [by a grand jury] whether you had taken certain steps to cover or conceal or hide the box when you removed it from the home?"

"Yes."

"Do you recall doing that?"

"Yes."

"In fact, when you took that box out, and concealed it, were you attempting to do that in a way so people didn't know what you were doing?"

"That's correct."

Jenkins said that the box weighed about forty pounds and smelled "skunky." She had assumed it contained marijuana. But when Bomberg asked her if she had looked inside of the box she said, "No."

When she was asked how she had disposed of it she said, "A dumpster."

When she was asked to be more specific she said, "I can't remember."

Over the course of ten hours of testimony, Shayanna had uttered the phrases "I can't remember," "Not that I can remember," "I can't recall," "I'm not sure," and "I have no idea," so many times they began to sound like a mantra.

CHAPTER 85

The following day, March 31, turned out to be every bit as dramatic, as Robert Kraft took the stand.

Contrary to all expectations, the story he told seemed to tilt the whole case on its axis.

The seventy-three-year-old billionaire was suffering from a head cold—you could hear it in his voice as the clerk swore him in. But Kraft's sense of humor remained intact.

On the stand, he seemed folksy, informal—more like your everyday Patriots' fan than their owner.

"Sir, do you work?" the DA asked.

Kraft chuckled and smiled.

"I think so," he said. "Yes. I work at One Patriot Place."

"And what do you do for work, sir?"

"Whatever they ask me to do."

"Do you run a business?"

"Yes. We're in [the] packaging and paper business, private equity. And we have two sports teams."

328 ■ JAMES PATTERSON

The DA asked Kraft about Wednesday, June 19, 2013. Did he recall going to Gillette Stadium on that day?

Kraft did. He remembered the news vans parked in the stadium lot, and helicopters hovering overhead.

"I went directly to the weight room," Kraft said. "I saw two of our strength coaches and Aaron Hernandez."

"At that time did you ask to speak with him?"

"Yes. There's an office connected to the weight room that I brought him into . . . I understood there was an incident that had transpired and I wanted to know whether he was involved. Any player that comes into our system I consider part of our extended family, and I wanted to get him help."

"Did you say this to the defendant?" the DA asked.

"Yes," said Kraft. "He said he was *not* involved. That he was innocent. And that he hoped that the time of the murder incident came out. Because, I believe, he said he was in a club."

There were gasps in the courtroom: jurors had already seen video surveillance footage of Hernandez, Wallace, Ortiz, and Lloyd, taken just before the murder. They had been at a gas station, not a club. No testimony the jurors had heard had placed Aaron at a club on the night of the murder.

Moreover, how did Aaron know *when* the murder had been committed?

It was obvious to everyone in the room that, if Kraft was telling the truth, Aaron had lied to him on June 19.

Lied stupidly, in a manner that actually seemed to *implicate* him now.

Afterward, Kraft said, Aaron "hugged and kissed me and thanked me for my concern."

"And after that," the DA asked, "did you see the defendant again?"

"No."

Kraft had been on the stand for ten minutes, about the length of his conversation with Aaron. But ten minutes was all it took to do lasting damage to Aaron's case. And on the following day, April Fool's, Alexander Bradley took the stand and drove several more nails into his former friend's coffin.

CHAPTER 86

Judge Garsh had ruled against telling the jury about Bradley's claim that Hernandez had shot him, and about the civil lawsuit that Bradley had filed.

The jury *did* get to hear about Bradley's own rap sheet: the drug busts, the shooting in Hartford. Within two and a half minutes of taking the stand, Bradley admitted to being a drug dealer.

Nevertheless, his testimony proved to be damning.

Bradley told the jury that Aaron had purchased as much as four ounces of weed from him, at a cost of $1,200 to $1,500, on a weekly basis starting in 2010.

According to Bradley, Aaron smoked as much as an ounce a day.

Hernandez was paranoid, and believed that he was being followed by helicopters, and the police, Bradley said.

Bradley also told the jury that, when he stayed at Aaron's

house in North Attleboro, which he did "quite often," he slept in a room in the basement.

During the course of one visit, two years earlier, in November of 2012, he'd gotten a look at a "small, black" lock box that Aaron kept by the bar area in the basement, or in a closet next to a trophy case.

Aaron's defense team hoped the jury had the conclusion, from Shayanna's testimony, that the box she had gotten rid of contained nothing more than forty pounds of marijuana. They had also tried to block Bradley from testifying, filing a motion that claimed that the risk of a mistrial was "unacceptably high."

But the motion had failed, and what Bradley said next helped to undermine the idea that Shayanna had only helped Aaron get rid of some weed.

"This black box," Bradley was asked. "Did you ever see it in an open condition?"

"Yes," Bradley said.

"And who opened it?"

"Mr. Hernandez."

"And when it was in an open condition, did you ever see any of the contents inside?"

"Yes."

"And what did you see inside?"

"There was a firearm. Money. Marijuana joints."

Bradley described the firearm: it had been a semi-automatic pistol, he said, "silver-grayish colored, with a brown handle."

Bradley also said that, in the course of a trip to Miami, he had seen Aaron holding a Glock pistol.

Oscar "Papoo" Hernandez had been in the room at the time, Bradley said, tying Aaron to a gun prosecutors believed to be the murder weapon, and to the man prosecutors believed had furnished him with that gun.

CHAPTER 87

By the end of the trial, prosecutors had all but proven that Aaron had been in the clearing on the night of the murder.

With closing arguments approaching, Aaron's lawyers felt that they had no choice but to admit it.

Aaron *had* been present, James Sultan explained, shocking everyone in the courtroom—but *only as a witness* to Odin Lloyd's murder.

Ernest Wallace or Carlos Ortiz had killed Lloyd while out of their minds on PCP, the lawyers claimed. But neither Wallace nor Ortiz had been called to testify. In the end, Aaron's defense lasted less than one day, with only three witnesses called to the stand:

Dr. David Greenblatt, a professor of pharmacology at Tufts, who described the behavioral effects of PCP. (Aaron's cousin Jennifer Mercado had testified, previously, that she had seen Wallace and Ortiz smoking PCP.)

Eric Carita, a forensic consultant who had swabbed the Bubblicious chewing gum that one of the shell casings had stuck to, and sent to Texas for processing.

Jennifer Smith, the forensic analyst who had processed the sample and established a link to Aaron's DNA. Smith explained that DNA can be transferred from one object, then onto another, then onto a third object—a process known as "secondary transfer." It was "extremely likely," Smith said, that DNA on the gum could have been transferred onto the shell casing.

On the following day, April 7, James Sultan presented his closing argument in Aaron's defense.

The approach that the lawyer adopted now was low-key, but eloquent. Sultan's late father, Stanley, had been a writer, a college professor, and a colleague and close friend of Sylvia Plath's.

Now, Stanley's son brought the measured tones of the seminar room into Judge Garsh's courtroom.

"It's been a long trial," Sultan told the jury. "We started back in January. Slogged through those mountains of snow. And now, it's spring."

"There's plenty of evidence," Sultan said. "You heard from more than 130 witnesses. There are more than 430 exhibits, some of them voluminous. I submit to you, there are really two ways you can go about analyzing the evidence: The right way. And the wrong way."

The right way, Sultan said, was to start with the presumption that Aaron Hernandez was innocent.

Hernandez and Lloyd had been friends, Sultan said.

"Aaron and Odin shared a passion. A passion for marijuana. Odin was very skilled at rolling blunts. Odin would roll blunts for Aaron and they'd smoke together...On the first weekend of June 2013, Aaron and Odin were together at Club Rumor in Boston, where they went for Shayanna's birthday party...The following weekend, Aaron and Odin were together at a club in Providence. And on Friday night, June fourteenth—a night you've heard a lot about—Aaron and Odin went, again, to Club Rumor in Boston. Were they friends? Obviously, they were friends. They were future brothers-in-law. But the prosecution wants to deny the obvious. The prosecution has presented, through its evidence, a number of possible theories of why Aaron would want to murder Odin. Let's go through those, and see if they make any sense."

Theory #1, Sultan said, was that Aaron had killed Odin because Odin had been rude to his friend Alexander Bradley.

The lawyer did not even bother to point out how ridiculous this theory was.

Theory #2 was that Aaron and Odin had argued at Rumor.

But, according to Sultan, this theory rested entirely on the testimony of a single, unreliable witness.

Theory #3 was that Aaron was worried about Odin telling Shaneah about their misadventures with Jennifer Fortier and Amanda DeVito.

But hadn't Aaron already told Shayanna about their trip to his "other spot"?

"What about infidelity?" Sultan asked. "Is Aaron worried that Shayanna's going to find out that he was out chasing after other women? What did Shayanna tell you? She told you she knew all about Aaron's interest in chasing other women. She didn't like it. But she hoped he'd outgrow it."

Then, shifting gears, the lawyer asked the jury to consider whether Aaron could really have been stupid enough to kill Odin Lloyd himself.

"If Aaron planned in advance to murder Odin, why would he do so in his own town...in an open location less than a mile from his home? If Aaron had planned in advance to murder Odin, why would he leave keys to a car he had rented in Odin's pocket? Along with Odin's cell phone and wallet? And for that matter, why did Odin still have his cell phone? If Aaron had planned in advance to murder Odin Lloyd, why would he bring along two witnesses? And if Aaron had planned in advance to murder Odin Lloyd, why was a blunt found at the scene? A blunt shared by none other than Aaron Hernandez and Odin Lloyd, two friends who shared an interest in marijuana?"

As for the box that Shayanna had removed from the house: Had the police found any marijuana during their searches of Aaron's house? Given how much Aaron smoked, didn't it stand to reason that they had not because the heavy box that Shayanna had placed in a black bag and removed from the basement, after the murder, was full of marijuana, and nothing but marijuana?

"Is it possible that the murder weapon was inside that bag that Shayanna removed that day?" Sultan asked. "Of course it's possible. Of *course* it's possible. *Anything* is *possible*. But a murder charge, a murder conviction, can't be based on possibilities, on guesswork, on speculation. That's not good enough."

Had Aaron made all the right decisions? Sultan readily admitted that Aaron had not. "He was a twenty-three-year-old kid," the lawyer said. "Who had witnessed something. A shocking killing. Committed by somebody he knew. He really didn't know what to do, so he just put one foot in front of the other. Keep in mind, he's not charged with being an accessory after the fact. You couldn't even find him guilty of that if you wanted to. He's charged with murder. And that he did not do."

CHAPTER 88

James Sultan used the full ninety minutes that he had been given to deliver his closing statement.

Now, William McCauley took his turn.

There were no witnesses to the murder. There was no clear motive, or murder weapon. But the DA took his time sorting through the evidence that he did have, step by step.

Hours after the murder, McCauley told the jurors, Ernest Wallace, Carlos Ortiz, and Aaron Hernandez had all been captured, on video, lounging around Aaron's swimming pool, drinking smoothies that Shayanna brought them.

If Wallace or Ortiz had just killed Odin, the DA asked, would it make sense that Aaron would be hanging out with them, so casually, so soon after the murder?

Again, and again, the DA pointed out that, in every piece of video evidence that they had seen, Aaron had "controlled" the actions of everyone around him.

"The defendant controlled every aspect of that trip,"

McCauley said, referring to the drive that culminated in Odin Lloyd's murder.

Then, switching from a scalpel to a blunter instrument, McCauley started to hammer away.

"He's the one," the DA said. "He's the one . . . He's the one."

The jury deliberated for more than six days before they returned with their verdict.

Sitting next to each other in the courtroom's front row, Terri Hernandez and Shayanna Jenkins embraced each other and burst into tears.

It was as if all the air had been sucked out of the courtroom.

The jury had convicted Aaron Hernandez of murder in the first degree.

"Madam foreperson," the clerk asked. "By which theory or theories—deliberate premeditation and/or extreme atrocity or cruelty?"

"Extreme atrocity or cruelty," the foreperson said.

Sitting across the aisle from Terri and Shayanna, Shaneah wiped tears away.

Odin's mother, Ursula Ward, cried and started to rock back and forth.

Standing between Sultan and Fee, dressed in a gray suit, a white shirt, and a polka-dot tie, Aaron licked his lips and mouth the word "unreal," but betrayed no outward emotion. He sat down while the jury convicted him of the additional charges—none of which mattered, as he would already be sentenced to life.

Judge Garsh took a few moments to thank the jury.

"This truly is a people's court, with you, the people, ruling," she said.

As she did so, a court bailiff knelt down and placed shackles around Aaron's wrists and his ankles. Then, Aaron was made to stand again.

Turning to his mother and his fiancée, he mouthed the words, "It will be okay."

"Stay strong," Hernandez told Shayanna as he was led out of the courtroom.

CHAPTER 89

L ater that day, Judge Garsh heard impact statements by Odin Lloyd's uncle, one of his sisters, and Ursula Ward.

"It doesn't feel like Odin is not here," Odin's sister Olivia Thibou said in her statement. "It feels like just a bad dream and I'm stuck between living and reality and this dream world where he's just not here and I haven't had a chance to speak with him."

"A lot of people won't see from outside the value and riches he had," said Odin's uncle. "It wasn't material, the wealth he possessed."

Ursula Ward, who had dressed Odin up all in white for his funeral, and had the words GOING HOME stitched into the side of his casket, said, "The day I laid my son to rest, I felt my heart stop beating for a moment. I felt like I wanted to go into that hole with my son...I'll never get to dance at his wedding. He will never get to dance at my wedding. I will never hear my son say, 'Ma dukes. Ma, did you cook? Ma, go to bed. Ma, you're so beautiful. Where are you going, Ma? Did you get my permission to go out? I love you, Ma.' I miss my baby boy, Odin, so much. But I know I'm going to see him someday again. That's giving me the strength to go on. We wore purple in this courtroom every day because it's my son's favorite color. I forgive the hands of the people that had a hand in my son's murder, either before or after. I pray and hope that someday everyone out there will forgive them also. May God continue to bless us."

Then, less than five hours after the jurors had delivered their verdict, the court handed down its state-mandated sentence: "You're committed to MCI–Cedar Junction for the term of your natural life, without the possibility of parole."

Hernandez stood, stoically, throughout his sentencing. He knew the word on Judge Garsh: Remarkably, no case that had come before her had ever been overturned on appeal. He knew that his finances were dwindling: His salary was gone; his lawyers had been expensive; Ursula Ward and her lawyer, Doug Sheff, were still pursuing a wrongful death lawsuit against him.

But Aaron's spirit had not been broken.

"They got it wrong," Hernandez said, as he was transported from the courthouse to the state prison. "I didn't do it."

PART ELEVEN

CHAPTER 90

During Aaron Hernandez's first week at Cedar Junction, the Department of Corrections learned that he had five enemies ("keep-aways," in DOC terminology) at the prison. As a result, Hernandez was kept in isolation. Before the week was out, he was relocated.

This time, he ended up Souza-Baranowski Correctional Center, a maximum-security facility in Shirley, Massachusetts.

Souza-Baranowski was the state's newest prison. It was also crowded, with ninety inmates crammed into cell blocks designed for sixty, and extremely violent.

"Fights, slashing, and suicide attempts cause the whole institution to freeze up on a regular basis, if not daily on a bad week," says Leslie Walker, who runs Prisoners' Legal Services, a nonprofit in Massachusetts.

At first, Hernandez was housed in the prison's Orientation

Unit. Corrections officers conducted hourly rounds, but there was time to interact with other inmates.

Within a few days, one of those inmates had given Aaron a new tattoo.

Tattoo guns at the prison were primitive: Motors came from typewriters. (In the absence of motors, inmates sometimes used homemade waterwheels.) Hollowed-out BIC ballpoint pens served as shafts. Needles were just straightened-out paper clips. Ink (always black) was made from pages torn out of thin-paged Gideon Bibles. Inmates burned the pages, caught the soot, scraped it together, and mixed it with water—a painstaking operation. But in Aaron's case, the process resulted in an elaborate, professional-looking five-pointed star on his neck. The words written across it— LIFETIME LOYALTY—were commonly associated with the Bloods.

Out of the prison's 1,100 inmates, 750 were confirmed gang members. When a corrections officer was asked how prisoners were supposed to survive in such an environment, the officer thought for a moment, then said, "Affiliate."

Prison officials spotted the new tattoo quickly, and disciplined Hernandez for getting it. But in most respects, Aaron presented himself as a model prisoner. After a month in Orientation Block, he was eager to find his place among the regular inmates.

Aaron wrote the administration several letters pleading his case.

"I have been here over a month and have no yard, $30 canteen, no gym etc," he wrote in one letter. "I know I really cant be bunked…because people could easily steal my shit, letter, law paperwork, and sell it and could do anything to get money and publicity which will continue to kill my cases like media has already done."

All that Aaron wanted to do was get comfortable, "start his bid," and find his proper place in the prison, he said. Since entering prison, in 2013, he had been trying to enter general population. He had no enemies at Souza-Baranowski. In fact, he knew and trusted a few inmates he'd known on "the streets."

With no further infractions on his record, Aaron's request was granted and he was moved into "pop." But despite his appeals and assurances, Aaron was soon reverting to his old ways.

aron's first fight at the prison was a "two-on-one" fight. According to prison officials, Hernandez was part of the two. According to another source, the fight was gang-related.

Afterward, Hernandez was taken to a segregation cell. A corrections officer visited him to check for marks and bruises, only to find that Hernandez had blocked the door.

When the officer finally managed to enter, he saw that Aaron's knuckles and one of his elbows were red.

As he put Aaron in restraints to take him down to see medical staff, Hernandez became "agitated and insolent."

"You just making up shit," he said to the officer. When the medical check was complete, Aaron became agitated again. "This place ain't shit to me," he told the guards. "I'll run this place, and keep running shit. Prison ain't shit to me!"

*   *   *

All in all, between May of 2015 and October of the following year, Hernandez racked up a dozen disciplinary offenses. The list included three fistfights, two offenses related to smoking, two prison tattoos, and the possession of a sharpened, six-inch metal shiv.

But, for Aaron, there was more to the prison than fighting. There were books to check out of the library. K2, synthetic marijuana, wasn't too hard to get in the prison. It was odorless, colorless. It didn't show up in urine tests. K2 could cause paranoia, hallucinations, and psychotic episodes. But it also created a feeling of euphoria. If Aaron was using the drug, it would have helped him face the anxiety of his upcoming trial for double murder.

Aaron was a "normal" inmate—"which was weird," a corrections officer at the prison recalls. "He fit right in."

Before long, he had made a few friends.

A petty criminal named Kyle Kennedy was one of them.

Kennedy had used a butcher knife to hold up a Cumberland Farms in Northbridge, Massachusetts. He walked out with $189, but crashed his getaway car. Arrested immediately, he was put into an unlocked cell at the local sheriff's station—at which point, Kennedy simply walked out.

He got three blocks down the road before the police picked him up once again. Now, Kennedy had an escape on his record—a crime that would ultimately land him in the federal prison system. "He was brought down to a local police department in Central Mass, these small little police stations," Kennedy's attorney, Larry Army, explains. "The police, when they arrested him for that, didn't lock his cell the right way or they didn't lock it. The kid's all fucked up, realizes it, and basically opens up his door and walks out the front door of the police station. 'He's like, "What's your problem? Nobody told me I couldn't leave."' So, because of this 'escape,' he's classified as a Level 1 security risk. Out of 120 guys in his cell block, one hundred were in for life. The other ones are there for twenty-plus years. Then there's Kyle, this kid who's there for two or three years. And then enter Aaron..."

Hernandez had heard about Kennedy when Kennedy was imprisoned at Cedar Junction, the prison Aaron had spent a few days at after his trial. "There was an issue that occurred," Army says. "Kyle was in the middle of taking care of it. Aaron had heard about it. So, Kyle does something over here. Aaron hears about it over there. He writes a letter and basically gives his respect. Then, all of the sudden, Kyle is transferred to Aaron's prison. Completely happenstance. But nothing happens that shouldn't happen."

Though the pertinent prison records have been redacted, it appears that, not long afterward, Aaron petitioned prison officials to make Kyle Kennedy his bunkmate.

CHAPTER 92

Aaron's friends and his family adjusted, as best they could, to his incarceration.

Though they had never married, Shayanna changed her name to Jenkins-Hernandez. She continued to raise Aaron's daughter, Avielle.

Despite their fights, and the fact that he had stabbed her, Terri continued to live in Bristol with Jeffrey Cummings.

DJ, who had started in on a promising career as a college football coach, found his opportunities dwindling after his brother's arrest.

Although he refused requests to be interviewed for this book, DJ did spend several days with Michael Rosenberg, a writer for *Sports Illustrated*. In July of 2016, *SI* published a long profile.

By then, DJ had given up on the coaching career and started a roofing company in Texas. Now going by "Jonathan," DJ came off as responsible, sober, and thoughtful. Photographs that accompanied the profile underscored his physical resemblance to Aaron. But the similarities seemed to end there.

DJ/Jonathan did not have his brother's freakishly outsized talent—or his dark side.

"No one but Aaron Hernandez will ever fully grasp how a millionaire tight end came to gun down a friend three summers ago," the tagline that ran with the article read. "But Aaron's older brother Jonathan was there from day one, and witnessed all the little moments, all the poor choices, all the unwise associations that led to murder. That perspective cost Jonathan his way of living—but that's O.K. He understands."

DJ/Jonathan really did seem to understand. The profile described the tattoo over his heart—

D&A
THERE'S NO OTHER LOVE LIKE THE LOVE FOR
A BROTHER
THERE'S NO OTHER LOVE LIKE THE LOVE FROM
A BROTHER

—and went on to describe that love in detail.

"He had a very big heart," Jonathan said. "That's what's craziest about all this. There is a disconnect. He would open up his arms to anyone." But Aaron's brother admitted that, although Aaron had sworn to him that he was innocent, he had been "involved," at the least, in Odin Lloyd's murder.

"Drugs, and people who don't have the best intentions for you," DJ explained.

* * *

Aaron's agent, Brian Murphy, believes in Aaron's innocence to this day. But he, too, sees no way around the fact that Aaron was there, on the night of Odin Lloyd's murder.

During the call Aaron had made, on the day after Father's Day, with the police stationed outside his house, Murphy had asked him if he'd seen Odin Lloyd.

"Well, I partied with him a couple nights ago, but I hadn't seen him since then," Aaron had said.

"Is he missing?" Murphy had asked. "Is something wrong?"

"I guess they can't find him. I don't know."

"All right. If your friend's missing, why would they wait outside your house?"

"I don't know, man," Aaron had said. "They're tripping. But I think they're waiting for a search warrant."

"I have to tell you," Murphy says today. "That conversation, I've never repeated it to anyone. He was so unbelievably crystal-clear to me that he had done nothing wrong—which obviously wasn't true, because he admitted he was there. And as I told Aaron, 'I believe in my heart that you did not shoot Lloyd, but what the hell were you thinking leaving? And going back to your house?' I never understood why he did that.

"Aaron's smart as hell. He's super-smart. He's a survivor. A hustler. If he was going to kill someone, he would never drive up to Boston, pick the guy up, come back to a clearing a mile from his house, shoot him, and leave him where he would be found. That's the clumsiest murder of all time. That's why I personally don't believe that he did it. Because if he wanted to kill Lloyd, and I can't imagine why he would... It's insane. He got the best blunts of his life from Lloyd. And even the homosexual angle, which I don't buy—I'm not saying whether he was or not, but I don't think he'd kill Lloyd over that.

"I don't see it happening. I don't see a motive. But even if he did, even if he *wanted* to kill him, he'd do it in a much smarter way. What *I* believe is that Carlos Ortiz was high as a kite on angel dust, showing off for Aaron—some argument ensued—and Ortiz shot Lloyd. At that point, Aaron's code kicked in and, as much as I disagree with it, Aaron lived and died with that code. He would never rat someone out."

DJ said that he had been open with Aaron about his distrust of certain characters Aaron had gathered around him. He also described Aaron's reaction to the concerns that he voiced about each of those characters.

"What's the worst that can happen?" Aaron had told his brother. "He's my friend."

"I don't know," DJ explained. "I just know he cared about people. And some of the people he cared about, I wasn't too fond of. I didn't think they were the best for him at that stage in his life. But he cared so much. He really did. It's very interesting, how much he cared."

If not for a few crucial choices, Aaron's life might have turned out differently. If only he'd accompanied DJ to UConn. If only he had managed to pull away from the bad elements in Bristol. If only Dennis Hernandez had lived to see his son succeed in college, and the NFL, and keep him on the straight and narrow.

"That's the million-dollar question, how my father—if he was still alive, how everything would have changed," DJ told *Sports Illustrated.* "I think it would have been completely different.

"But," he added, "I don't know. That's a fairy tale."

CHAPTER 93

On January 9, 2017, Alexander Bradley was sentenced to five years in prison and five on parole for his role in the 2014 nightclub shooting in Hartford.

Bradley had copped a plea: no contest to criminal possession of a firearm, first-degree criminal endangerment, and third-degree criminal mischief.

"I'm not the same person I was three years ago," he told the judge. "It was a tumultuous time in my life. I was going through some dramatic events."

Months earlier, prosecutors had granted Bradley immunity for the 2012 double murders in Boston in exchange for testifying against Hernandez. They had already indicted Hernandez for witness intimidation in connection with the 2012 Bradley shooting (the witness in question being Bradley himself). That, too, had given them leverage during the run-up to Aaron's next murder trial.

Now, after several delays, that murder trial was set to begin.

*   *   *

This time around, Hernandez had hired Jose Baez.

The high-profile Florida lawyer was famous—some would say infamous—for having represented an Orlando woman, Casey Anthony, in her sensational murder trial.

On or around June 16, 2007, Casey's two-year-old daughter, Caylee, had gone missing. Casey did not report the disappearance. A month later, on July 15, Casey's own mother, Cindy, finally called 911.

"There's something wrong," Cindy told the dispatcher. "I found my daughter's car today and it smells like there's been a dead body in the damned car."

Casey lied to detectives: the *babysitter* had taken her daughter, she said. When Caylee's body was found, several months later, Casey was charged with first-degree murder. Prosecutors pushed for the death penalty. *Time,* NBC, and other media outlets called it the "Social-Media Trial of the Century." Jose Baez was criticized for his defense, which seemed to change on a regular basis. Along with his client, he was savaged in the press. But in the end, Baez won. Casey Anthony was cleared of all serious charges.

Against all odds, Baez believed that he could pull off another miracle on Aaron's behalf.

On March 1, 2017, the lawyer delivered his opening statement in Hernandez's second murder trial.

CHAPTER 94

S ometimes," Baez said, "you want something so badly, that you're willing to make a deal with the devil just to make it happen. That is exactly what the Commonwealth did in this case."

The devil that Jose Baez had in mind was Alexander Bradley.

"It takes a lot of nerve to put that man on the stand and ask you all to believe him beyond a reasonable doubt."

Suffolk County Assistant District Attorney Patrick Haggen had less physical evidence to work with than Hernandez's prosecutors had had in 2015. The murders themselves had taken place five years earlier. The investigation had stalled, up until Aaron's arrest for Odin Lloyd's murder. And if Aaron's motive, in that case, was murky, the motive in this one was inexplicable: After playing in the Super Bowl, Aaron Hernandez had gone out and killed two men, simply because one of them had spilled a drink?

"There is no science that will connect Aaron Hernandez to this case," Baez told the jury. "What you do have is Bradley's story. An unbelievable, fantastic tale of lies."

If the jurors had known about Odin Lloyd's murder—if they had known that Aaron was already serving a life sentence, without the possibility of parole—they might have been more inclined to buy Bradley's story. But, ostensibly, despite the wall-to-wall coverage that Hernandez's 2015 trial had generated, none of the jurors knew about his previous conviction.

Aaron's lawyers in that case, James Sultan, Michael Fee, and Charles Rankin, had been solid, even exceptional. But Baez brought style and star power to the proceedings.

"Alexander Bradley is a three-legged pony," Baez would say, hopping up and down as if he were riding a horse. "You can't trust this man. You can't *ride him home.*"

And in many respects, Baez had an easier case to argue. In 2012, investigators had not paid as much attention to the murders of two obscure African men as they might have, had they known that an NFL player was involved.

Now, the prosecution's entire case rested on the testimony of an admitted drug dealer.

Patrick Haggen called the usual array of witnesses: first responders, detectives, forensic experts. Brian Quon, the security consultant from Underbar, testified. So did Ugochukwu Ojimba and Jaime Furtado, who were bouncers at Cure.

Aquilino Freire and Raychides Gomes-Sanches, who had been in the car with Safiro Furtado and Daniel de Abreu, described the shooting.

Members of the victims' families, who had filled the courtroom's first two rows for the duration of the trial, cried on the stand.

But Jose Baez did not dispute the fact that Daniel de Abreu and Safiro Furtado had been murdered. He simply argued that *Bradley* had murdered them, over a drug deal gone wrong.

On March 20, the thirteenth day of the trial, Bradley himself took the stand.

CHAPTER 95

Jose Baez had studied the testimony that Bradley had given, in the Odin Lloyd murder trial, carefully.

"I thought he could hurt us," the lawyer would say. "This was no ghetto superstar. He was going to come across well."

Bradley *did* come across well. He made no bones about having been a professional drug dealer. He described the night of the murders in great detail. He described the night Aaron Hernandez had shot him.

Bradley was wearing a button-down shirt and square, rimless glasses. The prosthetic eye in his right eye socket seemed to stare straight ahead, eerily, as he went, point by point, through the text messages that he and Hernandez had exchanged in the wake of that shooting.

When the prosecutor asked Bradley why he had refused to tell police in Florida who the shooter had been, he said, "I didn't want to tell. That's not the route I wanted to take. I didn't want to tell on Mr. Hernandez, I wanted revenge...I wanted to make it even."

Watching him testify, it was easy to understand Hernandez's anxiety and paranoia.

"I didn't want to talk to the police," Bradley said. "I wanted Mr. Hernandez. I wanted his life."

When it came to Alexander Bradley, Hernandez's paranoia had been justified.

Jose Baez began his cross-examination by calling Bradley a liar.

"Mr. Bradley, this whole spilled drink incident is something you're completely making up, isn't it?" he asked.

Bradley did not rise to the bait. He remained calm and polite, addressing the lawyer as "Mr. Baez" and "Sir" as he denied each and every allegation.

Hernandez pulled on his lip, nervously, as he followed along.

"Now," Baez asked, "after being shot in Florida, you did not cooperate with the police?"

"Correct," Bradley replied. "Correct."

"And that's because you didn't *know* who shot you."

"That is incorrect."

"You know who shot you?"

"Most certainly."

"And you knew the details of who shot you, and how?"

"Extensively."

"Okay. And you refused to cooperate with the police... You then consulted with a lawyer...and then you sent all those text messages that we went over, right?"

"At some point, yes."

"And your intent was to get money from Aaron Hernandez."

Bradley hesitated for a moment, then said, "At a point that became my intent, yes."

"And I know—we know—you wanted to kill him, too, right?"

Bradley hesitated again before he leaned into the microphone.

"Yes," he admitted, and Baez pounced.

"Because you're a *killer,*" the lawyer said.

The DA objected.

The judge said, "Sustained."

But Baez had made his point.

According to Baez, the Florida shooting was another example of yet another drug deal gone bad. Bradley denied it. But, he went on to concede, death was an occupational hazard in his line of work.

"Dealing drugs is a very violent business, is it not?" Baez asked.

"It can be," Bradley admitted.

All in all, Bradley spent three days on the stand. Before letting him go, Baez scored one more point that would resonate with the jury.

Had Bradley sent his lawyer a text: Now u sure once I withdraw this lawsuit I wont be held on perjury after I tell the truth about me not recalling anything about who shot me?

Bradley did his best to explain: There were no circumstances under which Bradley wanted to bring criminal charges against Hernandez. But how could he appear before a grand jury, and deny any knowledge of the shooting, after filing civil charges that contradicted the very same claim?

"I'm *not* perjuring myself," Bradley insisted. But a shadow of a doubt would linger over the drug dealer's testimony.

The prosecution called Bradley's baby mama, Brooke Wilcox, next. She told the jury that, in the wee hours of the morning, on the night of the double murder in Boston, Bradley and Hernandez had come to her door.

In the privacy of Brooke's bedroom, she said, Bradley had told her, "This crazy motherfucker just did some stupid shit."

"Could you tell who he was referring to?" the DA asked.

"Yes. To Aaron."

On March 30, Shayanna Jenkins took the stand.

"I played my role," Shayanna Jenkins told the jury. "I learned to keep my mouth shut."

Though she seemed to remember even less than she had at Aaron's trial in 2015, Shayanna did recall that she had never asked Aaron about Alexander Bradley being shot.

"I pick and choose my battles," she said.

A man named Robert Lindsey testified the next day. He described a phone call he'd gotten on Valentine's Day, 2013 — the day after the Florida shooting.

"It was my cousin…" Lindsey said. "Alexander Bradley. He told me—excuse my language—he told me that, 'This faggot-ass nigga Aaron shot me in the eye.'"

*　　*　　*

In the few days that followed, more forensics experts were called to the stand. So were a slew of witnesses who had come up from Belle Glade: Tyrone Crawford, Deonte Thompson, Je'rrelle Pierre.

They recalled even less than Shayanna had.

CHAPTER 96

There is absolutely no evidence," Jose Baez assured the jurors on April 6, "that Aaron Hernandez committed this crime. What is scary, is how easy it appears to be charged with such crimes."

It was the last day of Aaron's second murder trial, and Baez had just launched into his closing argument.

Alexander Bradley was "a three-legged pony," Baez said. A pony the DAs were going to ride to the finish, despite the lies he had told.

Every few minutes, the lawyer would break away to review another piece of evidence the prosecution had offered. But, every time, he circled back around to his main point: Who was the jury going to believe? The *drug dealer*?

"Lies from beginning to end, ladies and gentlemen. Lies from Boston to Florida. But they're going to ride him," Baez said, hopping in front of the jury as if he was riding that three-legged pony. "They're going to ride him all the way home!"

Bradley was a perjurer, a parasite in designer clothes. "We all have to get up sometimes and go to work... But this man can prance around in designer shirts and not earn a penny... They cleaned him up. He's got a nice Burberry shirt on. The glasses are a really nice touch."

It wasn't a legal argument, per se. But it was effective. And, in any case, that text that Bradley had sent to his lawyer? "You need not any more information than that alone," Baez told the jurors. "*That* is your reasonable doubt for the entire case!"

"You can't trust this man," Baez concluded, as he pointed to a photo of Bradley. "You can't *ride him home*. That's not justice."

Patrick Haggen began his closing statement by admitting that Aaron Hernandez's actions were senseless, illogical. If there *was* a motive, in the killings of de Abreu and Furtado, it would not have been one that the jury could have understood.

"No matter how many pieces of evidence we put before you, it will never make sense," the assistant district attorney said.

Haggen *did* have a murder weapon: the .38 Special that police had recovered from Jailene Diaz-Ramos's trunk. But Bradley had confused matters there, as well: the way he remembered it, the .357 Magnum that he had gotten for Aaron was the gun that had been used in the drive-by.

It wasn't. But Bradley's faulty memory cast doubt on the matter.

Haggen was not a theatrical lawyer. He did not hop around the courtroom as if he were riding a pony. He stuck to the evidence, putting one photograph after another up on the screen.

He ended with a close-up of one of the tattoos Aaron had gotten in Redondo Beach.

"'God Forgives,'" Haggen said. "What is he asking God to forgive?"

According to the DA, Hernandez was asking forgiveness for having shot Bradley, having shot Furtado, having shot de Abreu.

"'God Forgives.' *His* statements. *His* words. *That* is a confession. But this is not a church, this is a courtroom. What matters in *this* room is the truth. What matters in *this* room is accountability. What matters in *this* room is a fair and just verdict based on the evidence, and not based on wild speculation, conjecture, and conspiracy theories. It has been five years since Safiro Furtado and Daniel de Abreu were gunned down in cold blood. Their lives matter in this room as well...The time for accountability is right now. His time is right now. Speak the truth through your verdicts and find him guilty."

CHAPTER 97

The jurors deliberated for thirty-seven hours over the course of five and a half days.

On April 14, they returned to the courtroom.

Shayanna sniffled as the jurors entered. A few moments earlier, she had been crying.

Everyone stood. It was so quiet that you could hear the rustle of clothing as people swayed from side to side. One of the courtroom's pool cameras panned over Aaron, who was wearing a gray suit, a blue shirt, and a blue tie. It lingered on the victims' families, in the front rows. It found Shayanna, behind them.

Aaron pursed his lips. A clerk asked the foreperson if the jury had agreed on a verdict.

The foreperson said that they had.

"Will the jury and the defendant remain standing please?" the clerk asked. "All others may be seated."

The judge took a long moment to review the verdict. Then, with a sigh and a grimace, he set the proceedings in motion:

"What say you, Madam Foreperson, on Indictment 2014-10417, Offense 001, charging murder in the first degree, victim Daniel de Abreu? Do you find the defendant not guilty, guilty of murder in the first degree, or guilty of murder in the second degree?"

The foreperson's voice was firm and even: "Not guilty."

For the first time, in all of his hundreds of hours in court, Aaron allowed his feelings to show in his face. His closed his eyes, inhaled deeply.

The clerk continued: "What say you, Madame Foreperson, on Indictment 2014-10417, Offense 002, charging murder in the first degree, victim Safiro Furtado. Do you find the defendant not guilty, guilty of murder in the first degree, or guilty of murder in the second degree?"

"Not guilty."

Aaron nodded, and continued to nod as the clerk continued to read and the foreperson answered.

There were eight counts in all. Hernandez was not guilty of witness intimidation. He was not guilty of armed assault and attempt to murder.

The one charge that Aaron was found guilty of was illegal possession of a firearm.

Members of the victims' families broke down in tears. One by one, they rushed out of the courtroom. As they did, Aaron let his mask slip, a bit more. Dennis Hernandez had taught his boy not to cry in front of other men. But now, Aaron did cry. He cried in front of the judge. In front of the jury that had found him innocent—in front of the world that had doubted his innocence—Aaron Hernandez cried tears of joy.

He looked young, almost boyish. His other conviction was up for appeal.

With Jose Baez on his team, Aaron was halfway to freedom.

CODA

The phones in Souza-Baranowski's G2 General Housing Unit all looked the same: mounted on columns, they were silver-colored with black handsets. To use them, prisoners punched in the PIN numbers that had been assigned to them on arrival. But prison etiquette had to be followed. By general understanding, each phone was claimed by a different gang. The Latin Kings had their phones. The gangs from Boston and Springfield had theirs.

Aaron Hernandez used phones that were claimed by the Bloods.

In the days immediately following his exoneration for the double murders in Boston, he spoke with his lawyers, with family members. He'd stay on the line with his fiancée, Shayanna, until the last possible minute. Then, as nine-thirty neared, a corrections officer would call time.

"Five minutes to count!" the CO would shout.

Every night was the same: The inmates in G2 would

shuffle off, grudgingly, to their cells. Hernandez would climb a set of blue stairs to his cell—Cell 57, left of the corrections officers' desk, located one level below. The CO would flick a switch that caused all the doors in the unit to slam shut and lock for the night. Then the prisoners would stand, facing the window in their cell door, and the CO would walk, slowly, past each cell, eyeballing the prisoners and physically checking to make sure that each door was locked.

Some COs walked the ground floor first, then climbed the stairs to count the second. Some COs did the opposite.

It was as much variety as the system allowed for.

For Aaron Hernandez, this had been the routine for two years. But the past few days had been different. According to an internal prison report, "He was positive and even happily emotional, which was not usual of Hernandez."

Aaron told other inmates that he was looking forward to reuniting with his family, and with Shayanna. He was still young—twenty-seven. If Jose Baez could work his magic again, he might have a few years of football left in him.

"Since Friday's verdict he had been talking about the NFL and going back to play even if it wasn't for the Pats," an inmate would say. "He talked about his daughter and spending time with her."

Now, it was the evening of April 18, 2017. The Patriots, who had won the Super Bowl again that year, would be going to the White House the next morning to meet with President Trump. But, once again, Aaron stayed on the line with Shayanna, drawing out the last long minutes of the day.

Then the CO called time and Hernandez shuffled off to his cell, his dark brown eyes shining with purpose.

A few hours later, at around one in the morning, Aaron hung part of a bedsheet over the window cut into the door of his cell.

He jammed the rail the door ran on with ripped-up pieces of cardboard.

Then he opened his Bible to the Book of John and wrote "John 3:16," in red ink, on his forehead.

Slicing into his right middle finger, Aaron used his own blood to mark that same passage in his Bible. He wrote "John 3:16," in his own blood, on the wall of his cell, and drew a crude pyramid, like the one on the back of a one-dollar bill.

Beneath it, he wrote the word "Illuminati."

Leaving several handwritten notes by the side of the Bible, he made large, stigmata-like marks, in blood, on both of his feet. Then, stripped naked, he poured several bottles of shampoo from the prison canteen all over the floor and picked up another part of the bedsheet, which he had twisted, tightly, into a rope.

Hernandez tied one end of the twisted sheet to the top of one of the vertical slats on the window across from the door to his cell. But the crossbar was just five feet from the floor. There was a metal desk directly beneath it, a metal chair next to it. Both had been bolted right into the wall.

What happened next took doing and determination on Aaron's part.

First, he rolled up some towels and stuck them through

the crossbar, so that the twisted sheet wouldn't slide down the vertical slat. Then, he tied the other end of the sheet around his neck.

By the time the guards found him, Aaron Hernandez was cold to the touch.

EPILOGUE

Even in death—especially in death—Aaron Hernandez monopolized the news cycle.

Why had he done it? *Had* he even done it?

Brian Murphy and Jose Baez refused to believe that Aaron had committed suicide. "He was so positive, so excited to come home," Shayanna said. "He was so, 'Daddy's gonna be home, and I can't wait to sleep in bed with you guys, and I can't wait to just hold you and love you.'"

A few days before Aaron's death, a Boston reporter had gone on the radio and gabbed about rumors that Aaron had been leading a double life. Before long, tabloids were floating the idea that Kyle Kennedy had been his prison lover.

Rumor had it that one of the three notes Aaron had left behind was intended for Kennedy. The contents of that note would not be revealed. But a copy of the note Aaron left for Shayanna *did* make its way into a court filing.

"Shay," Aaron had written. "Your character is that of a true angel and the definition of God's love!"

Aaron asked his fiancée to tell his story fully, to always remember how much he loved her. His death was God's plan, he said. In parting, he told her:

"(YOU'RE RICH)"

A month later, on May 17, Shayanna Jenkins appeared on Phillip McGraw's television program. There was no note intended for Kennedy, she assured Dr. Phil.

"There's nothing for Kyle Kennedy," Shayanna said.

When Dr. Phil asked her if Aaron was gay, Shayanna assured him that Aaron was not. "He was very much a man to me," she said.

On May 24, DJ Hernandez released a statement—his first public comment since Aaron's death.

"From the bottom of my heart," DJ had written, "I want to thank everyone who has supported my mother and me during such difficult times. My younger brother Aaron was far from perfect, but I will always love him. Many stories about my brother's life have been shared with the public—except the story Aaron was brave enough to share with our mother and me. It's the one story he wanted us to share with the world. It is Aaron's truth."

But the statement was followed by months of silence on DJ's part. As of this writing, the story that DJ hinted at remains untold.

What did Aaron mean, when he told Shayanna, "You're rich"?

One inmate told prison officials that Aaron mentioned a

rumor that had been going around the prison: If an inmate had an open appeal, and died in prison, he would be acquitted of that charge and rendered innocent.

Incredibly, that rumor turned out to be true: According to a principle known as Abatement ab initio ("from the beginning") the moment of Aaron's last breath was also the moment in which his conviction for Odin Lloyd's murder was rendered void. And if Aaron was free and clear of every murder he'd been accused of, didn't it stand to reason that the Patriots—who had voided Aaron's contract guarantees after his arrest for the murder of Odin Lloyd—owed Shayanna and Avielle the millions they had refused to pay Aaron?

As of this writing, lawsuits filed by Jose Baez and several other lawyers are ongoing.

As the summer drew to its close, Aaron Hernandez made headlines again.

On September 21, researchers at Boston University announced the startling results of their thorough examination of Hernandez's brain: not only did the brain exhibit symptoms of CTE, it showed signs of Stage III CTE—the worst case ever seen in a player as young as Hernandez.

Aaron's brain was "totally mangled," one of the researchers would say.

No medical diagnosis could explain all of Aaron's decisions, in life or in death. Many professional athletes suffer from CTE. Very few commit murder.

There is no way to establish how badly Aaron's brain was

damaged at the time that he committed his various crimes. No single explanation exists for any of his actions.

Like all lives, Aaron's life was more complicated than that.

What we *do* know is that Aaron Hernandez was an escape artist. On the football field, no one could catch him. In Florida, he was a few steps removed from a terrible shooting that no one had answered for. In Boston, he almost certainly committed a double murder that he got away with.

And when Aaron *was* caught, and convicted, for Odin Lloyd's murder, he continued to find new ways to escape. By killing himself, he escaped a long life behind bars. He escaped his sole remaining murder conviction, while finding a way to provide for Shayanna and Avielle.

In the end, he escaped understanding.

ABOUT THE AUTHORS

James Patterson holds the Guinness World Record for the most #1 *New York Times* bestsellers, and his books have sold more than 375 million copies worldwide. A tireless champion of the power of books and reading, Patterson created a children's book imprint, JIMMY Patterson, whose mission is simple: "We want every kid who finishes a JIMMY Book to say, 'PLEASE GIVE ME ANOTHER BOOK.'" He has donated more than one million books to students and soldiers and funds over four hundred Teacher Education Scholarships at twenty-four colleges and universities. He has also donated millions of dollars to independent bookstores and school libraries. Patterson invests proceeds from the sales of JIMMY Patterson Books in pro-reading initiatives.

*   *   *

Alex Abramovich is the author of *Bullies: A Friendship*. He writes for the *London Review of Books* and teaches at Columbia University.

Mike Harvkey is the author of the novel *In the Course of Human Events*. He has written for *Esquire, Salon, Poets & Writers,* and other publications.

BOOKS BY JAMES PATTERSON

FEATURING ALEX CROSS

The People vs. Alex Cross • *Cross the Line* • *Cross Justice* • *Hope to Die* •
Cross My Heart • *Alex Cross, Run* • *Merry Christmas, Alex Cross* • *Kill
Alex Cross* • *Cross Fire* • *I, Alex Cross* • *Alex Cross's* Trial (with Richard
DiLallo) • *Cross Country* • *Double Cross* • *Cross* (also published as *Alex
Cross*) • *Mary, Mary* • *London Bridges* • *The Big Bad Wolf* • *Four Blind
Mice* • *Violets Are Blue* • *Roses Are Red* • *Pop Goes the Weasel* • *Cat &
Mouse* • *Jack & Jill* • *Kiss the Girls* • *Along Came a Spider*

THE WOMEN'S MURDER CLUB

The 17th Suspect (with Maxine Paetro) • *16th Seduction* (with Maxine
Paetro) • *15th Affair* (with Maxine Paetro) • *14th Deadly Sin* (with
Maxine Paetro) • *Unlucky 13* (with Maxine Paetro) • *12th of Never* (with
Maxine Paetro) • *11th Hour* (with Maxine Paetro) • *10th Anniversary*
(with Maxine Paetro) • *The 9th Judgment* (with Maxine Paetro) • *The 8th
Confession* (with Maxine Paetro) • *7th Heaven* (with Maxine Paetro) • *The
6th Target* (with Maxine Paetro) • *The 5th Horseman* (with Maxine
Paetro) • *4th of July* (with Maxine Paetro) • *3rd Degree* (with Andrew
Gross) • *2nd Chance* (with Andrew Gross) • *1st to Die*

FEATURING MICHAEL BENNETT

Haunted (with James O. Born) • *Bullseye* (with Michael Ledwidge) •
Alert (with Michael Ledwidge) • *Burn* (with Michael Ledwidge) • *Gone*
(with Michael Ledwidge) • *I, Michael Bennett* (with Michael Ledwidge) •

Tick Tock (with Michael Ledwidge) • *Worst Case* (with Michael Ledwidge) • *Run for Your Life* (with Michael Ledwidge) • *Step on a Crack* (with Michael Ledwidge)

THE PRIVATE NOVELS

Princess (with Rees Jones) • *Count to Ten* (with Ashwin Sanghi) • *Missing* (with Kathryn Fox) • *The Games* (with Mark Sullivan) • *Private Paris* (with Mark Sullivan) • *Private Vegas* (with Maxine Paetro) • *Private India: City on Fire* (with Ashwin Sanghi) • *Private Down Under* (with Michael White) • *Private L.A.* (with Mark Sullivan) • *Private Berlin* (with Mark Sullivan) • *Private London* (with Mark Pearson) • *Private Games* (with Mark Sullivan) • *Private: #1 Suspect* (with Maxine Paetro) • *Private* (with Maxine Paetro)

NYPD RED NOVELS

Red Alert (with Marshall Karp) • *NYPD Red 4* (with Marshall Karp) • *NYPD Red 3* (with Marshall Karp) • *NYPD Red 2* (with Marshall Karp) • *NYPD Red* (with Marshall Karp)

SUMMER NOVELS

Second Honeymoon (with Howard Roughan) • *Now You See Her* (with Michael Ledwidge) • *Swimsuit* (with Maxine Paetro) • *Sail* (with Howard Roughan) • *Beach Road* (with Peter de Jonge) • *Lifeguard* (with Andrew Gross) • *Honeymoon* (with Howard Roughan) • *The Beach House* (with Peter de Jonge)

STAND-ALONE BOOKS

Juror #3 (with Nancy Allen) • *Texas Ranger* (with Andrew Bourelle) • *Triple Homicide* (with Maxine Paetro and James O Born) • *The President*

Is Missing (with Bill Clinton) • *Murder in Paradise* (with Doug Allyn, Connor Hyde, Duane Swierczynski) • *Fifty Fifty* (with Candice Fox) • *Murder Beyond the Grave* (with Andrew Bourelle and Christopher Charles) • *Home Sweet Murder* (with Andrew Bourelle and Scott Slaven) • *Murder, Interrupted* (with Alex Abramovich and Christopher Charles) • *All-American Murder* (with Alex Abramovich and Mike Harvkey) • *The Family Lawyer* (with Robert Rotstein, Christopher Charles, Rachel Howzell Hall) • *The Store* (with Richard DiLallo) • *The Moores Are Missing* (with Loren D. Estleman, Sam Hawken, Ed Chatterton) • *Triple Threat* (with Max DiLallo, Andrew Bourrelle) • *Murder Games* (with Howard Roughan) • *Penguins of America* (with Jack Patterson with Florence Yue) • *Two from the Heart* (with Frank Constantini, Emily Raymond, Brian Sitts) • *The Black Book* (with David Ellis) • *Humans, Bow Down* (with Emily Raymond) • *Never Never* (with Candice Fox) • *Woman of God* (with Maxine Paetro) • *Filthy Rich* (with John Connolly and Timothy Malloy) • *The Murder House* (with David Ellis) • *Truth or Die* (with Howard Roughan) • *Miracle at Augusta* (with Peter de Jonge) • *Invisible* (with David Ellis) • *First Love* (with Emily Raymond) • *Mistress* (with David Ellis) • *Zoo* (with Michael Ledwidge) • *Guilty Wives* (with David Ellis) • *The Christmas Wedding* (with Richard DiLallo) • *Kill Me If You Can* (with Marshall Karp) • *Toys* (with Neil McMahon) • *Don't Blink* (with Howard Roughan) • *The Postcard Killers* (with Liza Marklund) • *The Murder of King Tut* (with Martin Dugard) • *Against Medical Advice* (with Hal Friedman) • *Sundays at Tiffany's* (with Gabrielle Charbonnet) • *You've Been Warned* (with Howard Roughan) • *The Quickie* (with Michael Ledwidge) • *Judge & Jury* (with Andrew Gross) • *Sam's Letters to Jennifer* • *The Lake House* • *The Jester* (with Andrew Gross) • *Suzanne's Diary for Nicholas* • *Cradle and All* • *When the Wind Blows* • *Miracle on the 17th Green* (with Peter de Jonge) • *Hide & Seek* • *The Midnight Club* • *Black Friday* (originally published as *Black Market*) • *See How They Run* • *Season of the Machete* • *The Thomas Berryman Number*

BOOK**SHOTS**

FOR READERS OF ALL AGES

MAXIMUM RIDE

Maximum Ride Forever • *Nevermore: The Final Maximum Ride Adventure* • *Angel: A Maximum Ride Novel* • *Fang: A Maximum Ride Novel* • *Max: A Maximum Ride Novel* • *The Final Warning: A Maximum Ride Novel* • *Saving the World and Other Extreme Sports: A Maximum Ride Novel* • *School's Out—Forever: A Maximum Ride Novel* • *The Angel Experiment: A Maximum Ride Novel*

DANIEL X

Daniel X: Lights Out (with Chris Grabenstein) • *Daniel X: Armageddon* (with Chris Grabenstein) • *Daniel X: Game Over* (with Ned Rust) • *Daniel X: Demons and Druids* (with Adam Sadler) • *Daniel X: Watch the Skies* (with Ned Rust) • *The Dangerous Days of Daniel X* (with Michael Ledwidge)

WITCH & WIZARD

Witch & Wizard: The Lost (with Emily Raymond) • *Witch & Wizard: The Kiss* (with Jill Dembowski) • *Witch & Wizard: The Fire* (with Jill Dembowski) • *Witch & Wizard: The Gift* (with Ned Rust) • *Witch & Wizard* (with Gabrielle Charbonnet)

CONFESSIONS

Confessions: The Murder of an Angel (with Maxine Paetro) • *Confessions: The Paris Mysteries* (with Maxine Paetro) • *Confessions: The Private School Murders* (with Maxine Paetro) • *Confessions of a Murder Suspect* (with Maxine Paetro)

MIDDLE SCHOOL

Middle School: Escape to Australia (with Martin Chatterton, illustrated by Daniel Griffo) • *Middle School: Dog's Best Friend* (with Chris Tebbetts, illustrated by Jomike Tejido) • *Middle School: Just My Rotten Luck* (with Chris Tebbetts, illustrated by Laura Park) • *Middle School: Save Rafe!*

(with Chris Tebbetts, illustrated by Laura Park) • *Middle School: Ultimate Showdown* (with Julia Bergen, illustrated by Alec Longstreth) • *Middle School: How I Survived Bullies, Broccoli, and Snake Hill* (with Chris Tebbetts, illustrated by Laura Park) • *Middle School: My Brother Is a Big, Fat Liar* (with Lisa Papademetriou, illustrated by Neil Swaab) • *Middle School: Get Me Out of Here!* (with Chris Tebbetts, illustrated by Laura Park) • *Middle School, The Worst Years of My Life* (with Chris Tebbetts, illustrated by Laura Park)

I FUNNY

I Funny: Around the World (with Chris Grabenstein) • *I Funny: School of Laughs* (with Chris Grabenstein, illustrated by Jomike Tejido) • *I Funny TV* (with Chris Grabenstein, illustrated by Laura Park) • *I Totally Funniest: A Middle School Story* (with Chris Grabenstein, illustrated by Laura Park) • *I Even Funnier: A Middle School Story* (with Chris Grabenstein, illustrated by Laura Park) • *I Funny: A Middle School Story* (with Chris Grabenstein, illustrated by Laura Park)

TREASURE HUNTERS

Treasure Hunters: Quest for the City of Gold (with Chris Grabenstein, illustrated by Juliana Neufeld) • *Treasure Hunters: Peril at the Top of the World* (with Chris Grabenstein, illustrated by Juliana Neufeld) • *Treasure Hunters: Secret of the Forbidden City* (with Chris Grabenstein, illustrated by Juliana Neufeld) • *Treasure Hunters: Danger Down the Nile* (with Chris Grabenstein, illustrated by Juliana Neufeld) • *Treasure Hunters* (with Chris Grabenstein, illustrated by Juliana Neufeld)

OTHER BOOKS FOR READERS OF ALL AGES

Cuddly Critters for Little Geniuses (with Susan Patterson, illustrated by Hsinping Pan) • *Unbelievably Boring Bart* (with Duane Swierczynski, illustrated by Xavier Bonet) • *Not So Normal Norbert* (with Joey Green, illustrated by Hatem Aly) • *The Candies' Easter Party* (illustrated by Andy Elkerton) • *Jacky Ha-Ha: My Life is a Joke* (with Chris Grabenstein, illustrated by Kerascoët) • *Give Thank You a Try* • *Expelled* (with Emily Raymond) • *The Candies Save Christmas* (illustrated by Andy Elkerton) • *Big Words for Little Geniuses* (with Susan Patterson, illustrated by Hsinping Pan) • *Laugh Out Loud* (with Chris Grabenstein) • *Pottymouth and Stoopid* (with Chris Grabenstein) • *Crazy House* (with Gabrielle Charbonnet) • *House of Robots: Robot Revolution* (with Chris Grabenstein, illustrated by Juliana Neufeld) • *Word of Mouse* (with Chris Grabenstein, illustrated by Joe Sutphin) • *Give Please a Chance* (with Bill O'Reilly) • *Jacky Ha-Ha* (with Chris Grabenstein, illustrated by Kerascoët) • *House of Robots: Robots Go Wild!* (with Chris Grabenstein, illustrated by Juliana Neufeld) • *Public School Superhero* (with Chris Tebbetts, illustrated by Cory Thomas) • *House of Robots* (with Chris Grabenstein, illustrated by Juliana Neufeld) • *Homeroom Diaries* (with Lisa Papademetriou, illustrated by Keino) • *Med Head* (with Hal Friedman) • *santaKid* (illustrated by Michael Garland)

For previews and information about the author, visit JamesPatterson.com or find him on Facebook or at your app store.